PROJECT HEAD START
Past, Present, and Future Trends in the Context of Family Needs

SOURCE BOOKS
ON EDUCATION
(Vol. 13)

GARLAND REFERENCE LIBRARY
OF SOCIAL SCIENCE
(Vol. 378)

Source Books on Education

1. Bilingual Education: *A Source Book for Educators*, by Alba N. Ambert and Sarah E. Melendez
2. Reading and Study Skills in the Secondary Schools: *A Source Book*, by Joyce N. French
3. Creating Connections: *Books, Kits, and Games for Children*, by Betty P. Cleaver, Barbara Chatton, and Shirley Vittum Morrison
4. Gifted, Talented, and Creative Young People: *A Guide to Theory, Teaching, and Research*, by Morris I. Stein
5. Teaching Science to Young Children: *A Resource Book*, by Mary D. Iatridis
6. Microcomputers and Social Studies: *A Resource Guide for the Middle and Secondary Grades:* by Joseph A. Braun, Jr.
7. Special Education: *A Source Book*, by Manny Sternlicht
8. Computers in the Classroom . . . What Shall I Do?: *A Guide*, by Walter Burke
9. Learning to Read and Write: The Role of Languge Acquisition and Aesthetic Development, *A Resource Guide*, by Ellen J. Brooks
10. School Play: *A Source Book*, by James H. Block and Nancy R. King
11. Computer Simulations: *A Source Book to Learning in an Electronic Environment*, by Jerry Willis, Larry Hovey, and Kathleen Hovey
12. Day Care: *A Source Book*, by Kathleen Pullan Watkins and Lucius Durant, Jr.
13. Project Head Start: Past, Present, and Future Trends in the Context of Family Needs, by Valora Washington and Ura Jean Oyemade

PROJECT HEAD START
Past, Present, and Future Trends in the Context of Family Needs

Valora Washington
and
Ura Jean Oyemade

Howard University
School of Human Ecology

GARLAND PUBLISHING, INC. • NEW YORK & LONDON
1987

Library of Congress Cataloging-in-Publication Data

Washington, Valora, 1953–
Project Head Start: Past, Present, and Future
Trends in the Context of Family Needs.

(Source Books on Education; vol. 13) (Garland
Reference Library of Social Science; vol. 378)
Bibliography: p.
Includes index.
1. Project Head Start (U.S.)–History. 2. United
States. Head Start Bureau–History. 3. Head Start
programs–United States–History. I. Oyemade, Ura Jean.
II. Title. III. Series. IV. Series: Garland Reference
Library of Social Science; v. 378.

LC4091.W37 1987 371.96′7 87-11873
ISBN 0-8240-8521-3

Cover design by Alison Lew

Printed on acid-free, 250-year-life paper
Manufactured in the United States of America

Dedicated

to my son

Omari Washington-Smith

CONTENTS

PREFACE

Project Head Start is now celebrating its 22nd anniversary year. This project is one of the most successful and enduring programs from President Lyndon Johnson's War on Poverty. While Head Start has been written about and studied extensively, we still know very little about the impact of the project on families. Commonly perceived to be an educational program, other critical components of Head Start, such as parent involvement, have not been given the attention that they deserve.

This volume adds to the Head Start literature an explicit focus on past, present, and future trends in the context of family needs. The intended scope is comprehensive and embodies all of the major components of Project Head Start. However, this volume is unique in that we are particularly concerned with Head Start as a vehicle for helping poor families to achieve economic self-sufficiency. The unifying theme of this book is our assessment of how well Head Start has met, and continues to meet, the changing needs of the children and families that the project serves.

Developed as a reference tool, this book contains essays followed by a reference list and by evaluative bibliographic entries. This book is topically organized into seven parts which include eleven chapters. We examine many aspects of Project Head Start including its philosophical basis; the continuing appropriateness of its theoretical foundation; research on its overall effectiveness; program quality and content; and program adaptability to changing family, social, and national trends.

Our hope is that this book will help to create a more meaningful interface between academic research and public policy needs or perspectives. This book also aims to build a liaison of understanding, and to create a basis for more collaborative interaction, between public policies and the people who are actually affected by them.

It is not possible to recognize and acknowledge all of the families, Head Start directors, federal and regional office staff, and scholars who directly or indirectly gave of their time and energy in the preparation of a work of this scope. Special tribute, however, must be given to Mr. Clennie Murphy, Acting Commissioner for Head Start, and his Special Assistant, Dr. Trellis Waxler, who nurtured our ideas and provided us with invaluable guidance. Dr. O. Jackson Cole, Dean of the School of Human Ecology at Howard University, was an important contributor to our discussion of "Head Start Effectiveness" (Chapter 6). We are also appreciative of the advice and encouragement provided by participants in the "Minority Scholars" conferences in 1983 and 1985. (These persons are listed in Chapter 7). Ms. Carolyn Joyner has provided invaluable and essential administrative assistance through this and our other Head Start-related projects. Finally, we wish to thank our colleagues at Howard University for their support and assistance.

Valora Washington
Assistant Dean and Associate Professor
School of Human Ecology
Howard University

FOREWORD

At its inception, over two decades ago, Project Head Start was established as a nationwide demonstration project which had as its overt purpose the mandate to "interrupt the cycle of poverty" for America's poor families. During the past 21 years, Head Start has advanced far beyond the original experimental demonstration stage. A total of 9,597,070 children and their families have been served by the program since it began in the summer of 1965. Today, approximately one out of six of the eligible preschool children from low-income families are served by Head Start.

As a result of experience, research and evaluation we have amassed a great deal of information about those aspects of the Head Start experience which lead to a qualitatively enriching program. Additionally, we have also been able to identify unique aspects of the Head Start program, such as the parent involvement component, which have contributed to its continued success and distinguished it from other types of child care programs.

Bolstered with this information, Head Start is now ready to move toward an era where special emphasis will be placed on improving the quality of its experience for participating families by capitalizing on the unique Head Start characteristic of involving parents directly in their local program's operations. A major component of this new strategy will be to have parents as primary educators of their children. We also believe that by assisting parents in their efforts to reach economic self-sufficiency, we are accomplishing the initial Head Start mandate of interrupting the cycle of poverty.

Drs. Washington and Oyemade, two minority Early Child Development practitioners and researchers who have been involved in many aspects of the Head Start program over the past twenty years, have written a book which is very timely in that it addresses many of the issues we encounter as we attempt to emphasize quality service and education. Not only does their well researched book provide an excellent overview of the history of Head Start in the context of the needs of the family, but it goes beyond to identify current trends in family development which have tremendous implications for the effectiveness of Head Start in meeting those family needs.

As I visit Head Start programs around the country, I am constantly reminded by center directors, teachers and teachers aides that the family structure served by Head Start is indeed changing. When the project began in 1965, the average Head Start mother was older than she is today and single parent families in 1965 were infrequent while today the percentage of single parent families approaches 55%. Also reflecting the change in family is the current trend for more mothers to be employed today.

We have come to realize that Head Start cannot adequately address the goal of interrupting the cycle of poverty simply by providing educational opportunities for children. In order to qualitatively improve Head Start efforts, we must identify ways to strengthen those families who enter the program who have many other needs just as important to them as the education of their children. In order to strengthen these families, we must not only focus on the provision of social services to meet their current needs, but we must also adapt as a major goal new ways to prevent the recurrence of these and other problems within the current and the next generation of Head Start parents.

The authors, along with other scholars cited herein, have made many excellent recommendations which will be useful for local Head Start programs as well as the national Head Start office as we develop this new effort.

Clennie H. Murphy, Jr.
Acting Associate Commissioner
Head Start Bureau
400 6th Street, S.W.
Washington, D.C. 20013
February 1987

INTRODUCTION

As Project Head Start celebrates its 22nd anniversary year, it is clearly recognized as one of the most successful and enduring antipoverty programs in the United States. The widely heralded effectiveness of Head Start is particularly important because of the program's service to large numbers of poor and nonwhite ethnic group children.

As black researchers, we have been concerned about the minimal involvement of minority researchers in much of the published literature about Head Start. Therefore, in 1983 we co-convened a national conference on "Minority Perspectives on the Future of Project Head Start." At that meeting, black, Hispanic and Asian scholars grappled with three issues: the rationale for Head Start as a vehicle for upward mobility; the effects of Head Start on minority children; and the continuing appropriateness of Head Start for minority children. The conferees agreed that there was an urgent need to direct attention to parent involvement in Head Start as a means to assure a stable foundation for the educational, economic, and social progress of the poor families served.

Consistent with the recommendations from the 1983 meeting, we initiated several investigations of Head Start parents. Using a random sample of 5,000 households in the District of Columbia, we worked with a Head Start grantee to assess the community needs. In a pilot effort to understand the process through which parent involvement is, and can be, more effective, we studied Head Start families in Baltimore, Maryland, Columbus, Ohio, and Nashville, Tennessee. Moreover, in 1985 we reconvened our panel of minority scholars to join in a broad-based national study of Head Start parents.

In this context, we have been reminded of an important original mission of Head Start: to help children and their families to achieve economic self- sufficiency. We were startled to discover that little is known about the impact of parent involvement, a crucial aspect of Head Start. We are convinced that the effectiveness of Head Start programs today is hampered by the relatively limited attention to family development. Further, changes in family structures and functions since the founding of Head Start have altered the ability of many families to take advantage of traditional Head Start services.

Four trends in family life are particularly evident:

1. The feminization of poverty;

2. The rise in teen parenting;

3. The surge in the number of mothers of preschool children in the workforce; and

4. The increasing challenge for low-income families to attain economic self- sufficiency.

These trends are often interrelated: The female poor are frequently teen mothers who, in an attempt to attain economic self-sufficiency, seek employment while their children are young. These changes in families indicate an urgent need for complementary changes in the services Head Start provides.

These four changing conditions in American families create new demands on individuals and on the programs that serve them. Many observers agree that these dramatic changes are neither short term nor likely to be reversed (Cherlin, 1981). New family structures and roles are not automatically accommodated in federal programs, but the implications of these changes for Head Start must be explored by all professionals who are concerned about our nation's children. It is imperative that we consider possible changes because of Head Start's "recognition of the importance of the family, rather than the school, as the ultimate source of a child's values and behavior" (Zigler and Anderson, 1979, p. 14).

This book is our attempt to review Head Start as a comprehensive child development program in the context of changing family trends. This book contains essays, an extensive reference list, and an annotated bibliography. The unifying theme of the book is the assessment of how well Head Start has met, and continues to meet, the changing needs of the children and families the program serves. This book examines many factors including:

1. The philosophical basis for Project Head Start;

2. The continuing appropriateness of its theoretical foundation;

3. Research on Project Head Start;

4. Program quality and content; and

5. Program adaptability to changing family, social, and national trends.

A major goal of this book is to create a meaningful interface between academic research and public policy needs or perspectives. The book aims to build a liaison of understanding and create a basis for interaction between science and policy; science and program consumers; policy and program consumers; and among advocacy, science, and policy.

This book is divided into seven parts. Part A contains three chapters. This part presents an overview of Project Head Start including a background of the program, a description of its administrative structure, and an outline of the programs, budgets, and the children served.

Part B presents an overview of program effectiveness including a critical assessment of the evaluation efforts; a look at economic self-sufficiency as an original rationale for Project Head Start; an analysis of its continuing relevance and appropriateness; and recommendations from the minority scholars conferences held in 1983 and 1985.

Part C contains four chapters which assess changing family trends and their implications for Project Head Start. The trends discussed are the feminization of poverty, adolescent parenting, and parental employment issues.

Part D examines the increasing challenge of economic self-sufficiency. Responses that Project Head Start can make to these challenges are outlined.

Parts E, F, and G present a reference list, including annotated bibliographies, an author index, and a subject index.

As Head Start moves into its third decade, it is timely to analyze its past and present and to offer a proactive approach to addressing the issues of Head Start and the public policies which affect them. The book is interdisciplinary, holistic, and comprehensive in scope. The book also has a developmental emphasis: Head Start programs and policies will be described from the view of how they influence family or child growth. Furthermore, the book highlights the cultural, historical, and ecological factors which affect Head Start programs and policies.

TABLES

TABLE

ABBREVIATIONS

ACYF	Administration for Children, Youth, and Families
AFDC	Aid to Families with Dependent Children
CDA	Child Development Associate
CDF	Children's Defense Fund
CPR	Current Population Report
CRS	Congressional Research Service
GAO	General Accounting Office
NCSS	National Center for Social Statistics
OCD	Office of Child Development
OEO	Office of Economic Opportunity
OHDS	Office of Human Development Services
USDC	United States Department of Commerce
USDHEW	United States Department of Health, Education, and Welfare
USDHHS	United States Department of Health and Human Services
USDHUD	United States Department of Housing and Urban Development

PROJECT HEAD START
Past, Present, and Future Trends in the Context of Family Needs

PART A:

AN OVERVIEW OF PROJECT HEAD START

CHAPTER 1

A BRIEF BACKGROUND OF PROJECT HEAD START

To understand the context in which changing family trends are important in the analysis and implementation of Head Start, we begin with a brief history of Project Head Start.

(Several references are useful in reviewing the history of Project Head Start including Ross, C. 1979; Zigler and Valentine, 1979; Greenberg, 1969; Jones and Fowler, 1982; Richmond, Stipek, and Zigler, 1979; and Shriver, 1979.)

In the early 1960s, Americans and the Kennedy administration rediscovered what Michael Harrington labeled "the other America," in which it was estimated that nearly one-quarter of the American people lived in poverty. The impoverished lacked adequate food, housing, and health care, and their isolation from the mainstream of American culture had an equally devastating but less obvious effect on their economic status (Harrington, 1962).

In response to this concern, President Kennedy suggested that "the prevention of adult poverty and dependency must begin with the case of dependent children." This concept was based on the culture-of- poverty notion that poverty and welfare dependencies are transmitted intergenerationally largely because values and motivations deemed vital to economic achievement--education, independence, ambition, concern for the future--are not reinforced during a childhood spent in poverty and dependence on welfare (Hill and Ponza, 1983).

Based on this view, the Economic Opportunity Act of 1964 created the Office of Economic Opportunity (OEO), which was the major weapon in an "unconditional war on poverty." President Johnson declared a war "not only to relieve the symptoms of poverty but to cure it; and, above all, to prevent it." Although the legislation did not mandate Head Start or any similar program, it did direct OEO to pay special attention to the needs of young people (Zigler and Anderson, 1979).

Research and public policy coincided to create the impetus for the development of the Head Start program. Two classic volumes were influential in redirecting empirical thought about child development. In the first, J. McVicker Hunt's *Intelligence and Experience*, published in 1961, concluded that experience programs the development of the human brain and affects the rate of early development in human infants. In 1964 Benjamin Bloom's classic work, *Stability and Change in Human Characteristics*, concluded that important human characteristics showed a pattern of very rapid growth in the early years which steadily declined. For general intelligence, Bloom surmised that about 50 percent of the variation possible for any particular child was established by age four. In sharp contrast to belief in predetermined and fixed development, Bloom's work set the stage for a decade of vigorous insistence of the predominate role of the environment in development. Moreover, since the environment can be adjusted, Bloom willingly addressed himself to the question of social responsibility for disadvantaged children (Steiner, 1976).

However, these volumes did not directly translate into public policy. Rather, Steiner suggests that, whatever their importance for later efforts to effect social change, the short-run importance of these books was the coincidence of their timing with the political needs and purposes of the Kennedy and Johnson presidencies. President Kennedy's original antipoverty task force did not pinpoint preschool children in their proposed community-action program. Indeed, Head Start was not invented until six months after enactment of the Economic Opportunity Act, presumably with the hope of developing a more comprehensive program and one that would show quick results (Steiner, 1976).

Head Start was proposed by an interdisciplinary panel chaired by Dr. Robert E. Cooke, professor of pediatrics at Johns Hopkins University School of Medicine, a man with close ties to the Kennedy family. The panel, charged with considering the kinds of programs potentially effective to increase achievement and opportunities for the poor, targeted the preschool population for assistance. The panel recommended that the preschool effort be comprehensive, including health, education, and social services to compensate for the children's lack of the kinds of experiences and opportunities available to economically advantaged families (Steiner, 1976).

As part of the OEO efforts to implement the community-action provision of the act, Head Start was suggested as a program that would be "a microcosm of community action." It would offer major advantages beyond the services it would provide to children and their families. It would have a visible emotional impact as a symbol of OEO's potential. The program would fulfill community-action obligations by involving parents in planning the centers. Parents and youth could also obtain jobs as aides. Shriver hoped that Head Start would "bring together all of the different resources within different local agencies on one target--the child that is poor, and his family" (Ross, C., 1979).

The special importance of Head Start was said to be its provision of a unique range of services. It combined day care with medical and dental treatment, emphasized both the child's psychological development and school readiness, and introduced "social services into the child's home environment plus education of the parents" (Ross, C., 1979).

Steiner (1976) concluded that the preexistence of the antipoverty program provided the environment for creating Head Start. Once in place, the project expanded interest in early childhood. Child development experts, Steiner adds, too readily acquiesced as Head Start moved from experiment to institution without wide-ranging debate about likely costs, benefits, or alternatives. Only after evaluation studies questioned the investment value of Head Start (see Cole and Washington, 1986) did many Head Start planners speak publicly about "the naive environmentalism which caused Head Start to be oversold in the early days" (see Steiner, 1976, p. 29).

Thus, Project Head Start was launched during the summer of 1965 with the expectation of spending about $17 million for about 100,000 children. However, the demand was far greater than anticipated due largely to the massive manner in which the program was advertised. As a result, the Office of Economic Opportunity decided to support a much larger program than originally planned, despite the Cooke panel's warning that it would be preferable to have comprehensive programs for fewer children than to reach vast numbers of children with limited programs. Finally, 561,359 children were enrolled in 11,068 centers in the summer of 1965.

Head Start was extremely popular in contrast with some of the OEO's other programs (Steiner, 1976). Steiner (1976) asserts that Head Start achieved its instant and continuing popularity by focusing essentially on one model of service -- organized centers serving preschool children. This focus was adopted as a matter of administrative policy, not of statute. The Economic Opportunity Act of 1964, and the subsequent amendments to it which wrote a Head Start program into law, anticipated maximum community group freedom in choosing services such as prenatal care, child development training for parents, and in- home services. However, the amassing strength of the program made it quickly apparent that it would be virtually impossible to alter the program either by administrative action or by statutory authorization for alternative models -- even in the face of early evidence which cast doubt on the model's effectiveness in cognitive development. Throughout the Johnson administration, however, the value of Head Start as an effective instrument of early education was widely accepted by the public, by Congress, and by social scientists.

However, by 1969, during the administration of President Richard Nixon, a massive evaluation of Head Start by the Westinghouse Learning Corporation began to raise important questions about the lasting benefits of Head Start. Among the nine major findings of the Westinghouse Report, the most positive dealt with parents' strong approval of the program and its affect on their children.

Response to the Westinghouse report was mixed, far-reaching, and controversial.[1] President Nixon's planned strong endorsement of Project Head Start was transformed into an ambiguous statement describing the effort as still "experimental" (Steiner, 1976).

Edward Zigler says that the negative impact of the Westinghouse Report was so powerful, his first job on taking over Head Start in 1970 was to fight to keep the program alive (Zigler and Rescorla, 1985; see Chapter

[1] See Chapter 6 for detailed discussion about assessments of Head Start.

3). The program was still on a tentative footing when the "fade-out" assessment of Head Start outcomes was widely acclaimed by 1975. From 1975 - 1978, several national media sources reported that Head Start had been terminated, as the program faded from view (Zigler and Rescorla, 1985).

Nevertheless, Head Start was staunchly defended, and it remained popular among participants and acceptable to Congress. Presently, Head Start is enjoying a resurgence in public confidence. In fact, recent Congressional action to expand the program suggests that it has retained its favored position of the past. The present status is no doubt largely due to the fact that credible program data and favorable evaluation studies about preschool education are now available and widely publicized (e.g., Berruetta- Clement et al., 1984). The project is widely acclaimed by members of both major political parties in the United States (Subcommittee on Human Resources of the Committee on Education and Labor, House of Representatives, 1980, 1982, 1984). Importantly, the project maintains wide popularity in local communities.

Edward Zigler's (1979) observation about Head Start is quite clear: Head Start is less a static program than an evolving concept constantly in need of evaluation. It is critical to recognize Head Start's evolutionary nature. Further, Head Start plays an important role as a national laboratory for early childhood education.

At present, Head Start's future seems secure. Indeed, funding and pupil enrollments have increased markedly since 1980. Dr. Edward Zigler lists five forces that have kept Head Start alive in the 1980's during a Republican administration:

1. Effective support by parents, staff, and advocacy groups, such as the Children's Defense Fund;

2. A positive image in the media;

3. Strong bipartisan Congressional support;

4. Robust, reliable research demonstrating the long-term cost-effective benefits of Head Start; and

5. Powerful converts to the program within the Reagan Administration who, after working with Head Start, have become advocates--a sequence of events which Zigler notes is quite common (Zigler, 1985).

Similarly, Peter Skerry (1983) observed that the Head Start program has led a "charmed life." It has survived periods of budget cuts in other service programs and is often cited as an example of a successful federal program.

Nevertheless, careful observers of the Head Start program urge caution and continued vigilance in monitoring Head Start's success. There are a number of issues involving Head Start which remain unresolved. For example, budget and enrollment "increases" may mask questions about administrative changes and service delivery (see Chapter 5). Other issues involve program effectiveness (Chapter 6), program administration (Chapter 2), and its ability to meet the changing needs of families (Parts C and D).

CHAPTER 2

THE ADMINISTRATION OF PROJECT HEAD START

Sharon Stephan (1986) of the Congressional Research Service describes Project Head Start as a federal matching grant program with funds allocated to states on the basis of a formula that takes into account the states' child poverty population and other factors. The Secretary of the Department of Health and Human Services distributes funds to eligible Head Start agencies within the state. With certain exceptions, federal funds are limited to 80 percent of total program costs; there is a 20 percent non-federal matching requirement. About 13 percent of Head Start appropriations are reserved for Indian and migrant programs, payments to the territories, training and technical assistance and discretionary payments. Federal law prohibits Head Start programs from charging fees for participation although parents who wish to pay may do so.

Head Start is a federal matching grant program which provides over a billion dollars each year for services to help improve poor children's social and learning skills as well as their nutrition and health status. About two-thirds of the children are members of ethnic minority groups; about 12 percent are handicapped; and a majority are aged four. In 1986, 452,080 children were served in 1,305 Head Start Programs at a cost of $2,339.00 per child.

Since 1965, the program goals of Project Head Start have remained virtually unchanged, but the program's administration and operating structure have been modified over time. For example, in contrast to the early years of Head Start, today 82 percent of the Head Start programs are half-day. The average program provides services 34 weeks per year.

As Harmon and Hanley (1979) point out, decision- making in Head Start is shared between the federal Head Start agency, regional offices, grantees, and delegate agencies. The role of these units in the administrative structure of Head Start is discussed here.

Federal Head Start Agency

As one of the programs funded by the Economic Opportunity Act of 1964, Project Head Start was initially administered by the Office of Economic Opportunity (OEO) created by the Act. The director of Head Start was not subject to Congressional confirmation. The intent of the legislation was that Head Start would be located in OEO only until it demonstrated its workability and effectiveness at which time, like other OEO programs, it would be transferred to an unspecified cabinet department. Thus, OEO actively generated the initial community public interest which led to the massive summer "experiment" of 1965 and to support of the idea that child care programs could contribute to the development of human potential.

By 1968, however, concern about combining community action with preschool education and child care led to a directive from the President to study the feasibility of moving Head Start from OEO to another government agency. A month after his inauguration, President Nixon announced his intention to delegate the operation of Head Start to the Department of Health, Education, and Welfare (HEW), although he did not specify which office in HEW. As Richard Nixon began his presidency, there were also perceptions that, while OEO was facing an uncertain future, HEW was on the upswing.

Faced with a choice of offices within HEW, there was little enthusiasm for the prevailing three options: the Office of Education, the Children's Bureau, and the Social Rehabilitation Service (SRS). There were misgivings about the involvement of professional educators, and concern that SRS's preoccupation with public assistance and work training programs would overshadow child development considerations. An obvious logical possibility was the Children's Bureau, which staffed social work concerns such as foster care and adoption services. However, the

Bureau -- perceived as traditional, maternalistic, non-aggressive, noninnovative, and out of touch with the issues of poor and black children -- discouraged child development activists of the 1960's from using it as a focal point for an expanded program of federal intervention in early childhood.

Consequently, the decision was made to delegate Head Start to a new agency of HEW: an Office of Child Development (OCD) to be housed in the Office of the Secretary. Moreover, OCD was endowed with "high prestige and visibility" as it became the focal point of both new initiatives in child development and for programs it acquired from the Children's Bureau. Dr. Edward Zigler, a Yale University psychologist, served as OCD's first director, a position which he held for two years. By this time, the growth of Head Start had come to an end as the number of individual projects, enrollment totals in full year programs, and federal appropriations stabilized. However, increasingly less sure of the national administration's commitment to children, Zigler tried to innovate by encouraging the idea of a credential for semi-skilled child development associates, and by varying the Head Start service delivery model. Nevertheless, OCD was, in the final analysis, degraded in the HEW hierarchy; its new responsibilities were limited to making grants to combat child abuse. According to Steiner (1976), OCD proved to have no more political influence than the old Children's Bureau.

In 1977, OCD became the Agency for Children, Youth and Families (Harmon and Hanley, 1979). Today, Head Start is administered by the Administration for Children, Youth, and Families (ACYF), a part of the Office of Human Development Services in the United States Department of Health and Human Services (USDHHS). Regional office staff are also utilized.

Grants are awarded by the USDHHS Regional Offices and the Indian and Migrant Program Division to local public agencies, private nonprofit organizations, and school systems for the purpose of operating Head Start programs at the community level. Head Start funding is provided competitively to "grantees" (the public or private nonprofit organization) to carry on all or part of the work.

Regional Offices

Within Head Start, as in most federal grant programs, field administration is decentralized into ten regional headquarter cities. Regional office responsibilities have traditionally consisted of developing and processing grants, monitoring grantee operations, and providing technical support to local grantees. In theory these regional functions are carried out within the broad policy guidelines and operational directives established in the federal office (Harmon and Hanley, 1979).

Harmon and Hanley (1979) report that when Head Start was managed by OEO, regional personnel reported to Community Action Program (CAP) regional administrators, who in turn reported to OEO regional administrators. When Head Start was moved to OCD, the position of assistant regional director (ARD) for OCD was created in each region, with the ARDs operationally responsible to the HEW regional directors while receiving program guidance from OCD. Each region has a core staff of program specialists and a team of community representatives who oversee and support the activities of local Head Start grantees.

TABLE 1
LIST OF HEAD START REGIONAL OFFICES

Region I
Administration for Children, Youth and Families
OHDS/DH & HS, Room 2000, Federal Building Government Center,
Boston, Massachusetts 02203 (617) 233-6450
(Connecticut, Maine, Massachusetts, New Hampshire, Vermont, Rhode Island)

Region II
Administration for Children, Youth and Families
OHDS/DH & HS, Room 3900, Federal Building,
26 Federal Plaza, New York, N.Y. 10007 (212) 264-2974
(New York, New Jersey, Puerto Rico, Virgin Islands)

Region III
Administration for Children, Youth and Families
OHDS/DH & HS, 3535 Market Street (P.O. Box 13716),
Philadelphia, PA 19101 (215) 596-6676
(Delaware, Washington, D.C., Maryland, Pennsylvania, Virginia, West Virginia)

Region IV
Administration for Children, Youth and Families
OHDS/DH & HS, Room, 358 Peachtree-Seventh Building,
50 7th Street, N.E. Atlanta, Georgia 30323 (404) 221-2134
(Alabama, Florida, Georgia, Kentucky, Mississippi, North Carolina, South Carolina, Tennessee)

Region V
Administration for Children, Youth and Families
OHDS/DH & HS, 13th Floor, 300 South Wacker Drive,
Chicago, Illinois 60606 (312) 353-1781
(Illinois, Indiana, Michigan, Minnesota, Ohio, Wisconsin)

Region VI
Administration for Children, Youth and Families
OHDS/DH & HS, 20th Floor, 1200 Main Tower Building,
Dallas, Texas 75202 (214) 767-2976
(Arkansas, Louisiana, New Mexico, Oklahoma, Texas)

Region VII
Administration for Children, Youth and Families
OHDS/DH & HS, Room 242, Federal Building, 601 E. 12th Street,
Kansas City, Missouri 64106 (816) 374-3282
(Iowa, Kansas, Missouri, Nebraska)

Region VIII
Administration for Children, Youth and Families
OHDS/DH & HS, Room 7417, 1961 Stout Street,
Denver, Colorado 80202 (303) 837-3106
(Colorado, Montana, North Dakota, South Dakota, Utah, Wyoming)

Region IX
Administration for Children, Youth and Families
OHDS/DH & HS, Room 143, Federal Building,
50 United Nations Plaza, San Francisco, California 94102 (415) 556-7460
(Arizona, California, Hawaii, Nevada, Pacific Trust Territories)

Region X
Administration for Children, Youth and Families
OHDS/DH & HS, Third and Broad Building, 2901 Third Avenue,
Seattle, Washington 98121 (206) 399-0482
(Alaska, Idaho, Oregon, Washington)

Grantees

Grantees--the public or private nonprofit agencies granted assistance by the federal government to carry on a Head Start program--by law have responsibility for the actual operation of Head Start programs. It is federal policy to continue to leave the responsibility for Head Start with an existing grantee so long as it remains "viable" and conforms to Head Start performance standards (Harmon and Hanley, 1979). Thus, barring major expansion of the project, there is little change on the composition of the grantee network.

Delegate Agencies

While grantees can and do operate Head Start programs directly, they often delegate some or all of the operational responsibility to other organizations. These organizations, known as "delegate agencies," are private or public nonprofit associations.

Thus, while there is a single Head Start policy, there are over 2000 locally administered Head Start programs of varying quality. Head Start remains essentially a collection of locally run, autonomous programs (Zigler, 1985).

Head Start Program Goals, Component Areas, and Performance Standards

Richmond, Stipek, and Zigler (1979: 137) have restated the seven goals of Head Start exactly as they were set forth in the recommendations of the Planning Committee in 1965. These seven goals were to:

1. Improve the child's physical health and physical abilities.

2. Help the emotional and social development of the child by encouraging self-confidence, spontaneity, curiosity, and self-discipline.

3. Improve the child's mental processes and skills, with particular attention to conceptual and verbal skills.

4. Establish patterns and expectations of success for the child that will create a climate of confidence for future learning efforts.

5. Increase the child's capacity to relate positively to family members and others, while at the same time strengthening the family's ability to relate positively to the child.

6. Develop in the child and the family a responsible attitude toward society, and encourage society to work with the poor in solving their problems.

7. Increase the sense of dignity and self- worth within the child and the family.

Richmond, Stipek, and Zigler (1979) have concluded that the most innovative idea found in these seven recommendations is that effective intervention can only be accomplished through involving parents and the community.

Current official documents about Head Start list two primary goals and premises of the program:

> "The first goal describes the premises of the project: That all children share certain needs, and that poor children, in particular, can benefit from a comprehensive, interdisciplinary developmental program to meet those needs. Moreover, the child's entire family and community must be involved in the program: The family is the principal influence on the child's development. Local communities are permitted latitude in developing creative programs if their programs are consistent with the basic goals, objectives and standards of a comprehensive program.
>
> "The second goal is to increase social competence in children of low income families. The term social competence is used to refer to the child's everyday effectiveness in dealing with both the present environment and later responsibilities on school and life. Social competence takes into account the interrelatedness of cognitive and intellectual development, physical and mental health, nutritional needs and other factors. Thus, this concept offers

a wholistic approach to child development."

The goals of Head Start are related to four component areas around which grantees devise their programs: educational services, health services, social services, and parent involvement.

It should be noted that, in the early years of Head Start, the project was reluctant to issue specific program guidelines in these component areas except in areas like parent participation and career development (policy documents in these areas were seen as necessary to force compliance by the public school delegate agencies). This reluctance, Harmon and Hanley (1979) point out, was out of respect for "local control" and the notion that the programs were accountable primarily to parents except in matters of fiscal integrity. Thus, by 1970, Head Start administrators did not have accurate data as to how many children were served or what services were actually provided at what cost or benefit.

However, as a result of criticisms fueled by the Westinghouse Report, and the development of Head Start as a large, fairly stable program that could no longer be excused for uneven performance, broad programs of management and programmatic reforms were initiated. Chief among these reforms was the development and promulgation of program standards which were carefully drawn to mandate program quality without being prescriptive in terms of program design (Harmon and Hamley, 1979). Stephan (1986) states that the regulations governing Head Start now provide detailed guidelines about program objectives, performance standards, and operation (45 CFR 1303-1304).

Grantees and delegate agencies are required to develop written plans covering the implementation of the program according to detailed performance standards. The term "Performance Standards" refers to Head Start program functions, activities, and facilities required and necessary to meet the objectives and goals of the Head Start program as they relate directly to children and their families. Grantees must meet or exceed these standards. While compliance with the performance standards is required as a condition of federal funding, and programs not in compliance may be terminated, ACYF expects that the standards will be largely self-enforcing, drawing upon the official document describing Head Start performance standards (USDHHS,1984B). The performance standards were published in the Federal Register dated June 30, 1975, Volume 40, Number 126, Part II.

If a USDHHS official discovers that a Head Start program fails to meet the performance standards, the grantee is notified of the deficiencies in writing and advised that compliance must be attained in a period not to exceed 90 days. The grantee reports in writing in detail its efforts to meet the performance standards. USDHHS officials are expected to assist grantees by furnishing or recommending technical assistance. If compliance is not attained, the grantee is notified in writing that termination proceedings will begin or that refunding may be denied. The time period for correcting certain deficiencies, such as the space per child provided, may be extended to a maximum of one year.

In the next pages, we summarize the objectives, services, and implementation strategies which Head Start requires in the areas of education, health services, nutrition, social services, and parent involvement.

Education

There are five objectives of the educational service component of the Head Start Program:

1. Provide children with a learning environment and the varied experiences which will help them develop socially, intellectually, physically, and emotionally in a manner appropriate to their age and stage of development toward the overall goal of social competence.

2. Integrate the educational aspects of the various Head Start components into the daily program of activities.

3. Involve parents in educational activities of the program to enhance their role as the principal influence on the child's education and development.

4. Assist parents to increase knowledge, understanding, skills, and experience in child growth and development.

5. Identify and reinforce experiences which occur in the home that parents can utilize as educational activities for their children.

To meet these objectives, performance standards are established in the areas of program operations and facilities.

There are seven guidelines with respect to program operations that Head Start grantees are advised that they must meet. Grantees must:

1. Specify strategies for implementing the objectives, including curriculum approaches, teaching methods and classroom activities;

2. Provide for an environment which is socially and emotionally supportive; develops intellectual skills and promotes physical growth. In this context, grantees are urged to "build ethnic pride" and to "avoid sex role stereotyping";

3. Meet the special needs of children from various populations through curriculum considerations, staffing patterns reflective of the racial and ethnic population of the children and parent involvement;

4. Continually observe, record, and evaluate each child's growth and development for the purpose of planning activities to suit individual needs;

5. Participate in staff and staff-parent conferences and make periodic (no less than two) home visits;

6. Train staff and parent in child development and the behavior problems of preschool children;

7. Train staff in identifying and working with special needs children and their parents and in coordinating relevant referral resources.

With respect to facilities, grantees are advised to:

1. Provide a physical environment conducive to learning and reflective of the different stages of development of the children, including space, light, ventilation, heat, water, and other physical arrangements consistent with the health, safety, and developmental needs of the children;

2. Provide appropriate and sufficient furniture, equipment and materials to meet the needs of the program, arranged in a manner which facilitates learning, encourages a child's self-reliance, and assures a balance of structured and spontaneous activities.

Evidence that a Head Start center meets or exceeds state or local licensing requirements for similar kinds of facilities for fire, health, and safety are accepted as prima facie compliance with the requirements of item one.

Health Services

There are three general objectives for health services:

1. Provide a comprehensive health services program which includes a broad range of medical, dental, mental health and nutrition services to preschool children, including handicapped children, to assist the child's physical, emotional, cognitive, and social development toward the overall goal of social competence.

2. Promote preventive health services and early intervention.

3. Provide the child's family with the necessary skills and insight and otherwise attempt to link the family to an ongoing health care system to ensure that the child continues to receive comprehensive health care even after leaving the Head Start program.

To comply with the performance standards related to these objectives, grantees must:

1. Establish a Health Services Advisory Committee to assist with the planning, operation, and evaluation of this component. The committee should meet at least twice each year; must have Head Start parents, and community health services providers as members; and should include representation of the medical, dental, mental health, and nutrition professionals.

2. Assure that for each child enrolled in the Head Start program, a complete mental, dental and developmental history is obtained and recorded; a thorough *health screening* is given; and medical and dental examinations will be performed. The health screenings must include assessment of immunization status, growth assessment, vision testing, hearing testing, hemoglobin or hematocrit determination, tuberculin testing, a urinalysis and other tests such as sickle cell anemia, lead poisoning, and intestinal parasites may be appropriate. Head Start personnel are also advised to note speech problems and identify the special needs of handicapped children.

3. Provide for medical and dental treatment and follow-up services.

4. Handle the child's medical and dental records, insuring that they are established, forwarded when the child leaves the program, provided to parents.

5. Provide for an organized health education program for staff, parents, and children.

6. Meet mental health objectives such as providing services to children with special needs; providing for prevention, early identification, and early intervention.

7. Provide mental health services including the provision of a mental health professional, at least on a consultation basis, as well as using other community resources.

Nutrition

There are five objectives related to nutrition, which are part of the health services component:

1. Provide food which will help meet the child's daily nutritional needs in the child's home or in another clean and pleasant environment, recognizing individual differences and cultural patterns, and thereby promote sound physical, social, and emotional growth and development;

2. Provide an environment for nutritional services which will support and promote the use of the feeding situation as an opportunity for learning;

3. Help the staff, child, and family to understand: The relationship of nutrition to health, factors which influence food practices, and a variety of ways to provide for nutritional needs. Help the family to apply this knowledge in the development of sound food habits even after leaving the Head Start program;

4. Demonstrate the interrelationships of nutrition to other activities of the Head Start program and its contribution to the overall child development goals; and

5. Involve all staff, parents, and other community agencies as appropriate in meeting the child's nutritional needs so that nutritional care provided by Head Start complements and supplements that of the home and community.

The performance standards related to nutrition advise that Head Start programs:

1. Identify nutritional needs and problems of Head Start children and families;

2. Assist children in meeting their daily nutritional needs (for part-day children, at least one-third of the needs should

be met; for full-day children, one-half to two-thirds of the needs should be met);

3. Ensure that the nutrition services contribute to the development and socialization of the children in ways such as offering a variety of foods, providing family style service, and not using food as a punishment or reward;

4. Organize a nutrition education program for staff, parents, and children;

5. Involve parents and appropriate community agencies in planning, implementing, and evaluating the nutrition services;

6. Ensure that the programs of their vendors and caterers comply with applicable local, state, and federal sanitation laws and regulations for food service operations;

7. Provide for the direction of the nutrition services by a qualified full-time staff nutritionist or for periodic and regularly scheduled supervision by a qualified nutritionist or dietician as defined in the Head Start Guidance material. All nutrition services staff must receive preservice and inservice training as necessary to demonstrate and maintain proficiency in menu planning, food purchasing, food preparation, storage, sanitation, and personal hygiene;

8. Establish and maintain records covering the nutrition services budget, expenditures, menu uses, numbers and types of menus served with separate recordings for children and adults, inspection reports, recipes and other information deemed necessary for efficient operation.

Social Services

Five objectives guide the social services component of the performance standards plan:

1. Establish and maintain an outreach and recruitment process which systematically incurs enrollment of eligible children;

2. Provide enrollment of eligible children regardless of race, sex, creed, color, national origin, or handicapping condition;

3. Achieve parent participation in the center and home program and related activities;

4. Assist the family in its own efforts to improve the condition and quality of family life;

5. Make parents aware of community services and resources and facilitate their use.

The performance standards require that the social services plan:

1. Provide procedures for: the recruitment of children taking into account the demographic composition of the community and child/family needs; the recruitment of handicapped children; providing or referring for appropriate counseling or crisis intervention, advocacy, family contracts, and identifying and meeting the social service needs of families;

2. Close cooperation with existing community resources;

3. Provide for the establishment, maintenance, and confidentiality of records on children and their families.

Parent Involvement

The parent involvement objectives are as follows:

1. Provide a planned program of experience and activities which support and enhance the parental role as the principal influence in their child's education and development;

2. Provide a program that recognizes the parent as:

A. Responsible guardians of their children's well-being.

B. Prime educators of their children.

C. Contributors to the Head Start program to their communities.

3. Provide the following kinds of opportunities for parent participation:

A. Direct involvement in decision making in the program planning and operations.

B. Participation in classroom and other program activities as paid employees, volunteers or observers.

C. Activities for parents which they have helped to develop.

D. Working with their own children in cooperation with Head Start staff.

The parent involvement plan should address four areas: parent participation; the development of parenting skills; communications among program management, program staff, and parents; and communications among parents, area residents, and the program. These areas are specified as follows:

1. Assure the voluntary participation of parents in accordance with the Head Start Policy Manual, Instruction 1-31, Section B2, The Parents (ACYF Transmittal Notice 70.2 dated August 10, 1970). This part of the Policy Manual also appears in the Federal Register, Volume 40, Number 126, on Monday, June 30, 1975. The parent policy contains:

A. An introduction which highlights the belief that the gains made by the child in Head Start must be understood and built upon by the family and the community;

B. An outline of at least four major kinds of parent participation.

1). Participation in the decision-making process about the nature and operation of the program through the creation of Head Start policy groups as the formal structure for parent participation.

2). Participation as paid employees, volunteers or observers.

3). Activities for the parents which they have helped to develop.

4). Working with their children in cooperation with the staff of the center.

2. Provide methods and opportunities for involving parents in experiences and activities which enhance the development of their skills, self-confidence, sense of independence, their role as the primary influence in their children's lives, their roles as educators of their children, their ability to identify and use community resources, their opportunities for self-enrichment and employment, and their understanding of health, mental health, dental, and nutritional needs.

3. Ensure effective two-way communication between staff and parents on a regular basis throughout the program year.

4. Establish effective procedures by which parents and area residents can influence the character of programs affecting their interests.

Program Options

According to Steiner (1976), Head Start achieved its instant and continuing popularity by focusing essentially on one "model" of service: organized preschool centers. This exclusive focus was adopted as a matter of administrative policy, not of statute. Indeed, Head Start centers were so popular in both public and Congressional circles that it became virtually impossible either by statutory authorization or administrative action to implement alternative models. A traditional classroom-based program in which educational activities were enriched by other services was vigorously promulgated. Alternative forms of delivering services to children, such as in-home services, parent education, and prenatal care, were viewed as attempts to undercut the "model" (Harmon and Hanley, 1979).

Yet, by the period of 1968 to 1972, Head Start had lost its innovative character and had evolved into a fairly rigid delivery system committed to a single, classroom-based design--whether or not that design was most appropriate for a particular child or community. Partly as a response to criticisms of the project resulting from the Westinghouse Report, program options were initiated as part of Head Start's "improvement and innovation" efforts (Harmon and Hanley, 1979).

Beginning in April 1973, Head Start programs were permitted to consider several program models in addition to the standard Head Start model. Grantees were encouraged to select the program option best suited to the needs of the children served and the capabilities and resources of the program staff (USDHHS, 1984B). OCD stated that it could support any option or design provided that the community could demonstrate that it would result in a quality child development program at reasonable cost and meet Head Start guidelines.

Five program options were identified: the Standard Head Start Model; variations in center attendance; double sessions; home-based models; and locally designed variations.

The *Standard Head Start Model* was defined as a continuation of the present five-day per week, center-based classroom format. In 1973, grantees were advised to carefully assess their needs and capabilities to determine whether another program option might be more effective.

In the *variations in center attendance* option, Head Start programs may elect to serve some or all children on a less than five-day per week basis. All children who attend Head Start on a partial basis must receive the same comprehensive developmental services as full-day children. It was suggested that shortened hours in the classroom may be supplemented by a parent education program or another option which would assist parents in developing their role as educators of their own children. Examples of variations in attendance plans are split session schedules (two regularly enrolled groups each meeting two days per week with the fifth day set aside for activities such as inservice training or home visits), or the four-day week schedule with the fifth day used for special activities.

The *double sessions* option, it was cautioned, could not be required or permitted solely as a cost-saving device. In this option, different children are scheduled to attend morning or afternoon sessions. Provisions must be made to ensure high quality instruction, food, and individualization in both sessions.

Today, the average Head Start program provides services 34 weeks per year. Most Head Start programs (82 percent) are half-day, 10 percent are full-day, and eight percent are a combination of full- and half- day (Stephan, 1986).

Home-based models focus on the parent as the primary factor in the child's development and the home as the central facility. These programs must meet several conditions including the provision of comprehensive services, a curriculum and the requisite materials for each child, a parent program, weekend and evening services when needed, career development opportunities for staff, a service delivery system, a staff selection program in accord with the responsibilities, staff development, and opportunities for using volunteers.

In addition to the above four models, local programs could elect to design and propose an option which they felt was appropriate for their children and communities. These *locally designed options* must be derived from an analysis of the standard model, be consistent with good child development practice, be comprehensive, and be consistent with all performance standards.

Head Start Improvements and Innovations

Harmon and Hanley (1979) explain that program options were part of an overall Head Start Improvement and Innovation effort. Other innovations which were devised at that time were:

1. The performance standards.

2. Mandated self-assessment by local grantees as an integral part of the Head Start refunding cycle. In this way, OCD sought to create at the local level an impetus for improvement and innovation.

3. The creation of a program development and innovation staff at the national level. A primary focus was the integration of program components.

4. The conversion from summer to full-year programs.

5. Development and dissemination of program options.

6. Launching of the Child Development Associate (CDA) staff training program.

7. An enhanced emphasis on parent involvement (Harmon and Hanley, 1979; Collins and Deloria, 1983).

Despite marked improvement in performance in relation to minimum program standards, Harmon and Hanley (1979) conclude that neither local agencies nor OCD/ACYF regional staffs have fully exploited the opportunity to innovate. Moreover, while the Head Start goals and performance standards combine to form a single Head Start policy, there are over 2000 locally administered Head Start programs of varying quality (Zigler, 1985). The continuing variability in Head Start has its costs in terms of quality control.

Partly as a result of these improvements and innovations, Collins and Deloria (1983) assert that Head Start has grown more effective over the years. Research indicates that the impact of Head Start on children's intellectual development was roughly twice as great after 1970 as in 1969 and corresponds to the period in which several important improvements were introduced into Head Start. It is clear that effective program strategies can upgrade program quality.

Special Projects

In addition to program options, the new program development and innovation staff launched a series of national demonstrations to test and promulgate alternative designs. These special projects included Home Start, the Child and Family Resource Program, and Project Developmental Continuity (Harmon and Hanley, 1979; Valentine, 1979; Richmond, Stipek, and Zigler, 1979). Descriptions of some of these special projects are as follows:

1. *Parent and Child Centers* were launched in 1967 as a preventive program for children under the age of three (Work, 1972; Hamilton, M., 1972).

2. In 1970, three Parent and Child Centers became *Parent and Child Development Centers* (PCDC's) to develop and test models of parent-infant intervention.

3. *Home Start,* for children aged three to five, was funded from 1972 to 1975 (Deloria et al., 1974). Home Start provided Head Start services to children and families in their homes.

4. The *Child and Family Resource Program* was targeted to children and families from the prenatal period through age eight. A family advocate worked with each family to provide or make available prenatal care, developmental programs, pediatric care, programs to facilitate a smooth transition from preschool to

elementary school, and general supportive services (Child and Family Resource Program, 1973, 1975).

5. *Project Developmental Continuity* began in 1974 to offer Head Start related services to children throughout the first three years of primary school (Project Developmental Continuity (PDC), 1974, 1975, 1977). Special emphasis was placed on maintaining parent involvement and on the needs of handicapped and bilingual children.

6. *Health Start* which operated from 1971 to 1974, provided Head Start-like health services to children under the age of six who were not being screened through any other program (Vogt and Wholey, 1972; Vogt et al., 1973A, 1973B).

7. *Project Follow Through*, established in 1967 for school-aged children, was designed to continue and build on the cognitive and social gains made by children in Head Start or similar preschool programs (Abelson et al., 1974).

8. The *Child Development Associate* Credential and Training Program was initiated in 1972 to help child care workers achieve professional status (Trickett, 1979).

9. *Education for Parenthood* teaches Head Start parents and high school students about early childhood and human development through direct field experience in Head Start centers (Muenchow and Shays, 1980).

10. *Head Start collaboration with the Medicaid* Early and Periodic Screening, Diagnosis and Treatment Program (1974 to 1976) sought to make health services available to Medicaid eligible children.

CHAPTER 3

THE CURRENT STATUS OF PROJECT HEAD START: PROGRAMS, BUDGETS, AND THE CHILDREN SERVED

Today, Project Head Start is both broad in scope and services. In this chapter, we briefly review the number of programs, budgets, enrollments, the ages of the children served, the economic status of the children served, racial composition, multicultural services, and services to handicapped children. The statistics presented in this section are quotations from the annual "Project Head Start Statistical Fact Sheet" prepared by ACYF (USDHHS, 1985C and 1987).

Number of Programs

For fiscal year (FY) 1986, there were 1,305 Head Start programs, including 36 Parent and Child Centers, 106 Indian, and 24 migrant programs. About 39 percent of the sites are urban, 31 percent are rural, and 30 percent are an urban/rural combination.

There are 24,120 Head Start classrooms. These classrooms are supported by 79,968 paid staff and 666,800 volunteers (USDHHS, 1987).

Budgets

The FY 1986 budget was $1,075,059,000. Of that amount $1,046,959,000 was distributed among local Head Start projects. About $26,800,000 was used for training and technical assistance. The remaining funds, $1,300,000, were allocated for research, demonstration, and evaluation programs.

The estimated average cost to serve each Head Start child during 1986 was $2,339.00. For 1987, the projected average cost per child is $2,445.00.

Stephan (1986) reports that in March 1984, the Office of the Inspector General (IG), Department of Health and Human Services, Region X, issued a report on enrollment and attendance issues within Head Start. The IG report found that Head Start agencies averaged 97 percent enrollment (of program capacity) and 82 percent average daily attendance; in over half of all the months sampled, programs were underenrolled and underattended. The IG projected that if the 100 percent enrollment and 85 percent average daily attendance requirements for Head Start were met, 13,500 more children could be enrolled under current funding (about a three percent increase) (see USDHHS, 1984A).

Overall Enrollments

The total enrollment for Head Start in Fiscal Year (FY) 1986 was 451,732. As indicated in Table 2, Head Start enrollment between 1965-1969 was above 500,000 children. Enrollment levels dropped below 400,000 children between 1970-1982. Since 1982, enrollments have increased to levels above 400,000 children.

In 1965, the pilot year, Head Start was a summer program only. From 1966-1981, children were enrolled both full- and part-time. Since 1982, only full year services have been provided. Overall, a total of 10,048,800 children have been served by the programs since it began in 1965.

TABLE 2
ENROLLMENTS AND CONGRESSIONAL APPROPRIATIONS FOR PROJECT HEAD START 1965 to 1987

Fiscal Year	*Enrollment*	*Congressional Appropriation*
1965 (Summer only)	561,000	$ 9 6.4M
1966	733,000	198.9M
1967	681,400	349.2M
1968	693,900	316.2M
1969	663,600	333.9M
1970	477,400	325.7M
1971	397,500	360.0M
1972	379,000	376.3M
1973	379,000	400.7M
1974	352,800	403.9M
1975	349,000	403.9M
1976	349,000	441.0M
1977	333,000	475.0M
1978	391,400	625.0M
1979	387,500	680.0M
1980	376,300	735.0M
1981	387,300	818.7M
1982	395,800	911.7M
1983	414,950	912.0M
1984	442,140	995.75M
1985	452,080	1,075,059,000
1986	451,732	1,040,315,000*
1987 (projected)	451,732	1,130,542,000

*Post Gramm-Rudman

Source: USDHHS. *Project Head Start Statistical Fact Sheet.* Washington, D.C.: ACYF, 1985C and 1987

Ages of the Children Served

For FY 1987, the ages of the children served were reported as follows:

5 year-olds and older..........	13 percent
4 year-olds......................	59 percent
3 year-olds......................	26 percent
under 3 years of age...........	2 percent

Economic Status of the Children Served

While Head Start primarily serves children with incomes below the poverty line, some nonpoor children are served. According to Richmond, Stipek, and Zigler (1979) the project's planning committee agreed that economic segregation was not desirable and that Head Start should provide opportunities for children from different income groups to learn from each other. Since 1965, Head Start has provided that up to ten percent of the children served could be drawn from above the poverty line. However, because of funding limitations, many local programs have found it difficult to meet the needs of the poor and at the same time promote economic integration.

Further, the most needy children appear to benefit most from Project Head Start (the most needy are defined as children from families whose mother had a 10th grade education or less, children of single- parent families and children with low cognitive scores when they entered Head Start). An exception to this pattern is that children from small families gained more than children from large families (Collins and Deloria, 1983).

Racial Composition

Since about 90 percent of Head Start families are below the poverty line, it is not surprising that Head Start serves a large number of minority children. While some surveys suggest higher minority enrollment figures (Royster et al., 1978) it is generally accepted that 42 percent of all Head Start children are black; 33 percent, white; 20 percent, Hispanic; 4 percent, American Indian; and one percent Asian. In addition, 3 percent are from migrant farmworker families. Thus, minority children comprise at least two-thirds of Head Start's enrollment.

Royster and his colleagues (1978) observed that the participation of minorities, especially blacks and Hispanics, is twice as high as their proportion of the poverty population, while the percentage of white children is approximately half their proportion in the poverty population. These rates of participation illustrate that social policy has served the children and families of the ethnic and racial groups that are overrepresented among the poor (Laosa, 1985).

For FY 1986, the racial composition of the children was reported as follows:

American Indian..................	4 percent
Hispanic..............................	21 percent
Black..................................	40 percent
White..................................	32 percent
Asian..................................	3 percent

There appears to be small (one to two percent) decreases in the proportions of black and white children and small increases if Hispanic and Asian children (see Slaughter, 1982; USDHHS, 1985C).

Research indicates that minority children generally demonstrate impressive gains in Head Start, although, according to Collins and Deloria (1983), this was not equally true in all Head Start program settings. Intermediate cognitive gains were greater for Head Start children "in classes with less than half or more than 90 percent minority enrollment" (CSR, 1985, p.9). Critics note that the "less than half" claim is based on only two experimental studies (Schweinhart and Weikart, 1986).

Multicultural Services

As indicated previously, there are 106 Indian Head Start programs and 24 migrant programs. About 68 percent of the children served are ethnic minority children. Appropriately, Head Start offers a number of multicultural services.

For example, the children of migrant workers have been of special concern to Head Start (Valentine, 1979). Since 1969, Head Start has established programs for migrant children, with their most important aspect being flexibility of programming. Migrant Head Start programs operate for very long hours, sometimes from 4:00 a.m. to midnight, and open enrollment to infants and toddlers as well as the four- and five-year-olds. Valentine further states that Head Start programs for migrants have reached only two percent of these young children. Health, education, and nutrition specialists follow children as their parents follow the crops.

Although these programs perform an important and useful function, Head Start migrant programs have not really expanded much since 1974. Further, migrant children experience greater difficulties than other Head Start children in being immunized and gaining access to other health services such as dental care (Collins and Deloria, 1983).

Given that Hispanic children now comprise about 21 percent of all Head Start children, special efforts are also made to meet their special developmental and cultural needs. Projects have been funded to develop curricula providing instruction in two languages for Spanish-speaking children and to establish resource centers providing technical assistance to Head Start grantees with programs for Spanish-speaking children and families (Richmond, Stipek, and Zigler, 1979).

TABLE 3

INFORMATION SOURCES FOR HEAD START AMERICAN INDIAN AND MIGRANT PROGRAMS

American Indian Programs

Head Start Bureau, ACYF
Department of Health and Human Services
P.O. Box 1182
Washington, D.C. 20013
(202) 755-7715

Migrant Programs

Head Start Bureau, ACYF
Department of Health and Human Services
P.O. Box 1182
Washington, D.C. 20013
(202) 755-8065

Handicapped Children

According to *The Status of Handicapped Children in Head Start Programs* (1980), Head Start is the largest program that includes sizeable number of preschool handicapped children on a systematic basis. In 1972 Congress mandated that at least 10 percent of Head Start's national enrollment consisted of handicapped children (on a statewide basis as of 1974). Handicapped children accounted for 61,898 children or 12.2 percent of all children enrolled in full-year Head Start programs in FY 1985. This number included dropouts and late enrollees. In 1985 to 1986, handicapped children were 12.7 percent of Head Start enrollment.

Valentine (1979) lists two objectives of the legislative mandate: to provide necessary services for individual handicapped children in a mainstreamed environment and to coordinate services with other agencies serving handicapped children. In Head Start, an interdisciplinary diagnostic team designs an individualized program plan for each child. Most programs provide preservice and inservice training for staff working with handicapped children but reported that further training was still needed. Handicapped children in Head Start have a range of disabilities including mental retardation, health impairments, visual handicaps, hearing impairments, emotional disturbance, speech and language impairments, orthopedic handicaps, and learning disabilities. Although Head Start is serving a number of severely and profoundly handicapped children, the majority are classified as mildly to moderately handicapped (Collins and Deloria, 1983).

The specific types of handicaps are listed in *The Status of Handicapped Children in Head Start Programs* (1980) as follows:

Speech impairment	53.2 percent
Chronic illness	12.4 percent
Serious emotional disturbances	7.3 percent
Orthopedic disabilities	7.0 percent
Mental retardation	6.6 percent
Specific learning disabilities	5.6 percent
Hearing impairments	4.0 percent
Visual handicaps	3.2 percent

Many Head Start children have multiple handicaps.

Head Start has been shown to improve the cognitive skills of children with certain kinds of handicaps (Collins and Deloria, 1983). Children diagnosed as speech-impaired outperformed their peers who were not in Head Start or other preschool programs. Children with learning disabilities or emotional disturbances also performed better on some measures of intellectual achievement. Head Start did not appear to have a measurable effect on the cognitive development of mentally retarded or physically handicapped children. Overall, however, Head Start services to the handicapped compare favorably to those of non-Head Start programs even though the latter tend to have larger per pupil expenditures.

PART B:

A REVIEW OF PROGRAM EFFECTIVENESS

CHAPTER 4

ECONOMIC SELF-SUFFICIENCY AND HEAD START FAMILIES: AN ORIGINAL RATIONALE FOR PROJECT HEAD START

Any attempt to evaluate Head Starts' effectiveness must begin with an understanding of its theoretical and philosophical foundation. This chapter examines the initial premises which guided the development of the program and the major criticisms of the resulting approach in an effort to formulate more effective strategies and recommendations for future directions of Project Head Start.

Gil Steiner (1976), one of our nation's foremost analysts of social policies, suggested that Project Head Start was initiated as a result of a number of factors which included:

1. The belief that the child could serve as a mechanism for mobilizing community participation and hence bring about social change;

2. Publication and popular acceptance of scholarly findings on the formativeness of early childhood, and the importance of learning experiences early in life; and

3. The view that child care programs which serve the children of the poor are public investments in human development which can help maximize human potential.

With these factors providing the theoretical and political foundation, Project Head Start was conceived as a large scale social action experiment which could interrupt the sequence of poor parenting which leads to children with social and intellectual deficits which in turn leads to poor school performance, joblessness, and poverty leading again to high risk births, inappropriate parenting and a continuation of what has been termed the poverty cycle (Zigler and Valentine, 1979).

On the one hand, there was little difficulty in convincing the public that child care programs could contribute to the development of human potential. On the other hand, the premise that preschool intervention would lead to the elimination of poverty was viewed as an overly simplified solution to a very complex problem. The ambiguity with respect to the rationale assumed added significance when it became necessary to assess the impact of the intervention in relation to the stated objectives of Head Start (see Chapter 6). As the debate over the objectives of Head Start continues, the questions of the validity of the conceptualization and operationalization of Head Start as an antidote for poverty remains to be answered (see Chapter 4).

While the concept of a comprehensive early childhood program has been favorably received, Project Head Start has been fraught with criticisms which stem from:

1. Its focus on the culture-of-poverty theory and deficit approach to impoverished people;

2. Its adherence to the concept of transgenerational poverty;

3. Its assumption that education and enrichment would lead to economic mobility;

4. The use of culturally biased and inadequate assessment techniques; and

5. The feasibility of accomplishing the objective of upward mobility of the entire family through the program components of Project Head Start.

After examining each of these concerns, we will review the effectiveness of the parent involvement program in increasing economic mobility. Suggestions for enhancing the effectiveness of the goal of economic mobility are offered.

Culture of Poverty

Schiller (1980) presents two perspectives with respect to the causes of poverty which he termed the "flawed character" view and the "restricted opportunity" view. The "restricted opportunity" view holds that the poor fail to achieve due to the limited access and other barriers which are usually manifested in the form of racial and sexual discrimination, particularly in the job market. On the other hand, the "flawed character" view suggests that ample opportunities are available to the poor; however, they do not take advantage of these opportunities due to disorganized behavior which is exhibited through strong feelings of fatalism and belief in chance, strong present-time orientation, inability to delay gratification, feelings of inferiority, acceptance of aggression and illegitimacy, and authoritarianism. The "flawed character" view is the basic tenet of the culture of poverty and the more recent "underclass" theories.

On the assumption that the culture of poverty or flawed character was the major cause of poverty in America, Project Head Start and other poverty programs were designed to correct the problems of the deficient environment of the child through enrichment. Head Start, like other programs, assumed that the life-style of the poor was complex and defined by characteristics of dependency, illegitimacy, instability, psychological deficits, and behavioral deviance (Miller, 1965). As a result of this family disorganization, the poor child was said to be deprived not only of health and nutritional care but of adequate parental attention. Lower-class mothers were said to spend less time interacting with the child and to provide less verbal stimulation. Children from these homes were also said to receive less positive and more negative reinforcement (Bee, Van Egeren, and Steissguth, 1969), few situations for learning in the home (Dave, 1963), earlier relaxation of close parental supervision, and less sensory stimulation (Hunt, 1968).

More recently Auletta's (1982) widely discussed book, *The Underclass*, suggests "that whether it is a cause of an effect of poverty and unemployment, the underclass often exhibits abnormal behavior -- hostility, poor work habits, passivity, low self- confidence, alcoholism, and drug addiction." And moreover, this underclass, though it represents a minority -- not a majority -- of the poor, threatens to become permanent.

Criticisms of the Culture of Poverty

The culture of poverty arguments and the deficit model have been opposed by many scholars during the past two decades. On a conceptual level, Oscar Lewis (1968) suggested that although there was a culture of poverty, it was the result, not the cause, of the poor's response and adaptation to their lack of resources. Rainwater (1970) argues that the poor have similar beliefs to other Americans about what *ought* to determine success in life, but lack the means and resources to actualize their beliefs.

Similarly, Vernon Allen (1970A and 1970B) asserts that behavior cannot be equated with values; just because some poor people behave a certain way does not mean they desire to do so, or do so because of their beliefs or values. Allen further asserts that most of the studies on poverty are not useful because values are generally inferred from behaviors and are also used to explain the same behavior.

From a methodological perspective most of the criticisms of "culture of poverty" research are aimed at either the methodology used or the interpretation of the data. Many studies are correlational, making it improper to infer cause and effect. For example, though the black child may not perform well in school, it has not been demonstrated whether the "fault" lies in the child or in the school (Baratz, 1968). There is also an absence of longitudinal experimental studies that identify the critical variables and follow their effects over a period of time.

Another methodological flaw deals with sample selection. Auletta (1982) included in his study subjects selected for participation based on such behaviors as having criminal records, drug addiction, and long-term welfare dependence. These same factors were later used in his description of the characteristics of the underclass.

Studies on the "culture of poverty" have also relied on maternal antecedent behaviors (measured by verbal reports from mothers) and child consequent behaviors (measured from mothers' reports of children's behavior at home, and ratings made of children's behavior in school) (Yarrow, Campbell, and Burton, 1968). In their extensive methodologic critique of such research, Yarrow and her colleagues suggest that the validity of this reliance on interview responses must be determined by the correspondence between interview responses and observed behavior. When such validation attempts have been made for the same population, results often have shown quite low correlations (Radke-Yarrow, 1963).

Another limitation of "culture of poverty" research is the implication that children have little or no effect on their socializing environment. As Yarrow et al. (1968) state, "The view that the child's behavior results from maternal causes is so commonly held that it firmly fixes the interpretation of interview data in such directional terms."

Further criticism of the deficit model is leveled against the sensory deprivation hypothesis by Baratz and Baratz (1970). Research on the ghetto environment has revealed that it is far from a vacuum; in fact, there was so much sensory stimulation (at least in the eyes and ears of the middle-class researcher) that a contrary thesis was necessarily espoused; that theory argues that the ghetto sensory stimulation is not as "distinctive" for the lower-class child as it is for the middle-class child (Rosser and Oyemade, 1980).

On the matter of maternal interaction with the child, Baratz and Baratz (1970) point out that despite the fact that no study has ever indicated the minimal amount of stimulation necessary for the child to learn language, and despite the fact that the child has in fact developed language, the "ghetto mother" is still accused of causing language retardation in her infant. Of course, it is interesting to note here that except for those environments where social and sensory deprivations are extremely severe or totally absent, a condition certainly not characteristic of the black ghetto environment, there is no evidence to suggest that the black child is cognitively impaired by the level or quality of the maternal interaction. Also, there is no real evidence to support the theory that reading to the child and the number of books in the home are essential for learning to read.

Martha Hill and her colleagues (1983) further suggest that evidence which explicitly link attitudes of the parents to employment status of the child is sketchy. In a recent study of 1255 families over a 14-year span on the relationship between motivational orientation and economic outcomes, a consistent effect of only one motivational component was found: Black female household heads with a greater orientation toward challenge had higher earnings growth. Other variables such as future orientation, generalized expectancy, fear of failure, and need for achievement yielded no significant correlations.

Nevertheless, as a result of the deficit philosophy which was used as a rationale for the massive intervention effort, the subsequent programs of Project Head Start tended to reflect a deficit orientation. Intervention strategies were based on a middle-class model which tended to try to change the behavior of poor children to parallel the middle- class norms. While the Head Start program was aimed more at cognitive deficits, child spin-off programs such as Home Start attempted to modify the home environment in order to make it similar to the middle- class environment. Since the list of the founders of the Head Start Program included only a very few minorities (see Table 4), it is hardly surprising that the curricula, though well-intended, reflected the experiences with which they were familiar.

The criticisms of the culture of poverty outlined here emerged after most intervention programs had been developed. These criticisms rapidly discredited that theoretical orientation. However, as evidence of the latent harboring of the concept, similar ideas are now reported in discussions of welfare dependence and a new term has been introduced, the "underclass."

TABLE 4

PLANNING COMMITTEE FOR PROJECT HEAD START

Dr. Robert F. Cooke, Committee Chairman
Chairman of the Department of Pediatrics,
The Johns Hopkins University School of
Medicine, Baltimore, Maryland

Dr. George Brain
Washington State University

Dr. Urie Bronfenbrenner
Cornell University

Dr. Mamie Phipps Clark
Northside Center for
Child Development
in New York City

Dr. Edward Perry Crump
Meharry Medical College

Dr. Edward Davens
Maryland State Department
of Health

Dr. Mitchell Ginsberg
Columbia University

Dr. James Hymes, Jr.
University of Maryland at College Park

Sister Jacqueline
Webster College in St. Louis

Mrs. Mary King Kneedler
Associate Professior of Nursing
Western Carolina College
Cullowhee, North Carolina

Dr. Reginald Lourie
Children's Hospital
Washington, D.C.

Dr. John Neimeyer, President
Bank Street College of Education

Dr. Myron Wegman
University of Michigan at
Ann Arbor

Dr. Edward Zigler
Yale University

Intergenerational Poverty

Another major tenet of the War on Poverty was the view that poverty and welfare dependence are transmitted intergenerationally, largely as a result of deficient values inculcated in children which inhibit income mobility. Macauley (1977) maintains that welfare dependency is transmitted from one generation to the next since such traits as autonomy, independence, ambition, and coping are not reinforced in families that are on welfare and children are, therefore, less likely to exhibit these characteristics. In much stronger terms, Blanche Bernstein (1982) and Charles Murray (1984) argue that welfare has fostered dependency instead of reducing it, has encouraged the breakup of families, has weakened the sense of family responsibility, has led to a rejection of the work ethic, and has caused children raised in welfare-dependent homes to become dependent, lack a work ethic, not take responsibility for their own children, and engage in antisocial behavior.

The validity of the welfare dependency theory has been seriously challenged due to a lack of empirical evidence to support this view. There are few longitudinal studies which document the relationship between welfare status as a child and welfare status as adults. Maxwell (1985), however, suggests that black children born in poverty stayed in poverty for an average of ten years.

With respect to the effects of parent's attitudes on children's economic status as adults, Rosser and Oyemade (1980) point out that there is little evidence on the links between parental attitudes and subsequent achievement of the child. This is supported by Martha Hill and Michael Ponza (1983) who found that "Parental attitudes and values had little effect on children's later economic outcomes and welfare dependence."

Similarly, Frank Levy (1980), estimated the incidence of intergenerational poverty based on his analysis of the University of Michigan Survey Research Center study of about 5,000 families. Levy asserted that three out of ten poor adults and most new households formed by poor children -- about four out of five -- had incomes well above the poverty line.

Moreover, recent studies by Hill and Ponza (1983) suggest that impoverished families do in fact exhibit a substantial amount of income mobility. A majority (57 percent) of young adults from poor homes were not impoverished themselves after leaving home. Nor were these individuals clustered at the poverty line. It is, therefore, suggested that although children of the poor are at a greater risk of being poor as young adults, there is substantial upward mobility among these young adults from poor families. In a further analysis of the data, Hill and Ponza also found that long-term welfare dependency as a child does not cause long-term dependency as an adult, at least among blacks.

While the results of these studies do not support the theory of welfare dependency, it should be noted that the populations studied do not necessarily represent the current generation of welfare recipients. It is highly possible that certain factors such as the increase in teenage pregnancies and other social developments in our society (drug abuse, decline in education, and unemployment) may result in quite different behavioral patterns for the current generation.

Education As a Vehicle for Upward Mobility

In what was hailed as a major critique of intervention programs such as Head Start, Christopher Jencks and his co-authors of the highly controversial book *Inequality: Reassessment of the Effect of Family and Schooling in America* (1972), questioned the assumptions on which the War on Poverty were based. The fallacious assumptions cited (p.7) included:

> 1. Eliminating poverty is largely a matter of helping children born into poverty to rise out of it. Once families escape from poverty, they do not fall back into it. Middle-class children rarely end up poor.
>
> 2. The primary reason poor children do not escape from poverty is that they do not acquire basic cognitive skills. They cannot read, write, calculate, or articulate. Lacking these skills, they cannot get or keep a well-paid job.

> 3. The best mechanism for breaking this vicious circle is educational reform. Since children born into poor homes do not acquire the skills they need from their parents, they must be taught these skills in school. This can be done by making sure that they attend the same schools as middle-class children, by giving them extra compensatory programs in school, by giving their parents a voice in running their school, or by some combination of all three approaches.

They further assert that each of these assumptions is erroneous (p.7).

> 1. Poverty is not primarily hereditary. While children born into poverty have a higher than average chance of ending up poor, there is still an enormous amount of economic mobility from one generation to the next. Indeed, there is nearly as much economic inequality among brothers raised in the same homes as in the general population. This means that inequality is recreated anew in each generation, even among people who start life in essentially identical circumstances. (This view represents another challenge to the "intergenerational poverty" hypothesis previously discussed.)
>
> 2. The primary reason that some people end up richer than others is not that they have more adequate cognitive skills. While children who read well get the right answers to arithmetic problems, articulate their thoughts clearly, and are somewhat more likely than others to get ahead, there are many other equally important factors involved. Thus, there is almost as much economic inequality among those who score high on standardized tests as in the general population. Equalizing everyone's reading scores would not appreciably reduce the number of economic failures.
>
> 3. There is no evidence that school reform can substantially reduce the extent of cognitive inequality as measured by tests of verbal fluency, reading comprehension, or mathematical skills. Neither school resources nor segregation has an appreciable effect on either test scores or educational attainments.

Jencks and his colleagues grounded these assertions on data on the effects of schooling on the economic achievements of the child. In doing so, they are rather convincing in the argument that the *total* variation in incomes cannot be substantially reduced by improving education. However, they were less clear about whether *anything* could be done through education to improve the relative position of children who are now poor (Rivlin, 1973).

Thus, critics (Rivlin, 1973) of the Jencks' view acknowledge that it may be more efficient to reduce poverty by increasing the earnings or incomes of low income people directly, rather than to embark on the long, risky, and problematic process of raising the future income of poor children through school reform. However, critics also argue that education and development programs such as Head Start may be more feasible politically than direct income redistribution. Moreover, the side effects of education reform, such as altering the power alignment in a city by giving poor parents a voice in the schools, may be more valuable.

Inadequate Measures of Effectiveness

Since the premise on which Head Start was founded was based on the cultural-deficit model, initial attempts to assess the impact of the intervention on the development of the child reflected the same bias and suffered from similar problems. One goal of Head Start was to modify children's intellectual performance so that they would perform according to the middle-class norms. Thus, outcome measures were based on these middle-class norms and were, therefore, biased against the population being tested. It was impractical and also unrealistic to expect that Head Start could have such a dramatic impact after one or more years in an essentially part-time program. Measurement issues in Head Start are detailed in Chapter 6.

The Child as a Vehicle For Family Mobility

Education of the child has been accepted as a mechanism for reducing poverty in future generations, though not necessarily the most efficient. However, the notion that children's education may result in the upward mobility of their parents and other family members remains far less convincing.

It was anticipated that Head Start would facilitate economic self-sufficiency for Head Start children *and* their families. The parent involvement component of Head Start was viewed as the key to this aspect of the Head Start program. Through this component, parents would have access to opportunities to learn childrearing techniques as well as how to be "teachers" in their own home.

These parent involvement strategies were presumably based on the three theories of poverty presented in Table 5 (Midco, 1972):

TABLE 5

THEORIES OF POVERTY AND THE ROLE OF HEAD START PARENTS

THEORY	*CAUSE*	*CURE*	*PARENTS ROLE*
Personal Deprivation	Disadvantaged	Rehabilitation and Services	Learner
Social Structures	Disenfranchised	Institutional Change	Decision-making
Buying Power	Inadequate Money	Improved Buying Power	Jobs (No income supplement)

Source: Midco (1972)

As one might surmise from the culture of poverty theory, originally there was a high commitment to the theory of "personal deprivation" with respect to Head Start parents. There was extensive emphasis on education for parents in child development, parenting, self-improvement, and skill development in subsequent local practices. A major fallacy of this aspect of the training was the assumption that the parents lacked knowledge of appropriate childrearing practices and that the parenting styles they exhibited were inferior.

Focus on the presumed deprivation of Head Start parents reduced interest in this aspect of the program. Moreover, since the link between parental values and childrearing and subsequent achievement has not been clearly documented, that approach as a means to enhance economic mobility has been consistently challenged. We suggest that more appropriate educational programs might have focused more directly on factors related to economics such as management of resources, factors related to success on the job, and family relationships.

Subsequently, partly in response to criticism of the culture of poverty orientation and partly due to input from parents, there was increased recognition of the "social structure" theory of poverty in both policy and practice. This approach emphasized parent- involvement in decision-making within the Head Start programs in the areas of personnel, program, and policy. Parents also became involved in the policy councils and committees which share the decision- making authority for Head Start programs, thus affecting these institutions directly. Simultaneously, there were increasing references to the role of Head Start parents in influencing non-Head Start institutions such as public schools and welfare agencies.

Experiences related to the "social structure" theory may have been of benefit to a small number of Head Start parents who served on policy councils, resulting in greater visibility, power, and subsequent employment. However, it is unlikely that this aspect of the program could have benefited the large proportion of Head Start families who did not have these opportunities.

Efforts to train and assist parents in obtaining jobs outside of Head Start were very limited and were inevitably associated with other programs, either other components of OEO or the Comprehensive Employment and Training Assistance (CETA) Program. Thus the third component, buying power, was restricted mainly to preparation for the few available jobs within the OEO or Head Start program.

Effectiveness of the Parent Involvement Program in Increasing Economic Mobility

Evaluations of the impact of the Parent Involvement component of the program are rather limited and largely anecdotal. Valentine and Stark (1979) suggest that the effects of parent involvement have been as varied as the character of the parent involvement component of the Head Start program.

For example, in New York City, where parent involvement was interpreted as "parent control," a group of fathers of Head Start children got together and decided that what they needed were jobs. "They studied together to take the examination to be Sanitation Engineers to get jobs in New York City. They studied, got the manuals, got themselves a leader, passed the examination, and started getting jobs."

The case of a Head Start Program in the mountains of Central Pennsylvania is illustrative of parent involvement seen as "community change." These communities could not get TV reception. Eight members of the Head Start Policy Committee arranged to have a cable system put in the two communities. To these families, parent involvement helped them to realize that they could have an impact on their environment.

Another example is the Head Start Program in Mississippi operated by the Child Development Group of Mississippi (CDGM). With an emphasis on the fullest participation by the recipients, each one of the 84 centers was run by a local committee of poor people, which was responsible for the planning, program, hiring, administration, and ultimately, success or failure of the center. Through this program many of the parents, such as Fannie Lou Hamer, became formidable political figures.

In a 1983 issue of *Human Development News*, the case of "Loretta" highlights how one individual could benefit from parent involvement in Head Start. A high school dropout who was working in a snack bar at a college, involvement in her daughter's Head Start program lead to further work toward her GED and enrollment in college where she graduated with a degree in Human Services. Now she is employed as the Head Start Social Services/Parent Involvement Coordinator for her local Community Action Agency.

While these case studies reflect examples of how parent involvement could successfully mobilize parents, there are perhaps many more examples where the parent involvement component, either because of a lack of participation or the ineffectiveness of this component of the program, resulted in very little change in the families. In assessing the impact of Head Start families, it is clear that there exists a wide variation in the extent, type, and intensity of involvement in the program. These factors would, of course, affect the benefits from this component of the program.

As a result of this variation, many studies have focused on a comparison of the highly involved families with those who are less involved. Midco (1972), using the model of three different theories of poverty (personal deprivation, social structure, and buying power), studied the impact of Head Start with respect to anticipated outcomes for the child and family. (The overall goal of economic mobility was not assessed.) Midco found that, using the personal deprivation and social structure models, with Head Start parents playing the learner role and decision-making role, it was found that those parents who were more highly involved in these roles appeared most satisfied; showed more self-confidence and higher self-esteem; had a greater sense of internal focus of control and greater assurance about their future; were more involved in more efforts to change community institutions; and were more prevalent in programs having high quality. High involvement improved parent and child attitudes and behavior; it also improved program quality. Further, high involvement influenced positive changes in community institutions such as the social service and health programs. A major criticism of the study is that these differences could have existed between the highly involved and the less involved prior to the Head Start experience.

In another national study of the long-term effects of Head Start, Collins (1983) reports that seven percent of parents indicated that Head Start had helped them to find a job and nine percent indicated that Head Start had helped them to further their education. However, given the low percentage of those obtaining jobs, it is likely that these jobs were within Head Start.

Although these studies shed some light on the impact of the program on parental attitudes, we still know very little about the relationship of parent involvement to family members ability to obtain and maintain jobs; the impact of parent involvement on the career ladder movement of Head Start families; the impact of Head Start on family income patterns; or the impact of Head Start on the educational achievement of Head Start family members other than Head Start children.

Future Directions

The apparent limited success of Head Start in attaining the goal of economic mobility for poor families may be attributed to several factors including inadequate documentation and funding limitations. Other factors include the following:

1. The culturally deficit approach was based on faulty assumptions and therefore attempts to remedy poverty based on these assumptions were largely ineffective.

2. The focus on the education of the child was inadequate to meet the goal of economic mobility of the family.

3. The parent involvement component was based on a deficit model and did not address the skills that could enhance economic mobility.

4. The antipoverty approach failed to incorporate issues which have been found to be related to the incidence of poverty, such as:

A. Increased unemployment, and lack of jobs particularly for low income minority individuals.

B. Persistence of racial and sexual barriers which limit access to jobs and economic mobility.

C. Reduction in the number of public employment and training programs for the low-skilled and hard to employ.

D. Increases in the number of female-headed households or the improvement in the economic status of female- headed households.

E. Identification of culturally relevant variables and factors within the various ethnic groups which lead to economic mobility in order to structure more appropriate and effective training programs for low- income minority families.

Although it may have been based partly on fallacious assumptions, Head Start is the most widely respected remnant of the antipoverty movement, primarily owing to the success of the child development component of the program. Though it may be criticized as being inadequate for achieving economic mobility for all families, a well-established program such as Head Start presents a perfect opportunity for advancing new strategies and techniques for improving the economic self-sufficiency of poor families who are participating in the program.

Given what we know about the weaknesses of the current program with respect to economic mobility, what strategies would be feasible within the budgetary constraints and guidelines of Head Start?

We propose that the parent involvement component be given greater emphasis and two of its components be revamped and augmented: personal deprivation and buying power. Suggestions for facilitating economic self-sufficiency are presented in each of these two areas.

From Personal Deprivation to Personal Enhancement

Moving from the concept of personal deprivation and toward the concept of personal enhancement, we suggest the following strategies for Head Start programs:

1. *Inculcate values endemic to the poor and minority communities which have been found to foster achievement (e.g., work, ethnic pride, discipline, persistence, religion, caring, faith, self-confidence, independence, and supervision).*

Research over the past decade by minority researchers has revealed a great deal about the functioning of black families which result in effective coping and adjustment of family members. Oyemade and her colleagues (1983) found that traditionally black socialization patterns of discipline and rules, and less emphasis on material possessions, differentiate between positive (i.e., high academic achievement) and negative behavioral outcomes (i.e., juvenile delinquency and teenage pregnancy) for children from middle- and lower-class families. Moreover, consistent with Robert Hill's 1971 study, the religious involvement of the family and strong kinship bonds were found to play a key role in the successful adjustment of the adolescent. Other researchers (e.g., McAdoo, H., 1981B; Nobles, 1978; and Allen, W., 1976) have obtained similar data.

2. *Emphasize strengthening the family structure through improved marital interaction with a view toward reduction of the divorce rate and the number of female- headed households.*

The dilemma of female-headed households is more fully discussed in Chapter 9. Three alternatives to this dilemma appear feasible:

A. Increased support from fathers of children in single parent families;

B. Identification of more jobs and raising the pay scale for women; and

C. Reduction of the dissolution of minority families.

In view of the data which indicate that because of economic isolation and discrimination, two incomes are often necessary for substantial upward mobility of poor families, we recommend that Head Start program efforts focus on male/female relationships and strengthening family structures and functions within the poor community. Greater emphasis should be placed on the importance of the two parent family structure for the development of all family members. Indeed a report by the Joint Center for Political Studies (1983) suggests that "family reinforcement constitutes the single most important action the nation can take toward the elimination of black poverty and related social problems" (p. 12).

3. *Reduce the incidence of teenage pregnancy.*

Adolescent parenting is more fully discussed in Chapter 10.

4. *Incorporate training programs which emphasize utilization of resources such as use of credit, budgeting, and management of resources.*

Edwards' (1982) Program for Family Resource Development proposes that "if families are to break from the poverty cycle, to leave AFDC rolls, their ability to help themselves to play functional roles in their own progress must be strengthened. This could be accomplished through a program which will help them cope with problems related to conservation of family resources and raising their standard of living. The basic techniques of wise marketing, budgeting, planning, infant and child care, conservation of resources, stress management, and the knowledge of nutrition, food preparation, sanitation, and health practices will improve health, increase productivity, lead to reduction in incidence of disease, extend the utility of family incomes, and motivate unemployed household members to prepare for gainful employment and to seek solutions to problem situations" (p.7). Programs based on this model are currently being implemented in Washington, D.C. and East St. Louis, Illinois.

Buying Power

In the final analysis, the overall solution to poverty is jobs and a decent income. According to William J. Wilson (1981), poor black Americans, heavily concentrated in inner cities, have experienced a worsening of their economic position on the basis of nearly all the major labor-market indicators. The unemployment rates for both black men and black women from 1955 to 1978 have increased more than those of comparable whites. Furthermore, the proportion of black men and women employed as laborers and service workers (occupational categories with a higher than average jobless ratio) is twice that of white workers employed in these jobs. Moreover, structural changes in the economy (such as the shift from goods producing to service producing industries; the growing use of industrial technology; and the relocation of industries out of the central city) have compounded the unemployment picture for blacks and other minorities.

In the final analysis, the lack of economic opportunities for blacks means they are forced to remain in poor economically depressed inner cities and their children forced to attend inferior schools after Head Start. This gives rise to a vicious circle and reverses the positive effects of such programs as Head Start. Male unemployment also leads to growth in female-headed families. As Lee Rainwater pointed out in 1970, unemployed men are more likely to abandon their families than are employed men.

What can we do? It is widely accepted that several areas must be addressed before the goal of increased employment can be attained. These include:

1. Identification of available jobs.

2. Improved access and reduction of barriers such as discrimination which affect hiring and employment practices.

3. Development of job search and interview skills to enhance the probability of being hired when a possible job is found.

4. Improved training in skills necessary for specific jobs.

5. Development of positive work habits and attitudes necessary for improving productivity on the job.

Keniston and his colleagues (1977) suggest that the employment of minorities and women can be increased, without preferential treatment, by measures designed to ensure minority and female applications, by the elimination of unnecessary requirements, and requiring an employer who has not traditionally employed minorities or women in particular job categories to make training opportunities available. Head Start could assist in reducing employment barriers and improve the buying power of its participants by working with parents in identifying those employers who do not conform to these guidelines and lobbying to have unfair practices with respect to minorities and women changed.

Moreover, a major emphasis could be placed on Human Resource Development Programs for Head Start parents which would improve their employability. These programs, if instituted on a systematic and well-planned basis, could be incorporated into new or existing Head Start programs with very little disruption to the overall operation of the program.

CHAPTER 5

HEAD START: HOW APPROPRIATE TODAY?

As we have seen, Head Start was launched as an effort to serve the needs of poor children *and* their families. To interrupt the predictive power of race and disabilities on children's lives, Head Start has made special efforts to reach out to minorities and to the handicapped. Seeking relevance and appropriateness, there have been tremendous changes in the ways that services have been delivered over the years. Also, the tone of assessments and opinion about Head Start has ranged considerably. As Edward Zigler (1979) has aptly pointed out, Head Start should be considered more as an evolving concept than as a program.

With its focus on the poor, Head Start services continue to be in demand. This decade has ushered in a new wave of crisis for America's children and families. Domestic poverty in 1982 reached its highest level since 1965. Over 34 million Americans, or 15 percent of the population, fell below the official poverty level for a family of four ($9,862). Among racial minorities, the news was even more startling: almost 36 percent of blacks, and 30 percent of Hispanics, fell below poverty in 1982 (Washington, V., 1985A and 1985B).

Millions of dependent children are affected by the increase in poverty. In 1982, 22 percent of our nation's children were members of poor families. Nearly half of black children, and one-third of Hispanic children, live below the poverty level. Black children are more than three times more likely than white children to be poor (U.S. Department of Commerce, 1979).

The federal response to this surge in poverty contrasts sharply with the 1960's War on Poverty. Now, following a myriad of programs which gave rise to the promise of a "Great Society," public confidence is diminishing amid skepticism about what role the government can and should play. Also, in the current atmosphere of economic uncertainties, there is increased attention to the cost of social programs. In this decade, America's most dramatic response to poverty and social programs has been twofold: to reduce spending in social programs and to consolidate categorical programs into block grants to states.

Nevertheless, the federal administration has pledged to cast a "Social Safety Net" of programs, including Project Head Start, to allow for the provision of basic needs while restructuring the federal system. Yet, over 1,000 counties in the United States do not participate in Head Start. Further, only a fraction (15 percent to 18 percent) of eligible children have been served by Head Start over the years (CDF, 1984; Rivlin and Timpane, 1975).

As Head Start enters its third decade, expectations for the Project remain high. At the same time, budget cuts, changes in federal-state relationships, and concern about the national deficit prompt reconsideration of Head Start's continuing effectiveness and appropriateness.

Four concepts of Project Head Start are of particular concern in the present era:

1. Community control;

2. Parent involvement;

3. Its comprehensive focus; and

4. Cultural diversity.

An overview of each of these four concepts is presented with a discussion of current issues. Following an overview of each of these four concepts and a discussion of current issues, this chapter presents conclusions concerning the continuing appropriateness of these concepts and recommendations for program consideration. Special attention is given to the needs and issues related to ethnic minority status, since two-thirds of the children served are nonwhites.

Community Involvement

The focus on community change has been a unique aspect of Head Start. One of the initial stated purposes of Head Start was to marshal and coordinate federal, state, and local resources to involve the poor in the process of finding solutions to their own problems (OEO, 1967). Consequently, administrative control of the Head Start programs was placed at the local community level, thereby enhancing responsiveness to community needs (Harmon and Hanley, 1979).

Head Start has been influential in making local community institutions more responsive to the poor (Datta, 1979; Kirschner, 1970; Midco, 1972; Social Research Group, 1977). Head Start jobs and services have contributed to the economic vitality of communities. Head Start has also encouraged the coordination of community social services, although it is unclear whether the program has increased actual utilization of community services (Hubbell, 1983).

Community involvement was an important initiative of Head Start, yet gains in this area have not always occurred without controversy. Early efforts to establish the project in some local communities engendered serious conflict with the social milieu in which the project developed. For example, black parents were threatened with job loss and some facilities were the object of vandalism and arson (Gordon, S., 1966). In addition to the tensions created by endowing a particular group in a community with money and political power (Shriver, 1979), there were conflicts about the very definition and implementation of community action. Did Head Start seek to empower poor people politically and economically or to simply provide services?

Perhaps the most controversial program was the Child Development Group in Mississippi (Greenberg, 1969). The CDGM maintained the necessity for a community activist posture while some local whites found it difficult to accept the idea of self- determination and management by local black people (Payne et al., 1973). Others, such as Senator John Stennis, alleged the CDGM consisted of "out-of-state" Civil Rights activists who used program funds for Civil Rights and other unauthorized activities. Eventually, CDGM funding was reduced and another community action program, made up of both local community residents and public authorities, was developed (Jones and Fowler, 1982).

Indeed, while community action agencies were not required to be operated by, or approved by, local or state authorities, it was not unusual for political tensions to develop in cases where local education or other public authorities were not included in program operation or oversight (Jones and Fowler, 1982). A series of Congressional actions specifically sought to legislate means to reduce conflicts between community action programs and local governments (Jones and Fowler, 1982).

Yet, throughout the controversies, Head Start has maintained its goal of involving the community in planning and executing the program designed to service them (Riley and Epps, 1967). Community involvement, according to the Congress of the United States, was the concept of "maximum feasible participation" by the poor in social programs (U.S. Congress Public Law 88- 452, 1964; Zigler and Anderson, 1979). In fact, federal law and policy originally gave preference to community action agencies in the allocation of Head Start grants (Harmon and Hanley, 1979).

Current Issues in Community Control

The idea of community control--the concept of "maximum feasible participation"--has undoubtedly strengthened the Head Start constituency and led to its continued political support. In this era of ideological change, this concept is, without doubt, of continuing relevance and appropriateness for Head Start.

To retain community involvement, it is now necessary to reassert the importance of "maximum feasible participation." As a beginning, Congress should be asked to reaffirm its commitment to the community flavor of Head Start, which is now assured by the fact that grants are given directly from the federal government to local communities. In FY 1982, Reagan's staff proposed that Head Start be repealed and placed in a block grant at significantly reduced funding levels. The administration also considered "streamlining" the program's regulations, including the performance standards. Public appeals were a significant factor in preventing the advancement of this proposal; over 5,000 letters were sent to the Reagan Administration protesting these changes (CDF, 1985).

With the circulation of the Reagan Administration's 1983 policy paper entitled, "Head Start: Directions for the Next Three Years" (Subcommittee on Human Resources, 1982), there has been vigorous and renewed concern about administrative efforts to dismantle community involvement under the guise of strengthening "local control." Generally, the Head Start parents and service providers have opposed efforts to change performance standards, or alter the compliance monitoring or regulations systems.

Nevertheless, the Children's Defense Fund (1984) reports that in 1983 the Reagan Administration instituted a new grant-making process, disregarding the existing process. This process was put into place without first allowing the Head Start community to comment on the criteria that would be used to evaluate grant proposals. After Congress directed USDHHS to provide a public comment period, the proposed competitive bidding criteria was grudgingly published for less than the required thirty-day period while USDHHS simultaneously urged programs to submit proposals based on the proposed criteria. Neither a letter to USDHHS Secretary Heckler from twenty members of Congress nor the receipt of over 1,600 comments led to a single change in the original criteria.

Another issue currently under debate is the extent to which Head Start programs can improve their coordination with other community groups in an effort to strengthen services to the "whole" child/family. While the Administration recommends this, and grantees support the concept, there is varied opinion about the feasibility of the implementation strategy: many groups with whom networks could potentially be developed are themselves experiencing decreases in expenditures, staff, and services. Further, some grantees assert that, as heavily volunteer organizations, many grantees have already successfully coordinated and used all community and state resources. Indeed, "increases" in the Head Start budget since 1980 have been greatly offset by the necessity to pay for services previously secured through "non-safety net" programs. This is discussed further in the "Comprehensive Focus" section of this chapter.

The concept of community involvement has obviously led to strong feelings of affiliation within the Head Start network. Many Head Start advocates are now concerned that this broad communication network is threatened by two administrative changes in Head Start (Stephan, 1986):

1. Beginning in 1982, ACYF began to decentralize the training and technical assistance delivery system.

2. In 1985, the Reagan administration allowed the funding of the four bilingual- multicultural resource centers that had operated since 1978 to expire. Funding was instead provided to 28 local groups.

Stephan (1986) notes that those opposed to decentralizing the Training/Technical Assistance (T/TA) are concerned about jeopardizing the broad communication network, resource linkages, resource sharing, and the quality of training. In a related concern, the National Head Start Association president identified reduced monitoring and training visits from regional offices as a major issue of the 1980's.

Parent Involvement

Integral to the concept of community control is Head Start's focus on parent involvement. Parent participation has been a key element of Project Head Start since its inception. The Cooke memo of 1965, which formed the philosophical basis of Head Start, emphasized the role of the family and the community. Recognizing that parents have a privileged role in child development, both the development and operation of Head Start programs have stressed parent participation and involvement. Parent involvement in the various aspects of the Head Start program is mandated by law.

Further, all of the program component areas (education, health, social services, and parent involvement) outlined in the 1972 Head Start Performance Standards address the role of Head Start parents. Indeed, over time, "recipient" participation, as required by Head Start guidelines, was interpreted to mean participation by the parent, rather than by representatives from the larger community (Harmon and Hanley, 1979).

Head Start can accurately be credited with launching the trend toward parent involvement in education and social services (Harmon and Hanley, 1979). The goal is to provide parents with the knowledge and services that would enable them to improve their economic status and to provide a favorable developmental environment for their children (Zigler, 1979). Indeed the opportunities which allowed Head Start parents to plan and operate programs contrast sharply with the lack of such opportunities in America's public schools.

There is a wide range of parent activities in Head Start: advisory board memberships; classroom teachers; volunteers and aides; participants in parent meetings; and participation in structured parent programs (Slaughter, 1982). Also, every Head Start program has a policy council, at least 50 percent of whose members are Head Start parents. Through the policy council, parents are involved in decisions about the operation of the centers, including personnel matters and the allocation of funds.

To facilitate parent involvement, the National Head Start Bureau has developed and disseminated various resources over the years, including:

1976 -Exploring Parenting (parent education curriculum)

1978 -A guide for involving parents in Head Start

1982 -Exploring self-sufficiency series

1985 - Parent involvement component videotape

1985 -Adult literacy demonstrations

1985 -Family needs assessment model instrument

1985 -Looking at life series (parent education curriculum)

1986 -Parent enrichment curriculum (see Johnson, R. 1986).

The actual extent of parent participation in Head Start has not been fully documented. Estimates of the extent of parent volunteers in Head Start varies from three parents for every four children enrolled to 10 parents per 15 children (CDF, 1984). Nevertheless, a smaller core of parents provide the majority of volunteer hours (Hubbell, 1985). Limitations to parent involvement have been identified as transportation, child-care, parliamentary procedure, and frequent rotation of parents (Payne et al., 1973). Critics also charge that, while the principle of parent involvement is widely accepted, the implementation varies greatly (Payne et al., 1973; Caliguri, 1970).

Research to date has also failed to identify the most productive kinds of parent involvement activities. Robinson and Choper (1979) have further charged that national evaluations have failed to assess the contributions of parents to Head Start programs or the benefits parents have received from their participation.

Research has clearly indicated, however, that parents approve of Head Start. Head Start has had a demonstratable positive impact on parent attitudes toward, and interactions with, their children. Further, parent involvement enhances the effectiveness of the program: the children of parents who have high levels of participation performed better on tests of achievement and development (Grothberg, 1969). Head Start parents also tend to remain involved in their children's education once the children enter elementary school (Midco, 1972), thereby illustrating that these parents want to be involved in the education of their children and that their children benefit when they do (Richmond, Stipek, and Zigler, 1979).

Current Issues In Parent Involvement In Head Start

Parent involvement in education can be an appropriate and effective means of advancing the skills and knowledge of Head Start parents. These skills and knowledge may extend far beyond child development information. Rather, the process skills which poor and minority parents may acquire through their involvement in Head Start -- practice in negotiating with public institutions, enhanced leadership experiences, exercising control over aspects of their lives -- may be, over the long term, even more important in disrupting the cycle of poverty.

Thus, the concept of parent participation in programs such as Head Start is of critical importance. As parent skills and knowledge are enhanced, children benefit. Networks of these parents and children may be better prepared to cope with a less-supportive public school environment. Parents may be more aware of, and better able to address, discontinuities between their home cultures and the expectations of the schools. Indeed, proponents of the War on Poverty expected that parents would be transformed into agents of social change (Knitzer, 1972).

While the concept of parent involvement is appropriate, the actual implementation of the idea may now need to be revitalized. Some grantees have a paternalistic attitude toward parents which prevents parents from playing a decisive role in the project (Richmond, Stipek, and Zigler, 1979). There is also concern that new Head Start innovations, related to new or existing grants, recognize the value of parent opinion. Who is in the best position to suggest innovations?

The 1983 policy paper, "Head Start: Directions for the Next Three Years," gave rise to concern that parent participation would be endangered by a proposal to limit all programs to part-day operation on an 8-month basis. This change was anticipated to impede the ability of working parents, particularly those in rural areas, to participate in Head Start or to achieve economic self-sufficiency. Since Head Start is designed around parent and local community needs, the Head Start workers generally opposed that proposal (Subcommittee on Human Resources, 1982).

To further address the needs of working parents, Head Start should further expand services to children under the age of three. Demographic trends show that mothers of very young children are the fastest growing segment of the labor force (Washington, V. and Oyemade, 1985, 1984). At all income levels, the proportion of black working mothers of children under age six exceeds the proportion of white working mothers (CDF, 1982A, 1982B). Further, black women return to work when their youngest child is at least age three, compared to over age six for white women (CDF,

1980). Thus, more black children need full-time child care, and at younger ages, than white children. Indeed, the poor infant or toddler may be at greater risk, and have greater potential for intervention.

Further, past and proposed reductions or changes in Training/Technical Assistance (T/TA) potentially limit parent involvement. One Head Start director testified before Congress that T/TA reductions prevented the program from providing mileage and babysitting reimbursements, thereby making it more difficult to maintain the parent involvement component (Roman, 1982).

Since Head Start is heavily dependent on often unskilled parent volunteers, a reduction in T/TA is of serious consequence. Despite recommending an overall increase in Head Start funding for FY 1984, the Reagan Administration also proposed a 50 percent cut in the portion of the Head Start budget targeted to training, technical assistance, research, demonstration projects, and evaluation. Since the Title XX training program was eliminated in FY 1982, there is no available substitute source of federal funding to meet the training needs of Head Start (CDF, 1984).

The Children's Defense Fund (1984) reports that in 1983 Congress directed the administration not to cut back on Head Start's research and training activities. However, this mandate was ignored.

Similarly, reductions in the Child Development Associate (CDA) credential also limits training opportunities for parents. Sixty-five percent of Head Start programs use the CDA to involve parents in the educational component of the program (CDF, 1984). Eighty-nine percent of Head Start programs use CDA as part of their career development plan for staff (CDF, 1984).

Head Start as a Comprehensive Program

Despite the public focus on cognitive gains for children, Head Start has always been a comprehensive program which sought to address the needs of the "whole child." Head Start's four components--social services, health, education, and parent involvement-- address family needs ranging from housing and health care to emotional support and family counseling (CDF, 1984, 1983B). About ninety-seven percent of Head Start families received social services from Head Start and/or through referrals to other agencies (USDHHS, 1985C).

According to the performance standards, Head Start programs must provide comprehensive health services to children, including medical and dental screening and treatment, immunizations, mental health services, health education, nutrition, and services to handicapped children. In fact, it has been found that Head Start centers do provide a range of health services--screening, immunizations, and treatment--for most, but not for all, children. Health services remain uneven across the country. Migrant programs are less successful than other Head Start centers in providing these health services (Hubbell, 1983).

The emphasis on a comprehensive child development program, emphasizing the health and nutritional needs of children is of special importance to minority children. Throughout childhood and adolescence, nonwhite children suffer more health problems and receive fewer health services than white children. For example, black women receive less prenatal care and receive prenatal care later than do white women (USDHHS, 1980). Nonwhite children have an infant mortality rate almost twice that of white children (USDHHS, 1979A, 1978B). Black children lag substantially behind white children in basic immunization rates (USDHEW, 1980). Nonwhite children are twice as likely as white children to have no regular source of medical care, and are five times more likely to depend upon hospital outpatient or emergency room services. Even within income groups, nonwhite children are twice as likely as white children to lack private health insurance coverage (USDHEW, 1977A, 1977B).

Given the documented health needs of poor minority children, the health and nutritional aspects of Head Start are the only areas in which its contributions have not been disputed (Payne et al., 1973; Hill, C., 1972). For example, Head Start children have been assisted in enrolling in Medicaid; Richmond, Stipek, and Zigler (1979) describe Head Start as the nation's largest deliverer of health services to disadvantaged children. They maintain that Head Start children have received immunizations at a rate about 20 percent higher than the national average for poor children.

According to the Head Start Bureau (USDHHS, 1987) in 1985-86, 97 percent of the children enrolled ninety days or more completed medical screening including all of the appropriate tests, and 97 percent of those identified as needing treatment received treatment. Ninety-five percent of the children enrolled ninety days or more completed dental examinations and 96 percent of those needing dental treatment received treatment. Also, 96 percent of the children had completed all of the required immunizations or were up-to-date in their immunizations. Recent data also show that 50 percent of the Head Start children are enrolled in the Medicaid/Early Periodic Screening Diagnosis and Treatment (EPSDT) program which pays for their medical and dental services.

Nevertheless, the impact of Head Start health care on poor children and the extent to which needed services have been provided has not been thoroughly researched. Available data, however, reveals lower absenteeism, fewer cases of anemia, more immunizations, better nutritional practices, and generally better health among children who had participated in Head Start (Hubbell, 1983).

Current Issues in Head Start as a Comprehensive Program

Given Head Start's mission, program advocates are particularly sensitive to perceived threats to its comprehensive focus. For example, in its early years, there was concern that placement in the Office of Education would result in a reduction in the medical, nutritional, social, and parent involvement components of the program if professional educators assumed control (Jones and Fowler, 1982).

Program advocates now feel that the comprehensive mandate of Head Start is being challenged despite its inclusion in the President's "Social Safety Net." The reduction or elimination of other federal programs that have provided crucial support for Head Start evades the Project's ability to fulfill its comprehensive mandate; many services that Head Start provides are funded through these programs (Jones and Fowler, 1982; CDF, 1983A). For example, a Minnesota state preschool screening program, which no longer exists, previously paid for health screenings for Head Start children (CDF, 1983A and 1983B). Further, in 1982 Head Start lost over $12 million from the Title XX Social Services Block Grant which funds a variety of Social Services (CDF, 1985).

Thus "increased" appropriations for Head Start as part of the "Safety Net" are misleading if they suggest that the programs now have more "discretionary" funds. Further, "increased" funding levels and decreased support from non-Head Start agencies have been accompanied by an increase in pupil enrollment. More than 53,000 children were added to the programs between 1980 and 1984; in 1983, gains occurred despite no appropriations increase (Subcommittee on Human Resources, 1984).

The Reagan Administration estimated that the same number of children could be served in 1986 as in 1985 at the same funding level, which was an $80 million increase over 1984 (Stephan, 1986). The actual appropriation for 1986 was a twelve million dollar increase.

Child advocates have argued for increased funding for Head Start so that a greater percentage of the eligible population can be served (only 15-18 percent are now being served). The administration argues that, with improved enrollment practices, a greater percentage of the eligibles can be served. The administration also points out that in the past funds have been earmarked for expansion grants and that Head Start enrollment has improved as a result (Stephan, 1986).

Zigler and Lang (1983) argue that if expansion of Head Start would provide services to more children while preserving and upgrading the good quality of current programs, "anyone who cares about children would be in favor of it" (p.5). Adding that they doubt this would be the case, they state that they would rather see fewer children served well than more children served poorly. "Tokenistic" efforts to serve children are dangerous, not so much because they damage children as that they give the appearance that something useful is being done and thus become the substitute for more meaningful efforts (Zigler and Valentine, 1979).

Program quantity has not been affected negatively as a result of changes in the Head Start program, which leads to concern about eroding quality in the comprehensive mandate. For example, Head Start programs receive the bulk of their food from reimbursements from the U.S. Department of Agriculture Child Care Food Program, which is automatically adjusted each year to reflect changes in the costs of food. In 1985-86, virtually all Head Start programs participated in the USDA Child Care Food Program (USDHHS, 1985C, 1987).

In 1982, federal subsidies for meals and snacks served under this program were reduced, a $20 million loss to Head Start in that year (CDF, 1985). Despite the fact that, in FY 1984 Congress rejected the administration's proposal to move the food funds directly into the Head Start budget and to deny the automatic adjustment, the administration re-proposed this plan for FY 1985 (CDF, 1984). Again, the proposed $80 million "increase" in Head Start funding would effectively freeze funds for food, resulting in about an eight and one-half million dollar loss to Head Start in 1984, the equivalent of slots for about 3,500 children (CDF, 1984).

Another example of Head Start's recent losses uncompensated for by the "safety net" is the elimination of the Comprehensive Employment and Training Act (CETA). During 1981 Head Start used about 6000 CETA workers to serve over 50,000 children; in 1982, all CETA public service jobs were eliminated (CDF, 1985).

As of FY 1982, "medically needy children" not on public assistance *could* be, at the State's option, discontinued from receiving Early and Periodic Screening, Diagnosis and Treatment under the Medicaid Program. If States opt to elect this option, Head Start programs, required by law to provide medical services, would have to find and finance other sources of care (Jones and Fowler, 1982).

Finally, the effectiveness of the comprehensive approach of Head Start diminishes when federal budget cuts erode families' ability to provide for their basic needs. Many Head Start families depend upon programs which have experienced budget cuts: Aid to Families with Dependent Children, food stamps, and the Special Supplemental Food Program for Women, Infants, and Children. These families have often turned to Head Start for assistance in solving, or coping with, their unmet human needs (Subcommittee on Human Resources, 1982, 1984).

Aside from budget cuts, administrative changes are also affecting the comprehensive mission. In the effort to "expand" Head Start through increased enrollment, programs which serve children for only one year are now normally scored higher in the grant process than programs which serve children for two years. Again, this approach increases quantity at the expense of providing services for the neediest children. According to Clarence Hodges, former Commissioner of the Administration for Children, Youth, and Families, "our problem is, if we had children that needed coats and we could give coats and sweaters to some, should we give coats to all or coats and sweaters to some?" Replied Representative Miller of California, "What concerns me is whether or not the coat you then give them keeps them from freezing to death" (Subcommittee on Human Resources, 1982).

Discussions in the Office of Management and Budget about possible changes in the definition of poverty could portend future challenges to Head Start's comprehensive mandate (Subcommittee on Human Resources, 1984). In 1984, the Census Bureau's annual report on poverty included, for the first time, nine alternative poverty measures. The alternative measures, including non-cash benefits, produced higher income levels, thus lowering poverty readings. In anticipation of poverty definition changes, there are already prospective bills which contain provisions to protect Head Start from the subsequent cuts indicated by these changes.

Head Start and the Issue of Cultural Diversity

Recognizing the importance of attending to the diverse experiences which children bring to the classroom, some Head Start programs have been specifically targeted to serve special groups of children. For example, by 1986, there were 106 Indian and 24 migrant programs of the 1,305 total Head Start programs. Also, the Head Start Strategy for Spanish- Speaking Children was initiated in 1975 to develop sound bilingual/bicultural programs. However, consistent with proposals from the Reagan Administration, the funding set-asides for Indian and migrant programs were frozen at the funding level for the program in 1985.

Issues of diversity surfaced in the early days of Head Start. The eligibility criteria provoked some initial resentment of Head Start programs in several southern states (Jones and Fowler, 1982). Despite parent and community enthusiasm about the goals of Head Start, the program has been criticized around the concept of cultural diversity. The proportion of minorities in staff positions and the cultural deficit approach to program implementation are two concerns frequently raised.

Use of Non-Minority Staff

Royster et al. (1978) found that the ethnic composition of Head Start staff has not reflected the composition of the children served. Whites were overrepresented among supervisory staff, teachers, and aides. Blacks were underrepresented among supervisory staff. Hispanics, Asians, and Indians were underrepresented in all three staff categories.

A similar staffing pattern was found in a Head Start related project, Home Start. Steiner (1976) observed that, contrary to program descriptions, the typical home visitor was not a community resident selected for her indigenousness and experience as a local mother. Rather, the vast majority were white females with preschool education experience.

In recent Congressional testimony, Assistant Secretary for Human Development Services, Dorcas Hardy (Subcommittee on Human Resources, 1984) testified that 29 percent of Head Start employees are parents of current or former Head Start children. Given the ethnic composition of children, these workers are likely to be members of minority groups. It is important that Head Start programs vigilantly examine and monitor their staffing patterns in order to ensure more proportional representation of ethnic groups.

Many observers, including Laosa (1985), have wondered whether "maximum feasible participation" of the community in Project Head Start has really been implemented. Steiner (1976) observed that, within the child development coalition, community control has not been "an ineradicable principle." Indeed, Huell (1976) has argued that although black children are no longer denied education, programs such as Head Start are created on the assumption that poor or minority people are "deficit people" whose problems can be remediated only by white/lower- or middle-class designed programs.

A Deficit Focus

Related to the absence of minorities in staffing roles is the charge that Head Start has promulgated a deficit view of minority children. Laosa (1985) defined the cultural deficit or pathology paradigm as indicating that inequalities are caused by inherent flaws in the individual members of cultural groups at the bottom of the socioeconomic order. Therefore, despite the strong environmentalist flavor of the Head Start philosophy, the solutions suggest that there was a need to change or rehabilitate the individuals and cultures who participated. According to Slaughter (1982), the parents received the message that somehow they have failed their children and that without the intervention of Head Start, the children would be unsuccessful in school and fail themselves, as had their parents.

Countless critics have challenged the view that poverty results from deficits located within the individual (Stipek, Valentine, and Zigler, 1979; Ryan, W. 1971; Datta, 1970). A critical issue remains as to whether, and how, preschool intervention programs can best prepare minority children for social institutions (such as schools) that still continue to perpetuate inequality and racism.

Toward Cultural Diversity

There have been many proposals to assure cross- cultural perspectives in preschool intervention programs. Vernon Clark and Frank Graham (1975) made a case for black college sponsorship of Head Start programs. Similarly, one study found that, while Head Start was a desirable project to American Indians, there was a need for teachers specifically trained in understanding the Indians and materials of the native culture (Small, 1979).

Like many poverty programs, Head Start faces the task of recognizing explicitly, and acting on the knowledge, that poor people are not a homogeneous group. Different ethnic groups, and individuals, have needs which should be addressed as a matter of public policy (Washington, V. 1985B). Cross-cultural differences in values and perspectives have been documented (Washington, V. and Lee, 1982). Indeed, the call for multicultural education and standards which have been mandated for teacher training and curriculum in public schools (Washington, V. 1982; Washington, V. and Woolever, 1979) should be examined for the preschool. The goal is to assist children to become bicultural or bilingual and to enhance their ability to function in different environments (Laosa, 1982). Since no single curriculum appears to provide a superior cognitive measure of Head Start effectiveness (Huell, 1976), the cross-cultural goals of Head Start can be implemented without affecting negatively other aspects of the project. Head Start must more vigorously respect and support the diversity of its participants and utilize cultural strengths in developing new competencies.

The Continuing Appropriateness of Project Head Start

This outline of Head Start's major concepts -- community and parent involvement, the comprehensive focus, and cultural diversity -- suggests that the program continues to hold promise for poor and minority children, although it has not been the panacea that early supporters of the programs imagined that it might be. Further, there are important continuing issues that must be addressed to assure the vitality of Project Head Start: monitoring administrative changes that may adversely affect community involvement; enhancing opportunities for meaningful parent participation; assuring that the comprehensive mandate of Head Start is not eroded; and expanding the focus on multicultural education. There is also an urgent need to expand benefits to migrant children and to children under three. While all children served by Head Start will be affected by these program or political adjustments, there is little doubt that minority children will be most deeply affected.

In the future, Project Head Start is likely to place less emphasis on the preschool years as a "critical period" that has irreversible consequences on the child's or family's destiny. This is partly due to the growing recognition of the needs of the poor and minorities at other phases of the life cycle, including adolescence and old age. The realization that education alone cannot solve the complexities of poverty has also reduced emphasis on the preschool years as a critical period.

As early as 1970 R. Fisher concluded that, because America is racist and competitive, it is impossible to equalize educational opportunity for the poor. Fisher argued that Project Head Start makes as much sense as initiating a "Project Slow Down" for middle-class children.

Disillusionment about Head Start's impact on education may lead to undue pessimism about the project's appropriate role in the lives of poor and minority children. For example, Omwake (1970) did not seem to envision Head Start as having a critical role in the decade of the 1970's. From time to time, many commentators have reported that Head Start is "dead" (Zigler, 1979). In 1969, Joseph Durham challenged the need for compensatory education and suggested that the real task was to provide a system in which all children will have access to quality education.

These criticisms fail to suggest appropriate alternatives to Head Start. If Head Start is eliminated, what will we have to offer poor and minority children? Clearly, young children cannot wait for macroenvironmental change. However, within the context of the existing "system," children can be effectively prepared to achieve social and intellectual competencies.

In a more favorable review, Slaughter (1982) asserted that Head Start has realized all its goals except equal education opportunity. Head Start continues to exist as a valid institutional form which, combined with other programs and political struggles, addresses the goal of equality.

While Head Start cannot be considered as a solution to poverty, it may help maximize the benefits of schooling for the child, whether or not the schooling itself contributes to the long-range economic status of the child. Stipek, Valentine, and Zigler (1979) asserted that Head Start provides meaningful social experiences, prepares children for elementary school, integrates parents into the social systems that affect their children's lives, and generally serves the needs of families and young children.

The 15th Anniversary Head Start Committee (Muenchow and Shays, 1980) concluded that, while Head Start is a successful program, it has not yet fulfilled its potential. The chief problems were identified as:

1. Insufficient staff, particularly at the regional level, to deliver technical assistance to local grantees;

2. Low teacher salaries;

3. The need to extend services to more children;

4. Uneven quality of services between Head Start centers with respect to the education component;

5. Too many shifts in the administrative structure of the program;

6. The need to strengthen the managerial resources at both the regional and national levels;

7. High inflation erodes program quality while increasing family needs; and

8. The inability to keep pace with the changing demographic characteristics of the target population.

As social programs, such as Head Start, are being reassessed in the context of economic uncertainties, child advocates and minority scholars must more actively articulate the strengths and needs of the program as they affect poor and minority children. We must continue to monitor the program for its appropriateness and to insure that the program reaches, as a priority, those children who are most likely to benefit from it.

How appropriate is Project Head Start for children and their families as we approach the 1990's? Most observers would agree with Dorcas Hardy's (Subcommittee on Human Resources, 1984) observation that Head

Start "has made a substantial contribution in providing equal opportunities, particularly to minority children and children with special needs" (p.25). The 1960's and 1970's were time periods in which we learned that a national program could be successfully designed, implemented, and fine-tuned. However, in recognizing the ingenuity, appeal, and resilience of Head Start, our challenge in the 1990's is to maintain, advocate, and monitor needed improvements in program quality. Head Start *works* and intervention can be successful. But, particularly in time of dwindling economic, political, or civil rights support, less than optimal conditions for program quality may prevail.

CHAPTER 6

HEAD START EFFECTIVENESS: A CRITICAL ASSESSMENT[1]

Although Head Start's comprehensive design and emphasis on the "whole child" and parent involvement set it apart as a clearly unique program, the effectiveness of the education component has been the focus of public debate. Debate about whether Head Start "works" has generally been limited to the program's academic benefits.

The measurement of Head Start's effectiveness has been complicated by several factors. The scope and breadth of the entire program has made it more difficult to assess than other social programs. Indeed, as Valentine, Ross, and Zigler (1979) observed, Head Start's comprehensive program was characterized by several factors, including a multiplicity of goals which were to be accorded equal emphasis; the absence of clearly-defined approaches for achieving each goal; the absence of a prioritized sequence of goal emphasis; and the built-in flexibility for programs nationwide to implement the program to suit the individual needs of the host community. These factors hindered both the achievement of any single aim and the evaluation of program effectiveness. To complicate the matter further, there was no reliable and valid instrumentation for evaluation by program personnel (Gordon, E.W., 1979). As a consequence, there was a rush to develop instrumentation overnight. Against this background, it is not surprising that Head Start's effectiveness has been questioned.

---

[1] Dr. O. Jackson Cole, Dean of the School of Human Ecology at Howard University, is coauthor of this chapter.

the country (Richmond, Stipek, and Zigler, 1979). This has never been true. Local programs have always had wide flexibility in planning educational curricula tailored to the needs of their children and communities, a freedom even more strongly encouraged since the improvement and innovation effort of 1973 (Richmond, Stipek, and Zigler, 1979). Nevertheless, despite this array of negative factors, there is concrete evidence that Head Start works, apparently in spite of its inherent limitations.

Yet, there are several issues about which an assessment of Head Start must be concerned. Chief among these concerns has been the overconcentration of evaluative efforts on the use of IQ and other standardized tests when assessing the effects of intervention, the narrow focus on children's cognitive and intellectual gains, the matter of appropriate definition and assessment of social competencies, and the underrepresentation of minority group members on committees that set and recommend policies bearing on these matters. The latter concern is especially critical, given the large proportion of minority children enrolled in Head Start and the apparent concomitant underrepresentation of blacks and other minorities as teachers and senior staff in Head Start programs (Royster et al., 1978).

This chapter has six objectives:

1. To summarize the major reports on the effectiveness of Project Head Start before 1980.

2. To review some of the issues raised by Head Start evaluations, particularly by the Westinghouse Report.

3. To present the results of studies from the Consortium on Developmental Continuity.

4. To summarize two major recent reports on the effectiveness of Project Head Start: The Perry Preschool Project, and the Head Start Evaluation, Synthesis, and Utilization Project.

5. To discuss the conflict between the child educative and parental development goals of Head Start (following the work of Omwake, 1979).

6. To explore the issue of social competency as a measure of Head Start effectiveness.

Reports on Head Start Effectiveness Before 1980

As Head Start was being designed, there was emphasis on opinion that the preschool years are a critical period for the development of many human characteristics, but especially for verbal ability, general intelligence, and general school achievement (Steiner, 1976). Steiner (1976) states that no cautionary word had been uttered in the early days of Head Start. Rather, President Johnson shared the hope of experts that preschool experiences would give poor children a boost in school. The President further asserted in a 1965 education message that preschool programs had successfully helped poor children to overcome educational deficits, citing programs in New York and Baltimore as evidence. From President Johnson's January 1965 education message to President Nixon's February 1969 message on the reorganization of the antipoverty program, Head Start's value as an instrument of early education was not in dispute (Steiner, 1976). While J. McVicker Hunt advised President Johnson's policy assistants in 1966 that the beneficial effects of Head Start could be lost without follow-through in the early elementary grades, the prevalent mood was that Head Start was effective (Steiner, 1976).

Zigler and Rescorla (1985) report that strong evaluation efforts were not part of Head Start's initial planning. An evaluation of the 1965 summer Head Start effort consisted of a hodgepodge of instruments culled from the literature; this created a strong negative reaction among Head Start staff and families and led to inadequate and inconclusive results. Yet, Head Start enjoyed good press and became a major social program the following year.

However, in the first weeks of the Nixon Administration, the results of a massive evaluation study conducted by the Westinghouse Learning Corporation and Ohio University became available, leading Nixon to change his plans for a strong endorsement of Head Start.

Overall, the Westinghouse Report found that there were no observable effects of the summer Head Start programs on the children when followed up three years later. The study was a post-hoc comparison of school children who had attended one of over a hundred Head Start centers across the country with a matched sample of control-group children from the same grades and schools who did not have Head Start experience. Both groups were administered a series of tests covering various aspects of cognitive and affective development (Steiner, 1976).

The Westinghouse Report (Westinghouse Learning Corporation, 1969) was of particular importance because it was the first large-scale national study to evaluate the impact of Head Start participation on later school achievement. Aside from a slight but significant superiority of full year Head Start children on some measures of cognitive and affective development, the Westinghouse Study concluded that Head Start children were not appreciably different from their non-Head Start peers in most aspects of cognitive and affective development. Among the nine major findings of the Westinghouse Report, the most positive dealt with the parents' strong approval of the program and its effect on their children rather than on measurable cognitive gains or social-emotional development (Steiner, 1976).

Further, the Westinghouse study recorded the lack of any long-term intellectual or academic impact from Head Start participation. The study reported that Head Start graduates showed only modest immediate gains on standardized tests of cognitive ability and that these gains disappeared after the first few years of school. The most publicized finding was that the cognitive gains made by Head Start children were lost after a few years of elementary school. The Westinghouse Report also made an important recommendation: short summer programs in Head Start should be replaced with programs of longer duration.

Steiner (1976) reported that responses to the Westinghouse study were mixed. While Nixon reacted to the study, in Congress the Westinghouse study produced very little reaction, and "no thoughtful reaction at all" (Steiner, 1976, p. 33). On the other hand, researchers produced several volumes of criticisms about the study's methods and findings (Smith, M.S. and Bissell, J.S. 1970; Campbell and Erlebacher, 1970A; 1970B).

Members of the initial planning committee for Head Start were unenthused and unimpressed by the Westinghouse findings. Urie Bronfenbrenner (1979: 87) called the Westinghouse proposed design "an overly mechanical and mindless plan..." (also see Lourie, 1979). Richard Orton (1979: 133) stated that "Most of us associated with Head Start believe that the blackest day in the history of the program was the day the Westinghouse Report results were prematurely released to *The New York Times*...the findings of the Westinghouse evaluation seemed to us staff members to be inconclusive at best and potentially damaging at worst...Our fears were realized; the (*Times*) story emphasized the word 'failure'...it has taken Head Start many years to recover from that release." Zigler and Rescorla (1985) state that the pessimism of the Westinghouse study pervaded the media and became the dominant public view of Head Start.

Yet, when the Westinghouse study was released, Head Start administrators could produce virtually no evaluation or even simple quantitative data to counter it. The only completed federally sponsored national evaluation of Head Start was the Kirschner Report (Harmon and Hanley, 1979).

Early in 1970, Kirschner Associates (1970) produced an evaluation of Head Start's impact in local communities. The Kirschner study involved 58 communities with full-year Head Start programs. Illustrating that Head Start was an important social force in American society, Kirschner recorded 1,496 institutional changes grouped into four categories:

	Number	*Percent*
Increased involvement of the poor at decision-making levels	305	20.3
Greater employment of the poor as paraprofessionals	51	3.4
Greater educational emphasis on the educational needs of the poor and minorities	747	50.0
Modification of health services and practices to serve the poor better and more sensitively	393	26.3

The Kirschner report concluded that Head Start effectively made local institutions more responsive to the poor.

A few months after the release of the Westinghouse study, OEO published its review of all Head Start research and evaluation conducted between 1965 and 1969 (Grotberg, 1969). That assessment concluded that Head Start children did not lose what they gained from the experience, but that they tended to level off to a plateau which allowed other children to catch up with them. Parental approval of Project Head Start was also confirmed; indeed, the children of parents who had a high level of participation performed better on achievement and developmental tests (Steiner, 1976).

In 1977, another federally sponsored review of Head Start research since 1969 was published (Mann, Harrell, and Hurt, 1977). This assessment of numerous evaluations of on-site Head Start studies has confirmed that Head Start graduates:

1. Enter primary school close to or at national norms on measures of school readiness;

2. Maintain this advantage during the first year of school; and

3. Fail to show substantially better performance in comparison with non-Head Start participants in grades two and three.

As we will see later, results from longer term follow-up studies, which began to appear around 1979, show that Head Start graduates are less likely to be placed in special education classes or retained in a grade. Also, Datta (1979) reports that there are some "sleeper effects" on attitudes and achievement measures, relative to non-Head Start comparison groups, but final levels of test performance are still woefully low for both groups.

A study by the General Accounting Office (1979) reviewed the need for and impact of early childhood development programs on low income families. GAO concluded that preschool programs that reach children during their first four years help them "perform significantly better in school" and produce "lasting, significant gains."

In contrasting these reports with the Westinghouse Study, Steiner (1976) concluded that in the 1970's Head Start had reached a standoff. The project remained popular among participants and acceptable to Congress. If it seemed not to be accomplishing a fundamental objective, its defenders argued that it accomplished other, nonacademic objectives. Head Start advocates complained that scant attention was given to the Kirschner report. A decade later, Edward Zigler continued to be dismayed: "Why does everyone quote the Westinghouse Report (1969), which allegedly definitively demonstrates the failure of Head Start, while no one notes the Kirschner Report which documents its success?" (Zigler, 1979: 371).

Zigler's question may be answered by Steiner's (1976) argument that the failure of Kirschner to capture attention was because the universe in favor of enhancing the cognitive development of children is enormously larger than that concerned with changing local institutions. As Harmon and Hanley (1979) point out, Kirschner's finding "was not relevant to the terms of the argument set in motion by the Westinghouse evaluation" (p.391).

Thus, Steiner concluded, the Westinghouse study put a brake on planning new children's programs.

By 1974, with Zigler's assessment that Head Start "was on a tentative footing" (p.66), there were a number of evaluations of Head Start but little coherence or consistency to the evaluation effort (Zigler and Rescorla, 1985). As Director of OCD, Zigler commissioned two projects to synthesize the evaluation research on Head Start. Both studies viewed the same evidence but came to different conclusions. The first study, by Urie Bronfenbrenner (1975B), an original planner of Head Start, concluded that the initial gains of Head Start children "fade out" after three or four years. The second study, by Sally Ryan (1974), had a more positive and optimistic view of the data. However, by 1975, the fade-out assessment of Head Start was widely accepted. From 1975 to 1978, Head Start faded from public view; *The New York Times* and the A.P. News Service even reported that Head Start had been terminated (Zigler and Rescorla, 1985).

Issues from National Evaluations of Head Start

Many of the bases upon which the Westinghouse study has been criticized apply to the findings from other national impact studies as well. These studies have been criticized for:

1. The narrowness of their outcome measures;

2. Possible selection biases in who attended Head Start itself;

3. The question of program continuity;

4. The failure to examine the effect of different curricula;

5. The failure to examine the role of family process variables.

Head Start, according to Zigler and Anderson (1979), was designed to influence a broad array of factors including children's physical well-being, formal cognitive development, more circumscribed academic achievement, and socio-emotional development. Zigler and Anderson warned that no one of these factors should be judged as preeminent; rather all should be viewed as interacting in order to enhance social competence.

Narrow Outcome Measures

A commonly held misconception about Head Start is based on the idea that its primary purpose is to develop the cognitive capabilities and improve the IQ's of disadvantaged preschool children (Richmond, Stipek, and Zigler, 1979). For example, Wesley Becker (1981) asserted that the true goal of Head Start is to increase the IQ and school achievement of disadvantaged children; since initial gains in these areas "faded out," it could be concluded that Head Start was a failure. Nevertheless, as has been noted, Head Start has been since its inception a comprehensive program to improve health, nutrition, social skills, and parent involvement in their children's activities.

Nevertheless, assessments of the program's effectiveness have been concentrated in the cognitive and academic achievement domains with particular focus on IQ. As E. Gordon notes (1979), IQ has come to dominate the discussions of Head Start impact data. Weikart (1982) argues that standardized tests simply are approximations of the real-world goals, and that it is unclear what early grade achievement correlates mean in terms of actual adult performance. Travers and Light (1982) applaud the use of highly practical indicators by the consortium on Developmental Continuity (Lazar et al., 1977) which combine academic motivation and skills, but they observe that the use of such measures deserves close scrutiny insofar as these measures are affected by school policies and other external factors that may obscure their interpretation as measures of long-term individual success.

Zigler and Anderson (1979) decry the minimal attention devoted to the parent involvement component and the comprehensive "whole child" approach in assessments of Head Start, and observe that apparently it was easier to give children IQ tests than to find out if they were healthy and happy, or if their parents participated in the programs. Further, IQ tests are well-developed instruments that have proved valid and reliable predictors of school performance whereas measures of social-emotional variables are few in number and not well-understood (Richmond, Stipek, and Zigler, 1979; Zigler and Rescorla, 1985).

Given that two-thirds of Head Start children are members of ethnic minority groups, the heavy emphasis on IQ measures in Head Start immediately raises concern about the cross-cultural fairness of tests. Jensen (1969) and others have argued that an individual's genetic potential contributes significantly more than the environment to his or her intellectual capabilities. On the other hand, Zigler, Abelson, and Seitz (1973) have demonstrated that "performance" in test situations is not necessarily related to the underlying "competencies" of the children being tested. Poor children very often lack the motivation to perform well in test situations. Further, research that does not use IQ as an indicator of intellectual ability has shown that poor children have a vast range of intellectual and social competencies.

Experts continue to take opposite sides on this issue (see Cole and Brunner, 1971). These criticisms are nonetheless sound and have raised significant challenges to the commonly held assumption that the poor child has a range of social and intellectual deficiencies.

Selection Bias

The issue of selection bias is important in interpreting evaluation results where randomly selected control groups are not available. As Datta (1979) explains, if one assumes that Head Start serves the neediest children first, the Westinghouse data reveal reliable and important value-added effects of Project Head Start on later achievement. Shipman's (1972) analysis of the data gathered for the 1969-70 national impact study demonstrates that Head Start clearly enrolls "least-advantaged" children. If generalizable, the Shipman data indicate that Head Start has reached out to children who are likely to have greater developmental lags than Head Start-eligible children who do not enter the program.

Program Continuity

Relative to the question of program continuity, the issue is whether the special attention received by Head Start participants should be carried through to the primary school setting. Weisberg and Haney (1977) reviewed percentile ranks on the Mathematics Achievement Test (MAT) annually from kindergarten to third grade for the same pupils and found that at each readiness level, Head Start children who continued in Follow Through had steadier and higher performance than those who did not continue. Stipek, Valentine, and Zigler (1979) argue that the idea that a one-shot preschool intervention can counterbalance the debilitating effects of inadequate inner-city school systems and the associated conditions of living in poverty must be subjected to intense scrutiny.

Curricula

Another issue raised by the national impact studies is the effect of different curricula. A frequent criticism of the Westinghouse study was that it failed to examine differences in both the nature and quality of either the Head Start programs or the elementary school classrooms as factors influencing children's performance (Datta, 1979). This would seem to be a critical variable that must be examined, given Zigler's (1979) observation that there is likely to be as much variation within Head Start as there is between Head Start and non-Head Start environments. Mann et al. (1977) report data from Featherstone who investigated whether planned variation in eight Head Start programs have differing cognitive effects on different kinds of children. Based on data of analysis of the first two years of planned variation, there is no one approach that will work for all children. Similarly, both Shipman (1972) and Zigler (1979) argue against the view that poor children are a homogenous group universally in need of a single type of intervention program.

Datta (1979) notes that while extensive research is currently underway on curricula, little is being done to assess the role of program quality (independent of curriculum philosophy). Her analysis of this research concludes that both implementation and outcomes are affected by variables related to quality in the classroom, the school, and the community.

Family Process Variables

The final major issue identified by Datta (1979) is the role of family process variables. Datta reports that parental formal schooling and the mother's educational aspirations and expectations for the child predict subsequent school performance. Dunteman et al. (1972) and Coulson (1972) report similar findings for the immediate effects of Head Start. From the findings it is reasonable to conclude that participation in Head Start may not explain any individual variation in children's later school performance, after the impacts of family situation, status, and process variables are partialed out.

As we mentioned, there has been considerable concern and speculation about whether Head Start's immediate effects on measures of intellectual performance "wash out" or "fade out" over time. Sally Ryan (1974) asserts that when parents are significantly involved in the project, gains can be maintained. The "wash out" effect has also been challenged by the Consortium on Developmental Continuity (Brown, 1979; Lazar et al., 1977; Palmer and Anderson, 1979). Moreover, the failure of children to have continued academic success may be viewed as reflecting deficiencies of elementary schools rather than inadequacies of the Head Start program. Zigler (1973: 372) argues that "Besides being erroneous, the worst danger of the fade-out position is that it provides ammunition to those in America who feel that expending money in an effort to improve the lives of economically disadvantaged children is a waste."

Related to this issue of parental influence, Zigler (1979) wondered if the development of leadership potential among the poor, as a consequence of parental participation in Head Start, might not be an important factor in optimizing children's development. The question which Zigler raised is whether a child's sense of control is affected by the leadership behavior which is modeled by the children's parents. The modeling formulations of the social- learning theorists would predict that children who develop a view that their parents can influence their own destiny should themselves develop similar behaviors. In view of the economic disadvantages experienced by Head Start-eligible children, especially those who belong to ethnic minority groups, we believe that "sense of personal control" is a fruitful area for the investigation of long-term effects in a nonintellectual area.

The Consortium on Developmental Continuity

Partly based on concern about the impact of the Westinghouse Report, in 1975 the Consortium on Developmental Continuity was formed by a group of investigators who conducted separate intervention studies immediately before and after the beginning of Project Head Start. These investigators decided to pool their efforts, locate the children in their earlier studies, and compare them on a common set of criteria to determine if there were long-term gains from early intervention. The following is an analysis of the results of the Consortium findings. We draw heavily in this enterprise from the reviews of studies by Datta (1979), Palmer and Anderson (1979), Lazar et al. (1977), and Mann et al. (1977).

Despite variations in design, when results from the Consortium on Developmental Continuity are considered as a whole, they not only answer the questions whether early childhood programs can be effective, but also provide strong evidence for the lasting effects of early intervention.

Palmer and Anderson noted that Head Start and intervention studies are not synonymous. While Head Start as a national program includes individual programs of varying effectiveness, the intervention studies were designed to ascertain whether an individual program had durable results. Hence, the variety of programs included in the various interventions permits conclusions which could not be derived from a single study and this suggests ways of assessing the persistence of preschool effects.

The collective results from the consortium studies identified long-term benefits in three areas for the experimentals relative to the controls: special education assignment, in-grade retention, and cognitive measures. In addition, the program improved cognitive skills into the primary grades as measured by the Stanford-Binet. Further, preliminary analyses indicated significant differences in attitudinal responses, such as program children rating themselves better than others in their school work compared to their controls and high parental satisfaction with the program.

Palmer and Anderson report that five of the consortium studies demonstrated significantly higher reading scores for children exposed to early intervention; two found that experimental children had higher reading scores but not significantly so; and one reported no differences. There was also strong evidence of increased arithmetic achievement.

As in all longitudinal studies, attrition was a consortium concern. Although there were instances of differential attrition for three studies, neither across nor within studies did attrition appear to have been biased in favor of experimental children.

No single study significantly affected all variables associated with elementary school performance, but all studies affected at least one, and some, several. However, the data from these studies are especially compelling with respect to percent retained in grade and assignment to special classes. In spite of the implications of these findings for actual scholastic performance, Palmer and Anderson contend that more longitudinal studies are needed to determine what kinds of intervention are best for what kinds of children. No single program, they maintain, will be found best for all children regardless of region, ethnic background, and community or family environment.

There was variability among the consortium studies in terms of type of program, amount of parental involvement in the training and amount of family support given, age when the original intervention occurred, duration of the intervention, intensity of the intervention, and theoretical persuasion of the principal investigator. In addition, subjects were drawn from widely varying geographical locations and were from both rural and urban populations. Moreover, all studies had not originally gathered data that would permit assessment of all the common follow-up parameters. Nevertheless, the consortium did reach conclusions about the effects of age; duration; type and intensity of interventions; and amounts of family involvement as considerations for assessing the effectiveness of early intervention and, by extension, Head Start.

Age When Intervention Occurred

Preschool education intervention is defined as any treatment imposed from birth to age five, when most children enter kindergarten. Although every age of intervention is represented by one or more of the studies, Palmer and Anderson state that the best evidence of this treatment is offered by those studies in which age of intervention was varied as part of the research design: those of Palmer (two to three years), Gordon (three months to three years), Beller (four to five years), and Gray (four to five years).

In summary, Palmer found that at grade six no differences existed for reading and arithmetic achievement retention in grade between those trained at ages two and three years. Gray found no significant differences at any time between the two experimental groups on IQ or achievement. At grade four Beller found differences in IQ and reading achievement for both boys and girls and in math achievement for girls. However, early training was confounded with duration of training, and attrition was a concern because those who dropped out had a significantly lower IQ than those in his final sample. At grade three, Gordon found two or three years of intervention beginning at three months to be more effective in promoting differences in reading and mathematics than one or two years of intervention beginning at ages one or two years. However, his study confounds age of intervention with length and continuity of intervention. Hence, from the studies which varied age of training as a research design feature, no definitive conclusions can be drawn with respect to the best age at which to initiate intervention.

A similar pattern of inconclusive findings emerges from consideration of the other studies which did not vary age of training as part of the research design. Moreover, few conclusions can be reached across studies about the most effective age of intervention because of the number of confounding variables when comparisons are made. Although intervention at ages two and three years generally gave stronger results for both achievement and IQ scores in elementary school than did intervention at age four years, when most of the investigations intervened, the only fair conclusion is that intervention at any age prior to school seems to benefit the child and that further evidence about age of intervention is needed.

Duration of Intervention

Duration of intervention refers to the number of years prior to elementary school that children received early intervention. Palmer and Anderson found that this treatment was varied systematically as a design feature only in the studies of Beller, Gordon, Gray, Seitz, and Levenstein, with duration of intervention ranging from zero to three years or pre- grade-one schooling.

Beller, Gordon, and Levenstein found stronger effects with longer intervention; Gray found no difference between durations of three and two years; and Seitz found significant effects for longer duration among one cohort of Head Start girls only. However, these positive results for studies of longer duration are counterbalanced by the studies which, with one year or less of intervention, produced as many significant effects. As Palmer and Anderson noted, although the Beller, Gordon, and Levenstein studies suggested the seemmingly reasonable hypothesis that "the more intervention the better," the other data failed to support that hypothesis.

Types of Intervention

Lazar and Palmer and Anderson categorized interventions grossly as home-based, center-based, and combination instruction programs. In addition, both have distinguished programs on the basis of group and individual instruction. The programs of Seitz, Deutsch, Beller, Karnes, Palmer, and Miller were center-based. The programs of Gordon and Levenstein were home-based. Gray's Early Training Project, Weikart's Perry Preschool Project, and Miller's study represent a combination of home- and center-based elements. It should be noted, as Palmer and Anderson pointed out, that type of program is confounded by the arbitrary nature of the groups examined. In addition, home-based programs are used more frequently for infant intervention while toddler and preschool interventions tend to occur in center-based and combination instruction programs.

Among the center-based programs, the studies of Palmer, Seitz, and Miller presented data on retention in grade. Palmer and Seitz found experimentals less likely to be retained. In the Miller study there were fewer retentions among controls than among experimentals. Among the combination studies, Gray and Weikert reported differences in favor of the experimentals. Finally, among the home-based studies, Gordon's results favored the experimentals while Levenstein's slightly favored the controls. The data were insufficient from these studies to permit determination of whether the home-based/center- based/combination variable produced differential retention rates.

The combined evidence from five projects, which examined whether the children had been assigned to special education classes, shows that early education significantly reduces the number of children assigned to special education. Relative to this variable, data from center-based programs are available only from the Miller study which reported an advantage for controls. In contrast, the four home-based or combination programs showed advantages in favor of the experimental children. Comparison of center-based with home-based or combination programs was not possible. As an aside, it is of interest to note that the data from the Miller and Karnes projects, which were designed to compare different preschool curricula, indicate no significant differences in the rate of assignment to special education as a function of the different curricula.

Overall, data from seven projects represent moderate evidence that early education can have an effect on the likelihood of children's retention. In addition, five studies present strong evidence that preschool intervention reduces the number of children assigned to special education during their school years. However, the projects that had significantly reduced the rate of assignment to special education classes did not reduce also the number of retentions in grades. Lazar concludes that the difference in apparent strengths of effects for the two variables could be partially due to the fact that policy with respect to retention varies more widely among school districts than does policy with respect to special education. Nevertheless, four of these projects produced significant or near-significant reductions in the rate of assignment to special education.

Similar to the pattern found for the special education and grade retention variables, the findings are mixed when types of programs are examined for differential outcomes among experimentals and controls on reading achievement, arithmetic achievement, and IQ tests. Palmer and Anderson stated that there seemed to be no reason to conclude that there were advantages for home-based, center-based, or combination programs.

Another concern is the relative impact of individual or group training on overall development. Palmer and Anderson found that the studies of Palmer, Levenstein, and Gordon are representative of individual training, while those of Deutsch, Beller, Seitz, Miller, Weikart, and Gray are representative of the group-training approach.

Among the individual training mode projects, significant effects for arithmetic and IQ were reported by each study. Palmer and Levenstein reported significant effects for reading while Gordon's results also favored experimentals, but not significantly. Palmer and Gordon reported experimental advantages in grade retention percentages, with Palmer's results being significant. Gordon and Levenstein reported significant special education placement effects for experimentals with the advantage particularly accentuated for Gordon's subjects who had two or three years of consecutive intervention; this strong result, however, reflects a confounding with duration of intervention.

Of the group-training programs, no data bearing on special education were reported by Deutsch, Beller, or Seitz. Only Weikart's study showed significant experimental effects. For retention in grade, only Weikart and Seitz presented significant results; no findings were reported by Deutsch or Beller. The studies of Beller, Seitz, and Weikart reported experimental IQ advantages while those of Deutsch and Miller did not. Seitz and Miller found no experimental advantages in reading and math achievement while Deutsch, Beller (for girls only), and Weikart did find such support.

Of all the dimensions analyzed thus far, the results reported here are distinctive and most convincing: individual training is superior to group training.

Intensity of Intervention

The intensity variable is assessed by examining the number of weekly hours that programs contacted children and their families, with contact ranging from two hours (Palmer) to 20 hours with the child and 90 minutes at home with the mother (Weikart). At these extremes of contact, consistent experimental advantages were reported for the five parameters we have reviewed--i.e., retention, special education, IQ, and reading and arithmetic achievement--by both Weikart and Palmer, with the exception of special education which was not assessed in the Palmer study. Moreover, as we saw above, Palmer's study produced the stronger effects among the individually-based designs while Weikart's was the most effective of the group- based types. Hence, no conclusions can be drawn about the relative effectiveness of the intensity of interaction.

In fact, Palmer and Anderson attribute the effects found more to the nature of the interaction rather than its quality. If their view is correct, it would seem to support the contention of Travers and Light (1982) that analysis of process measures--both gross measures of services provided and fine-grained measures of transactions between staff and clients--is critical to the assessment of the effects of intervention studies.

Amount of Family Involvement

Palmer and Anderson identified two dimensions of family involvement in the consortium intervention studies: (1) programs incorporating the active involvement of the parent in teaching the child through the use of home visitors who provided materials and advice on methods, and (2) programs that provided support services for the family, e.g., social workers. These two dimensions were not confounded in any of the studies.

Gordon, Levenstein, Gray, Weikart, and Miller utilized home visits. Beller, Deutsch, and Seitz provided support services, but not home visits. Palmer, Miller, and Karnes made no special provisions for parental participation or services. Some studies from each of the three levels of parental involvement reported significant effects for IQ, the achievement measures, grade retention, and assignment to special education classes. Unfortunately, studies from each of these three groups reported nonsignificant findings for these several variables as well. Thus, no conclusions can be reached about the effects of parental involvement. It should be noted that in the assessment of long-term intervention effects, no examination was reported bearing on the efficacy of different forms/patterns of parenting skills. This area is also almost entirely devoid from the Head Start literature in general. This is a serious omission and is an area demanding research in view of the paramount importance attached by Head Start to the role of parents in the education process.

The Consortium Findings in Summary

Considered collectively, the data reported from the different types of interventions refute the premature criticisms of Jensen (1969), Bronfenbrenner (1974), and Jencks (1972) that no long lasting benefits accrue to economically deprived children who attended several different early education programs.

However, the issue of whether these results are externally valid, as applied to Head Start, is not settled. Earlier, we noted Palmer and Anderson's observation that Head Start and early intervention are not synonymous. Hence, the extent to which the consortium intervention findings may be generalized to other programs must be investigated. Still, Palmer and Anderson observed that since many Head Start Programs incorporated elements similar to the consortium studies, it is reasonable to assume that some of them have benefited children as well.

Recent Evaluations: The Perry Preschool Project And the Head Start Synthesis Project

This chapter clearly illustrates that measuring the effectiveness of Project Head Start is a complex and demanding task. Although popular opinion since the late 1970's has held that Head Start is a success, there are still many unanswered questions about the short-, mid- and long-term effectiveness of Head Start and other intervention programs for poor children.

Recent attention to this issue has been stimulated by two major reports. The first, *Changed Lives: The Effects of the Perry Preschool Program on Youths Through Age 19*, was published in 1984. The second report, the product of the Head Start Evaluation, Synthesis, and Utilization Project produced by CSR, Inc., was titled *The Impact of Head Start on Children, Families and Communities* (McKey et al., 1985).

Changed Lives

This monograph extends data from the original consortium data from Weikart's Perry Preschool Project (see Berrueta-Clement et al., 1984). This study identified both the long-term and short-term gains for the participants in a non-Head Start preschool intervention program. Many media reports, however, did not clearly distinguish the fact that the Perry children were not Head Start children. An editorial in *The Washington Post* commended the Perry Study "as the long-term study of a Michigan Head Start program" (*The Washington Post*, Monday, September 17, 1984, page A14).

Since the Perry Project is not Head Start, the results of this study, like those of the Consortium on Developmental Continuity, cannot be directly translated into statements about Project Head Start. Nevertheless, since the Perry Project and Project Head Start share the goal of helping poor children to improve their social and intellectual skills, the study has clear implications for Project Head Start.

The Perry study was a longitudinal study of 123 poor black youths who spent two years, at ages three or four, participating in either an experimental "high quality preschool program" or a control group. The teachers "received extensive managerial supervision and inservice training," made weekly home visits and maintained a staff/child ratio of 1 to 5 or 6.

The Perry Preschool study reported long-term beneficial effects of preschool education including:

1. *Improved scholastic placement and achievement during the school years.* Although the initial increases in IQ and other tests of academic performance diminished over time and eventually disappeared, there was other evidence of school success such as standardized achievement test scores and the fact that the participants had fewer absences and were less likely to be placed in special education or retained in grade.

2. *Decreased delinquency, crime, use of public assistance, and adolescent pregnancy rates.* The program participants indicated more social responsibility although there were no participant/ control-group differences on variables such as general self-esteem, specific self-esteem, perceptions of health, and use of leisure time.

3. *Increased high school graduation rates, enrollment in postsecondary programs, and employment.* The Perry researchers concluded that the economic value of the program is more than seven times the cost of one year of the program.

Unlike Head Start's emphasis on parent involvement, the Perry study did not specifically address the degree of parental involvement or the effects of the program on parents. However, the report notes that, eleven years after the various stages of the program were initiated, there were no differences between groups on demographic measures such as father's employment; father's presence or absence; household density; neighborhood ratings by parents; or the number of family changes in residences (Stephan, 1986).

Head Start Synthesis Project

Within a year after the Perry report was issued, the CSR, Inc., review of Head Start research, commonly referred to as the Head Start Synthesis Project, was published. This review compiled a bibliography of 1600 documents (all published and unpublished *Head Start* research). Two hundred and ten of these research reports were examined using a statistical technique called meta-analysis to aggregate the findings (Stephan, 1986). Meta-analysis is a newly developed statistical technique for summarizing the findings of different studies that address the same question (Schweinhart and Weikart, 1986).

The CSR review addressed whether Head Start programs are meeting the legislative goals of improving the social and learning skills, and the nutrition and health status, of primarily low-income children, and whether the programs are complying with legislative mandates for program components. The review examined the impact of Head Start on children as well as on families and communities. This review did NOT address many of the factors covered in the Perry Preschool Project such as scholastic placement and achievement during school years, delinquency and crime rates, the use of welfare assistance, the incidence of teenage pregnancy, high school graduation rates, enrollment in postsecondary programs, and employment rates.

The Head Start Synthesis project concluded that:

1. The studies were "virtually unanimous" in finding that *Head Start has immediate positive effects on children's cognitive ability* but that the cognitive test score gains do not appear to persist over the long term (2 years after Head Start).

2. Based on "very few studies," *Head Start appears to affect the long-term school achievement of participants* in terms of being retained in grade or assigned to special education classes.

3. *There were immediate socioemotional gains* in the areas of self-esteem, achievement motivation, and social behavior,

with mixed results in the persistence of these gains over the long term (up to three years after Head Start).

4. There were positive findings in the areas of *improved child health, motor development, nutrition, and dental care* but mixed results on whether the home diets of the children were better than those of non-Head Start children.

5. There were *no significant differences in the health practices at home* between Head Start and non-Head Start parents.

6. It was *unclear whether parental involvement* in Head Start *is related to their children's cognitive test scores* or whether Head Start improves parental *childrearing practices.*

7. Whereas antidotal data indicated that Head Start improves the lives of many Head Start parents, no systematic research has been conducted on this topic.

8. Consistent with the Kirschner (1970) findings, CSR found that *Head Start generated increased use of education, health, and social services* and that Head Start programs serve linking and coordinating roles with such services.

Although the CSR study findings were generally positive, Head Start advocates were concerned--yet again--about the suggestion that the cognitive and socioemotional gains from Head Start do not persist over the long term. Indeed, the report elicited a flurry of attention in child-related and education media with headings such as "Head Start Gains Short Lived" (*Education Week*, September 11, 1985; see Bridgman, 1985) and "Cognitive Social Gains in Head Start Don't Last" (Stephan, 1986). Child advocates pointed to the Perry study as evidence of long-term gains; however, it is important to note that the Perry study dealt with long-term impact on school success, socioeconomic success, and social responsibility, NOT with cognitive and socioemotional gains.

Lawrence Schweinhart and David P. Weikart (1986), two researchers affiliated with the Perry Preschool Project, have criticized the CSR study on several grounds.

1. It overgeneralizes the findings of 210 studies of Head Start programs; those programs were neither representative of the many Head Start programs throughout its history nor of today's programs. Since Head Start operational strategies differ radically in many respects, such as number of months and/or hours of operation, the report's generalization cannot be justified.

2. The report did not distinguish between low quality of design and high quality of design studies. CSR claimed that the low quality of design studies added pertinent information and helped to create a larger data base for the meta-analysis.

3. The report discounts other relevant research such as those from the Consortium on Longitudinal Studies. CSR argues that those non-Head Start studies were better funded, had a more professional staff, and were more carefully monitored, directed, and evaluated than is typical for Head Start programs. Nevertheless, Schweinhart and Weikart argue that these programs should not be discounted because they shed light on the value of Project Head Start. Schweinhart and Weikart note that the Perry Preschool Project cost $5,000 per child (in 1981 dollars) with its 5 to 1 ratio. If the ratio were increased to 8 to 1 with trained staff, the cost per child would be reduced to $3,125, a cost that is within the range of today's Head Start costs. While these researchers admit that the consortium programs, including the Perry Project, probably were better implemented than is now typical for Project Head Start, the point is that their level of quality is attainable by Head Start programs.

Conclusion

Stephan (1986) points out that many observers assert that the CSR's findings on long-term cognitive and socioemotional gains from Head Start suggest the need for further assistance in the years following Head Start to assure that the effects of early intervention do not fade away. Acting Associate Commissioner of the Head Start Bureau, Clennie Murphy, notes that the Head Start Synthesis Project identified positive aspects of Head Start, but also identified areas where improvements are needed, including more effective planning of classroom activities, closer partnerships between parents and teachers, greater emphasis on school readiness skills, and closer linkages between Head Start and the elementary school to assure continuation of the growth that children demonstrate while in Head Start.

Schweinhart and Weikart (1986), noting criticisms of the "fade-out" views of Head Start, challenge the assertion that every Head Start program must demonstrate long-term effects. The evidence for short-term effects are abundantly represented by CSR. Evidence for mid-term effects comes from the Consortium on Developmental Continuity. Long-term effects are illustrated by the Perry Preschool Project. We do not know if all of Head Start's programs produce short-, mid- or long-term effects, "but we *do* know that all these effects are possible" (Schweinhart and Weikart, 1986, p.23). Preschool programs for the disadvantaged, they add, help our nation to provide equal educational opportunity for those children whose parents cannot afford to provide nonpublic schooling for their children.

Based on these findings, Schweinhart and Weikart assert that three levels of probability should be used in claims about preschool effects:

"Good preschool programs for children at risk of school failure do better prepare them for school both intellectually and socially, probably help them to achieve greater school success, and can lead them to greater life success in adolescence and adulthood" (Schweinhart and Weikart, 1986, p.23).

Head Start: Career Development or Child Development?

An assessment of the effects of Head Start on children cannot avoid the issue of the effect of the program on staff and parents, because of the direct and immediate impact which staff and parents may have on the educative functions of the program.

As in most day care settings, special training in child development or early childhood education is generally not a *prerequisite* to employment in Head Start. The "Project Head Start Statistical Fact Sheet" published in January 1987 states that 33.8 percent of the classroom staff have degrees in early childhood education *or* have obtained the Child Development Associate (CDA) credential (USDHHS, 1987). Zigler and Lang (1983) assert that Head Start has a better trained staff than any other publicly supported program for children with the exception of the public schools.

An important aspect of staffing in Head Start programs has been the use of those persons most familiar with the children and their backgrounds: parents. Omwake (1979) has suggested that with the emphasis on the use of parents and neighborhood residents as paraprofessionals, which emerged in 1967, the employment function of Head Start took precedence over the educative functions with deleterious consequences for the quality of the latter function.

According to the Children's Defense Fund (1984), Head Start has provided jobs for more than 415,000 Head Start parents and community residents since 1965. About 75,000 people, 29 percent of whom were the parents of current or former Head Start students, were employed in Head Start projects in 1982. The Project Head Start Statistical Fact Sheet (USDHHS, 1985C and 1987) states that 31.6 percent of the staff are parents of current or former Head Start children.

The assumption guiding the use of neighborhood residents as teaching staff is that local residents have a better understanding of the needs and nature of neighborhood children and their parents than do professionals. Thus, professional training is considered only one indicator of competence, with the consequence that Head Start staffs are composed of individuals with a wide variety of professional and nonprofessional competencies. The differences vary from program to program. Omwake argues that while it may be desirable to have varied competencies among staff, it is undesirable to permit variations in personal qualifications for working with the children. She regards it as particularly unfortunate and a serious defect that there are no definitive guidelines about qualifications for Head Start staff.

Omwake believes that Head Start's career- development program for adults has achieved the immediate objective of providing encouragement and opportunities for staff members to improve their skills and become suitable teachers for Head Start children. However, she maintains that improvements in staff education have not resulted in a consistently improved educational experience for children in all Head Start programs.

Aside from their parenting experience, most Head Start parents working in centers have minimal skills and preparation to "teach" children. Although 65 percent of Head Start programs use the CDA to involve parents in the educational aspects of the program (CDF, 1984), many Head Start parents/staff do not seek that certification for many reasons, such as the fees assessed. With funds for other Head Start training being slashed in recent years (CDF, 1984), the quality of both child care and instruction in Head Start is threatened.

Omwake also is critical of the effectiveness of staff training programs designed by planners. She argues that although the workshops are designed to meet individual program needs and staff participation is required, a brief series of meetings with a specialist is inadequate for an inexperienced staff person to learn how to apply child-development concepts to early-education practices. Omwake contends that the educational component of Head Start might benefit if the promise of career advancement were made only to those who demonstrate improved performance rather than to anyone who routinely proceeds through the training sessions.

Omwake's central point is whether it is appropriate in Head Start to accord equal emphasis to program quality and employment opportunity. However, from an assessment perspective her criticisms raise several questions to which answers should be provided. Does staff quality affect the quality of education received by the children in the center-based programs? What are the elements which constitute the core of an effective staff training program given that they have been assigned to meet individual program needs? In addition, Mann et al. (1977) observed that it is not clear which aspects of parental participation are associated with gains for both the child and the parent. Mann and her colleagues conclude that this area needs to be clarified with additional research.

The Issue of Social Competence

Zigler and Rescorla (1985) note that, in retrospect, Head Start probably had too many goals. The multiplicity of goals led to a failure to underscore what "should have been stated as the primary goal of Head Start: to enhance the everyday social competence of disadvantaged children of normal intelligence" (p. 68). Zigler (1979) laments the fact that the planners of Head Start even allowed the IQ score to achieve status as the ultimate indicator of compensatory education's success or failure, and did not make it clear from the beginning that cognitive functioning was just one of several criteria that was to be employed in the definition of social competence. The goal is to foster social and emotional adjustment, to kindle motivation for learning, and to bolster self-esteem" (Zigler and Rescorla, 1985).

While these ideas are clearly presented in the performance standards, Zigler and Rescorla (1985) recognize that critics see the attention to the concept of social competence as a fall-back position used to fill the vacuum created when the data showed that Head Start did not produce permanent gains in IQ and school achievement. Indeed, although enhanced social competence was a primary goal for Head Start planners, they did not stress this goal for the first ten or more years of the program (Zigler and Rescorla, 1985).

Research by Zigler and his associates suggests that the lack of social competence is the primary deficiency of disadvantaged children. Indeed, it is argued that IQ gains resulting from preschool experiences are due to changes in motivational factors (see Zigler and Rescorla, 1985).

With respect to assessing the effects of Head Start, an initial difficulty is defining the concept of social competence. Zigler (1973) defined social competence as follows:

> By social competence, we meant an individual's everyday effectiveness in dealing with his environment. A child's social competence may be described as his ability to master appropriate formal concepts, to perform well in school, to stay out of trouble with the law, and to relate well to adults and other children (p.3).

Definition of the concept of social competence was a first need. However, there still remained the task of systematically mapping on a rational basis the domains covered by the concept and the relationships among them, if the construct was to serve as a principal criteria for the assessment of the effectiveness of early education programs. The many problems involved in this task have been described by Anderson and Messick (1973). These investigators were part of a committee of experts that met in 1973 to define the term, resulting in the identification of seven conceptual distinctions important in defining social competency, and a list of twenty-nine statements that represent facets of social competency in young children. The experts, however, made little progress in developing a usable instrument for assessing social competence in children (Zigler and Rescorla, 1985).

However, there have been many attempts to develop measures of social competence such as those by Susan Harter (1982), Baumrind (1982), and L. Fisher (1980). Harter's instrument is a self-report instrument based on the assumption that children do not always feel equally competent in cognitive, social, and physical domains. Baumrind (1982) identified four major constructs: social agency (confidence, leadership); social maturity (cooperation, altruism, reciprocity); cognitive maturity (drive for mastery); and cognitive agency (verbal fluency, creativity). L. Fisher (1980) identified teacher's and children's scale factors. The children's scale had four factors: brightness/ compliance; intrusiveness (aggressive, egocentric behavior); dullness (academic failure); and friendliness.

Zigler and Rescorla (1985) found that Harter's and Fisher's instruments are similar to their definitions of social competence but lack the adaptive behavior component (e.g., daily living skills or independence) they feel is important. On the other hand, they found Baumrind's factors to be robust, yet lacking a methodology practical enough for general use.

Mediax Associates (1978; 1979; 1980; 1983) was awarded a large-scale instrument development project in the area of social competence. Using panels of experts as well as numerous workshops with Head Start personnel, more than 1,000 items listing discrete aspects of social competence were generated (Mediax, 1980). More recently, Mediax Associates (1983) outlined four broad domains (cognitive; social-emotional; health and physical; and applied strategies) and 21 subordinate dimensions of development in their approach to social competency.

The Mediax investigators argue that their measures are designed to assess the effects of the programs, or to compare groups of children, not to evaluate individual children. Although this is a notable position, we wonder what is to prevent the measures from subsequently being used for the latter purpose. We are too familiar with the misuses of the IQ tests among minorities to believe that practitioners follow faithfully the instructions of methodological specialists relative to data intrepretations once the measures are employed. Further, Zigler and Rescorla (1985) state that they prefer an indirect mode of assessment using teachers and parents as informants and using a brief rating scale appropriate for assessing individual children as well as group comparisons.

Given the awareness of concern about ethnic bias in defining social competence (Ogbu, 1982), it is critical to observe that Mediax Associates employed several steps in the measure-development process to derive measures which would allow for culturally diverse manifestations of development in a given dimension, including multiple appropriate responses to the same stimuli in most instruments. They also were careful to use illustrations with which children of different racial and social backgrounds could identify, and to provide instructions in both English and Spanish. In addition, their national panel of consultants, which exercised general project oversight, included child development specialists of various racial/ethnic backgrounds.

In the formulation of items, Mediax Associates indicated that specific characteristics identified as important by parents, staffs, and K-2 teachers were taken into consideration. Our only reservation about this procedure revolves around the fact that minorities tend to be underrepresented in head teacher and senior staff positions within Head Start.

A further innovation used by Mediax Associates was to distribute the measures to scholars with established expertise in areas of child development for the rating of items on a number of criteria, one of which was that the item was to be "free of bias toward racial, ethnic, sex groups." The reservation we have about this procedure concerns the lack of sufficient input of minority scholars in this process.

We have identified several commendable features of the approach adopted by Mediax Associates in its development of measures of social competency. However, if social competency is to replace IQ as the ultimate criterion for the assessment of educational intervention effects, then it is critical to insure significant minority participation at every step in the process.

Concluding Comments

Underlying the excitement of Head Start was a belief in education as the solution to poverty (Zigler and Anderson, 1979). Central to this belief was the idea that the preschool years were a "critical period" which, if properly addressed, would lead to the eradication of transgenerational poverty.

Initially, many Head Start supporters fully expected the preschool program to be the cornerstone of equal educational opportunity. As a form of primary prevention, Head Start was envisioned as a means of insuring that poor children would obtain the educational prerequisites necessary to take advantage of formal, traditional schooling (Slaughter, 1982).

Indeed, it was the unrealized expectation and focus of Head Start's educational objectives that has resulted in the severest criticism of the program. Although the thesis that a preschool innoculation would produce phenomenal cognitive gains is now characterized as "naive optimism" (Zigler and Anderson, 1979), this thesis is most frequently at the core of charges that the program has "failed." Yet, only one of the seven original Head Start goals deals specifically with cognitive or intellectual capabilities. Rather, as the first comprehensive, developmental, preschool intervention program, Head Start emphasized service to the "whole child": improving health, emotional/social development, mental processes, expectations for success, interpersonal/ intrafamily relationships, social responsiblity, and feelings of self-worth.

The objectives of the Head Start Program, although broadly conceptualized, were, for the most part, clearly defined. The program, however, has never been fully measured against those objectives for the variety of reasons identified in this paper, among others. Further research in a diverse array of areas will be required before a comprehensive and accurate assessment of the effects of the program will be possible. Perhaps it is time to consider again the possibility of creating "a few maximum effort projects in which the best of what we [know] would be implemented, monitored, and its impact on a specified population studied," as E. Gordon (1979: 400) indicated was an option at the outset of Head Start.

Yet, the results of decades of research on Head Start clearly show that quality programs produce clear and lasting gains for children and their families. However, not all programs produce such benefits, and several factors are related to program quality and effectiveness.

Diana Slaughter (1982) asserts that "Head Start has accomplished everything but what it was originally supposed to accomplish: equal educational opportunity" (p.3). Slaughter's analysis for this "failure" is that the causes of low academic achievement did not lie solely with the children's families, as it was originally implied by Head Start. Rather, these causes are multiply determined and shared by all the children's caregivers. Slaughter recommends short-term goals and an emphasis on continuity of care, coupled with a healthier respect for the children's role in their own learning and development.

CHAPTER 7

MINORITY SCHOLARS LOOK AT HEAD START: THEIR RECOMMENDATIONS

Previous chapters have reviewed the history, impact, and theoretical basis for Project Head Start. Although Head Start is regarded by most as a great social intervention, social scientists and politicians are still baffled by the inability of Head Start families to move into economic self-sufficiency.

In this book we have suggested several factors which account for the limited success in this area, such as fallacies in the theoretical basis of the program and lack of attention to parent involvement relative to other program components.

A critical question remains: what changes should be incorporated into the Head Start program to address the issue of upward mobility of families?

We convened two national conferences of minority scholars in 1983 and 1985 to address these issues. Our focus was on Asian, Hispanic, and black scholars for two reasons:

1. Minority scholars have been underrepresented in Head Start research, and

2. Minority children comprise over two-thirds of Head Start's enrollment, a proportion higher than their representation in the poverty population.

In this chapter, the two conferences are described with an emphasis on the recommendations offered. This chapter discusses the conference objectives, the conference issues, and the conference recommendations for both the 1983 and 1985 meetings. The list of conferees is presented in Table 6.

The 1983 Conference

Twelve minority scholars and several special guests convened in Atlanta on November 1-3, 1983, to discuss and to debate issues related to the future of Project Head Start. At the conference, titled "Minority Perspective on the Future of Head Start," participants were asked:

1. To examine from a minority perspective the rationale for the formation of Head Start.

2. To examine the appropriateness of Head Start programs for minority families.

3. To assess the effects of Head Start on minority children.

4. To assess the appropriateness of indices of success in Head Start programs.

5. To examine the programs of Head Start in relation to the objective of upward mobility of minority families.

6. To make recommendations for modifications in Head Start which would promote the upward mobility of minority families.

In addition to these objectives, participants were asked to consider the following questions:

1. Can Head Start be effectively used as a vehicle for economic mobility?

2. What innovations in Head Start would you recommend to enhance economic mobility in Head Start?

3. What are the appropriate goals of Head Start for minority children?

4. How can cross-cultural innovations be developed and implemented for Head Start programs?

5. How can parent and community involvement in Head Start be made more effective?

6. What research questions should be given priority?

7. What is needed to increase the participation of minority researchers in Head Start research?

8. How can continuity between home, Head Start, and the elementary schools be enhanced for minority children?

Conference Issues

Three panels with one presenter and three reactors were presented at the conference. Each scholar present was asked to review the paper prepared for one panel and to provide comments for the total group. The panels, including the names of the author/presenter and the reactors, were as follows:

PANEL I--

Minority perspectives on the rationale for Head Start as a vehicle for the upward mobility of minority families

Presenter: Dr. Ura Jean Oyemade
Howard University

Reactors: Dr. Lillian Phenice
Michigan State Univ.

Dr. Aline Garrett
Univ. of South-
western Univ.

Dr. Priscilla Hilliard

Institute for Educational Leadership, Inc.

PANEL II--

An examination of the appropriateness of Head Start programs for minority families

Presenter: Dr. Valora Washington, Howard University

Reactors: Dr. Vonnie McLoyd Univ. of Michigan

Dr. John Dill Memphis State Univ.

Dr. John Stevens Georgia State Univ.

PANEL III--

A critical analysis of the assessment of the effects of Head Start on minority children

Presenter: Dr. O. Jackson Cole Howard University

Reactors: Dr. Luis Laosa Educational Testing Service

Dr. Margaret Spencer Emory University

Dr. Asa Hillard, III Georgia State Univ.

Conference Recommendations

As a result of the panels and the discussion, a myriad of recommendations emerged. These recommendations, listed by each panel, were as follows:

Panel I: Head Start and Upward Mobility

Recommendations in the Paper.

Recommendations were made in two areas, both involving augmentation of the parent involvement component. It was suggested that the issues of personal derivation and buying power should be addressed further. In the area of personal deprivation, it was suggested that the focus move from the concept of personal deprivation to personal enhancement in the following ways:

1.01 Inculcate values endemic to the minority community which have been found to foster achievement (e.g., work ethic, pride, discipline, persistence, religion, caring, faith, self-confidence, independence and supervision);

1.02 Strengthen the family structure through improved marital interaction with a view toward reduction of the divorce rate and hence the number of female headed households;

1.03 Reduce the incidence of teenage pregnancy;

1.04 Incorporate training programs which emphasize utilization of resources such as use of credit, budgeting, and management of resources.

In the area of buying power, or helping minority families to obtain jobs and a decent income, there were five recommendations. These were:

1.05 Identify and improve access to available jobs;

1.06 Reduce barriers (i.e., discrimination) to hiring and employment;

1.07 Develop job search and interview skills;

1.08 Improve training in skills necessary for specific jobs;

1.09 Develop positive work habits and attitudes necessary for improving productivity on the job.

Recommendations from Reactors and the Discussion.

Among the many issues raised, those receiving the most attention in Panel I were the needs to:

1.10 Tailor programs to meet the needs of local communities;

1.11 Examine whether Project Head Start should be expected to improve economic mobility in addition to all of the educational and other objectives;

1.12 Upgrade the educational component of the Head Start program;

1.13 Examine issues of quality control within Project Head Start;

1.14 Improve decision-making skills within families.

Panel 2:Head Start: How Appropriate for Minority Families?

Recommendations in the Paper.

Recommendations are made in each of four areas: community control, parent involvement, the comprehensive program, and the issue of cultural diversity.

2.01 Reaffirm Congressional intent and commitment to the concept of community control which is now assured by the fact that grants are given directly from the federal government to local communities;

2.02 Analyze and monitor the effects of regulatory, administrative, and procedural changes (i.e., competitive bidding) on Project Head Start;

2.03 Revitalize the role of parents in Head Start Projects; enhance opportunities for meaningful parent participation;

2.04 Document the extent of parent participation in Head Start and the kinds of parent activities which are most productive for children and/or parents;

2.05 Specify and document the process skills that parents gain through Head Start (i.e., practice in negotiating with public institutions or enhanced leadership experiences);

2.06 Develop programs to more adequately serve the needs of migrant children;

2.07 Document the impact the Head Start health care component has on poor children and the extent to which needed services have been provided;

2.08 Monitor the impact of reductions in other federal programs (such as AFDC, WIC, Child Care Food Program) on Project Head Start to assure that the comprehensive mandate is not eroded;

2.09 Ensure that the composition of the Head Start staff reflects the ethnic composition of the children served;

2.10 Explore the issue of whether, and how, preschool Head Start can best prepare minority children for social institutions (such as primary schools) which perpetuate inequality and racism;

2.11 Develop and implement multicultural curriculum strategies for Head Start children;

2.12 Reemphasize the promotion of positive self-concepts through opportunities to learn about and appreciate one's own culture;

2.13 Reexamine the concept of "maximum feasible participation";

2.14 Expand services to children under three;

2.15 Ensure the provision of primary or supplemental health and nutritional services;

2.16 Invest more money in Head Start to boost enrollment, increase teachers salaries, reduce classroom size, and off-set "back door" budget cuts.

Recommendations From Reactors and the Discussion.

Most prevalent among the many issues and questions raised were the following:

2.17 How can Head Start prepare and promote parents to cope with a less supportive public school?;

2.18 Should we prepare parents and children to cope without changing the system?;

2.19 Is Head Start part of the problem or part of the solution?;

2.20 Enhance the Head Start curriculum in many ways, including social skills, language, math, etc.;

2.21 How can Head Start enhance the networking skills of parents, thereby enabling them to have their needs better served from agencies?;

2.22 Isolate and differentiate between the various kinds of parent involvement;

2.23 Assess the quality of parent involvement to determine which type of Head Start climate best promotes parent involvement;

2.24 Address the issue of staff training, salary, and benefits.

Panel 3:The Effects of Head Start on Minority Children

Recommendations in the Paper.

Evaluation strategies outlined included the need to:

3.01 Review the narrowness of traditional outcome measures;

3.02 Examine possible selection biases;

3.03 Examine the role of family process variables;

3.04 Examine the effect of different curricula;

3.05 More closely examine results with respect to the age, type, duration, or intensity of interventions and the amount of family involvement;

3.06 Clearly analyze, assess, and differentiate between the appropriateness of Head Start's equal emphasis on program quality and employment opportunities for parents;

3.07 Address the issue of staff training;

3.08 Define and develop measures for "social competence."

Recommendations from Reactors and the Discussion.

The discussion focused on the following issues and questions:

3.09 Develop ethnic perspectives on social competence and insure ethnic participation in every step of the process to define and measure social competence;

3.10 Design and implement follow-up studies and long-term assessments of Head Start children;

3.11 Focus on children in the context of their families and in the context of their ethnicity; look at outcomes in relation to the child's ethnic group membership;

3.12 Restructure our thinking on the rationale and expected outcomes of Head Start;

3.13 Specify and identify evaluation objectives; different audiences may need different data if they emphasize different aspects of the goals of the programs;

3.14 Follow-up parents of Head Start children to find out which are advocates and which are not; what is the impact on the children?;

3.15 Consider the possibility that developing strong "socially competent" minority children may result in children who are better prepared to pick up negative impact from their teachers when they enter elementary schools;

3.16 Consider the state-of-the-art problems which generally exist in early childhood education assessment instruments when looking at the impact of Head Start;

3.17 Reconsider the use of the word "minority," and the delineation of ethnic groups, for conceptual validity.

3.18 Develop more valid and reliable assessment instruments;

3.19 Describe early education in non-Head Start programs in order to have a valid basis for comparison of Head Start results;

3.20 Assess the problem of the validity of terms such as minority, social competence, and cognition which are used too vaguely and generally;

3.21 Investigate the relationship of parent behavior to parent outcomes;

3.22 Address the problem of bias since the evaluators do not represent the population being served; ensure that members of ethnic groups actually have academic experiences in that group.

Composite Recommendations

There were several major themes which united the three panels. These themes form the basis for the composite recommendations which we offer as the primary concerns emerging from this conference. The five priority issues are as follows:

1. *Define and enhance opportunities for parent involvement.* Project Head Start was formed as part of a comprehensive "War on Poverty" which sought to produce economic self-sufficiency for the families. This goal should be reaffirmed through efforts to document the extent of parent involvement; to isolate and differentiate between the various kinds of parent involvement; to determine which type of Head Start climate best promotes parent involvement; and to determine which types of parent involvement are more clearly related to pupil outcomes. In addition, the decision-making and process skills which enhance parental moves toward self- sufficiency, and advocacy for themselves and their children, should be explored.

2. *Assess the quality of Head Start programs and enhance the educational component of the project.* Throughout the conference there were questions about the variation in the quality of Head Start programs throughout the United States. There was also concern that, due to budgetary restraints, centers are utilizing a variety of attendance options for children which may adversely affect pupil outcomes. Several recommendations were made to improve the educational component. Most frequently suggested were calls to: inculcate ethnic values and heritage; facilitate the transition from Head Start to the public schools; enhance the teaching of academic subjects; and more closely examine results with respect to the age, type, duration, or intensity of interventions, and the impact of family involvement.

There was also concern about class size and staff-child ratios. Cuts in funds for staff training, coupled with budget cuts in support programs for Head Start, make the first priority to preserve the quality of Head Start services. Among the educational services needing preservation are the favorable staff-child ratios and reasonable class sizes enjoyed in the past (Zigler and Lang, 1983).

3. *Involve members of ethnic groups in Project Head Start as members of advisory panels, proposal reviewers, and principal investigators.*
   At the core of this recommendation is the lack of ethnic group representation in the research or evaluations of Project Head Start. This is of particular concern given that two-thirds of Head Start children are from racial minorities. The conferees recommended closer collaboration between federal or regional Head Start administrators and minority scholars.

4. *Address the issue of the training of Head Start staff, as well as the salary and benefits which they receive.*
   At the core of any reexamination of Head Start, or calls for innovations in the program, is concern about staff training, salary, and benefits. It is argued that the 19 percent staff turnover rate of Head Start programs negatively affects program quality (Stephan, 1986). Improvement in curriculum, parent involvement, or outcomes for children are related to the quality of staff. It was suggested that the salary scale for Head Start personnel be reevaluated.

Instead of improving the quality of training, and thus the quality of the educational component of the program, many centers have had to cut budgets for staff development. This affects not only the quantity of available staff in training, but also the quality of teacher preparation (Zigler and Lang, 1983). Both the number of staff and the appropriateness of their training have a tremendous impact on the outcomes of any program for children. The National Head Start Association

Director stated in 1985 that low teacher salaries attract unprepared workers who need intensive training; once the teachers are trained, they leave the programs--indeed, teachers with certification are often attracted to public schools where salaries and benefits are higher.

Specific recommendations for staff development also were outlined in the 15th anniversary report on Head Start (Muenchow and Shays, 1980). Among these recommendations is the call for at least one teacher in every Head Start classroom to have a nationally recognized credential in child development.

According to Stephan (1986) the Child Development Associate (CDA) program, a plan for training and credentialing the child care staff, was implemented by the Office of Child Development (ACYF predecessor agency) in 1975. Except for a brief interval, CDA has had continued support from ACYF since that time. In 1985, CDA responsibility was transferred to the private sector with the National Association for the Education of Young Children assuming leadership. Critics of private sector sponsorship feared that it would result in a substantial increase in candidate fees, pricing the credential out of the range of many interested people.

It was reported in 1983 that Head Start teachers receive extremely low salaries, averaging $7,500 a year (CDF, 1983B). If Head Start is to recruit and retain high quality staff, salaries and benefits must be improved. Zigler and Lang (1983) state that staff should have cost-of-living increases, salary incentives, and employee benefits at least comparable to those other personnel performing similar tasks in the same community. They further assert that, at every level of the program, job requirements and minimum salaries should be established; this attention to the conditions under which Head Start staffs work is of paramount importance because the high turnover rate in many programs undermines an essential element in the young child's development: continuity of care.

In February 1985, the Office of the Inspector General (IG), Department of Health and Human Services, issued a report on Head Start wage comparability to day care agencies. The report found that Head Start teachers' average *hourly* salaries of $5.41 was 27 cents an hour more than that of the day care teachers. However, the average annual salaries of Head Start workers was less ($7,473 compared to $9,135 for day care), partly because Head Start teachers worked fewer weeks per year and fewer hours per week. Further, Head Start staffs were found to have more extensive duties and responsibilities than day care staffs, including lesson plans, home visits, and parent education. Head Start staffs are required by law to be compensated at a rate that is not in excess of the rate paid in the local area for substantially comparable services or less than the minimum wage.

In another 1985 IG report, it was found (USDHHS, 1985B) that approximately three- fourths of all Head Start grantees drew unemployment compensation during the summer. The IG concluded that this practice is contrary to the intent of unemployment insurance laws. Of critical importance is the fact that in the past few years many states have made each employer more accountable for benefits paid to their employees. As a result, there have been substantial increases in unemployment insurance costs for Head Start programs in the past three years (from $9.8 million in 1983 to $15.6 million in 1985). The IG report stated that these costs drain funds that could be used for merit or cost-of-living raises and erode program quality by decreasing resources available for direct services to the children (USDHHS, 1985A).

5. *Improve the quality of services that regional offices provide to grantees.*
   Finally, Zigler and Lang (1983) suggest that the number of community programs assigned to regional representatives should be reduced so that they are not too overworked, can get to know individual programs well, and can help maintain the good quality of those programs.

Conclusion and Next Steps

Participants at the conference indicated that they were pleased with the discussion and the practical recommendations which emerged as a result of the conference. Several conferees revealed that the importance and timeliness of the issues, coupled with stimulating discussion and debate, resulted in this conference being one of the best meetings which they had ever attended.

However, it was felt that, during the one-and- one-half day conference, there was insufficient time to explore all of the issues. It was also the consensus that the group which was convened should act to seek solutions to the issues discussed. Consequently, there were nine "next steps" with which participants at the conference concluded:

1. There was the consensus that the group should "stay together" as a group and should reconvene in the future.

2. Individual members of the group, where possible, should seek to serve on the review panels for both the Head Start expansion grants and the discretionary funds.

3. Individuals should be available to consult with administrators of Project Head Start, where feasible.

4. Individuals, and/or teams from this group, should get involved with local Head Start centers.

5. Individuals, and/or teams from this group, should respond to the two then current federal register initiatives regarding project Head Start.

6. We should seek funding from the private sector, as well as from the federal government, to work in Head Start centers.

7. We should publish, and encourage other minority scholars to publish, findings about Head Start.

8. We should involve our graduate students in Head Start research.

9. As individuals we should disseminate widely the results of the conference.

1985 Conference Overview

At the end of the 1983 meeting, there was a strong consensus that the group should "stay together" to collaborate and build upon the momentum of the sessions. While that goal was achieved informally, there was an urgent and continuing need to devise a mechanism through which the ideas of the group could be translated into a specific, implementable research program.

With this idea in mind, a working group of minority researchers was convened at Howard University for a total of one-and-one-half days, October 14 - October 16, 1985. The objectives of the meeting were:

1. To review minority perspectives on the future of Head Start and outcomes of the 1983 meeting;

2. To critique indices of the success of Head Start programs;

3. To identify needed advances in Head Start research; and

4. To outline a collaborative study.

Each scholar attending the meeting was committed to reviewing, debating, and engaging in a collaborative research project to begin in 1987. It was expected that the project would concern the parent involvement component of Project Head Start; many recommendations from the 1983 meeting involved augmentation of the parent involvement component.

Conference Issues

A keynote address and three panels with one presenter and three reactors were presented at the conference. Each scholar was asked to review the paper prepared for one panel and to provide comments for the total group. The keynote address and panels, including the names of the author/presenter and the reactors were as follows:

KEYNOTE ADDRESS: Research and action strategies for minority scholars

Dr. Robert B. Hill
Senior Research Scientist
Bureau of Social Science Research and
Visiting Professor
University of Pennsylvania

PANEL I - Indices of the success of Head Start progress: A critical analysis

Presenter: Dr. Luis Laosa
Educational Testing Service

Reactors: Dr. O. Jackson Cole
Howard University

Dr. Sadie Grimmett
Indiana University

PANEL II - Future directions in Head Start research: Where do we go from here?

Presenter: Dr. Diana T. Slaughter
Northwestern University

Reactors: Dr. Aline Garrett
University of Southwestern
Louisiana

PANEL III - A proposal for a collaborative study of the parent involvement component of Project Head Start by minority scholars in various geographical areas of the United States

Presenters: Dr. Ura Jean Oyemade
Dr. Valora Washington
Howard University

Reactors: Dr. Lillian Phenice
Michigan State University

Dr. Patricia A. Edwards
Louisiana Tech University

Overview of Panels

Keynote Address: Dr. Robert Hill spoke on the topic of "Research and Action Strategies for Minority Scholars." He suggested several research and action strategies which should be targeted in conducting research aimed at strengthening minority families. These included:

Research

1. The need for family needs assessments to determine action strategies;

2. The need for research on the environmental impact of programs on families; and

3. The need for more policy-oriented research.

Action

1. Minority Scholars should meet periodically and communicate with each other;

2. Minority Scholars should monitor research funding involving minority

3. Minority Scholars should help young people to become more research oriented; and

4. Communities should focus on the coordination of self-help and government programs.

Panel I: Panel I focused on the indices of success of Head Start in achieving the goal of bringing about greater "social competence" in children of low-income families. Luis Laosa elaborated on the dearth of studies on the impact of Head Start on communities, the issue of measuring long-term vs. short-term effects, and the failure of most evaluation efforts to consider the processes that would explain the evaluation results.

Panel II: Focusing on future directions for Head Start research, Diana Slaughter addressed the factors in the home environment which affect the academic achievement of minority youth. Types of parental involvement that have been found to be positively related to achievement include supervision of learning activities at home; literacy enhancing activities such as reading, writing, and word games; and help with homework. Parent involvement in schools as teacher aides for tutors has also had positive effects on children's academic performance. It was suggested that the parent involvement component should be the focus of future research since the parent component is the major reason Head Start has survived politically.

Panel III: Panel III focused on a proposal for a collaborative study of the parent involvement component of Project Head Start. Valora Washington and Ura Jean Oyemade presented the training manual for a pilot project currently being funded by Howard University and conducted in Nashville, Tennessee; Columbus, Ohio; and Baltimore, Maryland. The goal of the study is to document those aspects of the parent involvement model which would optimize the achievement of the goals of economic and social self-sufficiency.

The discussion centered on the feasibility of the group of minority scholars replicating this study in their respective sites as a means of achieving a national sample.

Recommendations from Panels

As a result of the panels and the discussion, a myriad of recommendations, listed by panel, were as follows:

Panel 1: Indices of the Success of Head Start Progress: A Critical Analysis

1.01 More studies should focus on the impact of Head Start on the community.

1.02 Future evaluations of Head Start should focus on "Why?" questions: Why did programs fail to meet program objectives? Why were they successful? Can results be replicated? Are they generalizable?

1.03 Future evaluations should assess the unintended effects of the program.

1.04 There is a need for policies which coordinate early intervention with school policies in order to have a long-term impact.

1.05 There is a need to conceptualize a model which maps the program and the evaluation.

1.06 There is a need to ground research in the context of the situation.

1.07 There is a need to design a prospective study and follow the population over a period of time to study individual differences.

1.08 There is a need to distinguish between the parent component as implementor vs. the target of the intervention.

1.09 Evaluation studies must take into consideration the variation in operationalization of programs across sites.

1.10 There is a need to design a prospective study which takes into consideration the measure of the context and process using less traditional outcome measures.

Panel 2: Future Directions in Head Start Research: Where Do We Go From Here?

2.01 There is a need to define the developmental course desired from minority children.

2.02 Since norms are not universal, we need to define what kind of children we seek to produce.

2.03 There is a need to define what kind of child Head Start is trying to produce.

2.04 Head Start should also focus on teaching minorities to be more socially responsible to the minority communities.

2.05 Future Head Start research should not focus on education but parent involvement in order to maintain the parent involvement model.

2.06 There is a need to examine current research on the influence of the parent on the child.

2.07 There is a need to develop more effective models for involving parents in the educational process in the schools.

Panel 3: A Proposal for a Collaborative Study of the Parent Involvement Component of Project Head Start by Minority Scholars in Various Geographical Areas of the United States

The participants agreed on the value of a national collaboration to research the impact of the parent involvement component on economic self-sufficiency. In late 1986, we prepared a draft of the proposal for the group, and we have obtained funding under a Spring 1987 data collection schedule.

Conclusion

The minority scholars reached the same consensus that was reached in 1980 by President Jimmy Carter's 15th Anniversary Head Start Committee (Muenchow and Shays, 1980): our first priority is to maintain and improve the quality of Head Start programs. This can be achieved through performance standards, teacher certification, salary incentives, employee benefits, and parent involvement. Minority scholars expressed particular concern about building the family focus of Project Head Start and increasing linkages with public schools.

TABLE 6

PARTICIPANTS IN MINORITY SCHOLARS CONFERENCES

NAME	*MEETINGS ATTENDED*
Dr. O. Jackson Cole Associate Dean (now Dean) School of Human Ecology Howard University Washington, D.C. 20059	1983 & 1985
Dr. John Dill Associate Vice President Academic Affairs Memphis State University Memphis, Tennessee 38152	1983 & 1985
Dr. Patricia A. Edwards Assistant Professor Department of Education Louisiana Tech University 1509 Oakdale Street Ruston, Louisiana 71272	1985
Dr. Aline Garrett Chairperson Department of Psychology University of Southwestern Louisiana Lafayette, Louisiana 70504	1983 & 1985
Dr. Sadie Grimmett Professor Indiana University 10th & ByPass 46 Bloomington, Indiana 47401	1985

Dr. Robert Hill 1985
Senior Research Scientist
Bureau of Social Science Research
1990 "M" Street, N.W.
Suite 700
Washington, D.C. 20036

Dr. Priscilla Hillard 1983
Associate Director
Work & Education Programs
Institute for Educational Leadership, Inc.
1001 Connecticut Avenue, N.W.
Suite 310
Washington, D.C. 20036

Dr. Asa G. Hilliard, III 1985
Fuller E. Callaway Professor of Urban Education
Georgia State University
Atlanta, Georgia 30303

Ms. Carlethea Johnson 1985
Head Start Preschool Coordinator
227 St. Paul Place
Baltimore, Maryland 21202

Dr. Mildred Johnson 1983
Director
CABLE State Training Facility
North Carolina A & T University
Greensboro, North Carolina 27411

Mr. Richard H. Johnson 1983 & 1985
Head Start Bureau/ACYF
Post Office Box 1182
Washington, D.C. 20013

Dr. Shirley Jones — 1983
Dean
School of Social Work
University of Southern Mississippi
Hattiesburg, Mississippi 39406

Dr. Luis Laosa — 1983 & 1985
Research Scientist
Educational Testing Service
Princeton, New Jersey 08540

Dr. Vonnie McLoyd — 1983 & 1985
Associate Professor
Department of Psychology
University of Michigan
Ann Arbor, Michigan 48105

Mr. Clennie Murphy — 1983
Acting Associate Commissioner
Head Start Bureau
400 6th Street, S.W.
Donohue Building, Room 5163
Washington, D.C. 20201

Dr. Ura Jean Oyemade — 1983 & 1985
Chairperson and Associate Professor
Department of Human Development
School of Human Ecology
Howard University
Washington, D.C. 20059

Dr. Lillian Phenice — 1983 & 1985
Associate Professor
College of Human Ecology
Michigan State University
East Lansing, Michigan 48101

Ms. Margaret Shaw — 1983
Director of Extended Day Care
North Carolina A & T State University

101 Dudley Building
Greensboro, North Carolina 27411

Dr. Diana Slaughter 1985
Associate Professor
College of Education
Northwestern University
Evanston, Illinois 60201 ✓

Mr. Donald E. Smith 1983
North Carolina A & T University
107 Dudley Building
Greensboro, North Carolina 27411

Dr. Margaret Spencer 1983 & 1985
Associate Professor
Department of Psychology
Emory University
Atlanta, Georgia 30322

Dr. Joseph Stevens 1983
Associate Professor
School of Education
Georgia State University
Atlanta, Georgia 30303

Dr. Brenda Taylor 1983
Director
Dekalb County EOA
Head Start Program
2484 Bruce Street
Lithonia, Georgia 30058

Mr. Edward Vaughn 1983
Child Development Resource Specialist
Region IV
Department of Health and Human Services
101 Marietta Tower
Suite 903
Atlanta, Georgia 30323

Dr. Valora Washington Assistant Dean and Associate Professor School of Human Ecology Howard University Washington, D.C. 20059	1983 & 1985
Mr. Marvin H. Watkins Director, Research Administration North Carolina A & T State University 305 Dowdy Administration Building Greensboro, North Carolina 27411	1983
Dr. Trellis Waxler Head Start Program Specialist Administration for Children, Youth and Families Head Start Bureau Post Office Box 1182 Washington, D.C. 20013	1983 & 1985

PART C:

CHANGING FAMILY TRENDS: IMPLICATIONS FOR PROJECT HEAD START

CHAPTER 8

CHANGING FAMILIES: AN OVERVIEW

Political and administrative changes in Head Start, and in other programs which serve Head Start eligible families, are creating new challenges for poor children. Head Start, now in its 22nd year, continues to be the most successful and enduring program from President Johnson's War on Poverty. Head Start continues to be a comprehensive program that provides health, educational, and social services and aims to move preschool children and their families toward self-sufficiency.

The wisely heralded effectiveness of Head Start is particularly important in light of the project's focus on low socioeconomic groups. More than 90 percent of Head Start families have incomes below the poverty line. Minority children comprise at least two-thirds of Head Start's enrollment. Over 12 percent of the Head Start children are handicapped.

Nevertheless, only a fraction of eligible participants are served by Head Start. The 452,000 children now enrolled represent only about 18 percent of all qualified children. More than 1,000 counties in the country do not offer Head Start.

Not only are just a fraction of the families eligible being served, but the need for Head Start services is increasing. This decade has ushered in a new wave of crises for America's families. In 1983, domestic poverty reached its highest level since Head Start began in 1965. More than 35 million families, or 15 percent of the population, fell below the official poverty level (U.S. Bureau of the Census, 1983A; 1983B). Millions of dependent children are affected--in 1982, 22 percent of our nation's children were members of low-income families.

Attitudes Toward Family Support in the United States

Generations of American Presidents, both Democratic and Republican, have pronounced the importance of children and the family for a strong government. For examples:

Lyndon B. Johnson (1967) observed: "The family is the cornerstone of our society. More than any other force it shapes the attitudes, the hopes, the ambitions, and the values of the child" (p.130).

Richard Nixon (1972) affirmed a "national commitment to providing all American children an opportunity for a healthful and stimulating development during the first five years of life" (p. 1174-1187).

As a Presidential candidate Jimmy Carter (1978) stated: "There can be no more urgent priority for the next administration than to see that every decision our government makes is deigned to honor and support and strengthen the American family" (p. 463,464).

Yet, there is little in American social policy, aside from the public school, which commits the resources of the United States to fulfill these lofty promises for children and families. Indeed, care for children and family support have generally been considered a private matter.

This contrast between political rhetoric and actual policy poses the American dilemma which surrounds public policy toward young children. A distinction must be made between a general cultural piety about the family and specific social policies directed to family concerns. The two need not be complementary; most often, in American experience, they are in conflict (Moynihan, 1973).

Nevertheless, this dilemma raises a myriad of questions for public consideration: Should we routinely provide for the care of young children using public resources? Should public care be targeted to particular groups, such as the poor or handicapped? Should care be preventative or rehabilitative? How can our government reconcile our laissez-faire traditions toward children with increasing calls for comprehensive policies for all children? (Moroney, 1976).

In any country, societal taboos and beliefs influe
life and shape the ecological perspectives of young childre
States, the societal posture has been one of restraint and non
The care of children is considered to rest in the private domain
Gilbert Steiner (1976), a noted analyst of child and family policy
rearing "the least regulated important aspect of American life" (p.1,

The American tradition toward restraint in family matters has its roots in the eighteenth-century liberal or "laissez-faire" philosophers. The doctrines of Adam Smith, John Locke and others stressed individual freedom and free enterprise in a truly competitive market. Thus, the best government was the one that governed least. In the 1980's, such beliefs are labelled "conservative," yet they are still rooted in the notion that individuals can, in the prevailing social order, provide for their own needs through work, savings, investments, and acquisitions of property (Gil, 1976; Keniston et al., 1977).

Property rights have been ascendant in American values, and historically children have been considered the property of their parents. Thus, Condry and Lazar (1982) claim that when policy decisions raise conflict between property rights and the needs of children, property has usually won. As an example, they observe that pressure toward developing and enforcing strict federal day care standards in the 1970's was reduced because these standards would have increased the cost to private day care providers.

The tendency to insist on parental rights over children's needs (Sponseller and Fink, 1982) may also be related to the multiethnic character of our country. America's multiplicity of cultures and religious values lead to alternative childrearing styles. It would be difficult, at best, to "choose" from among the alternatives.

Further, suggestions that the government might provide general services to children and families have often been viewed with alarm. There is a historical tendency to fear "big government" as an invasion of the privacy and the sanctity of the individual family.

The primacy of the family in our country is such a strong ideological view that attempts to develop non-educational policies affecting children are subject to intense political attacks. For example, President Richard Nixon (1972), when vetoing proposed legislation, echoed the sentiments of millions of Americans when he asserted that "for the federal government to plunge headlong financially into supporting child development would commit the vast moral authority of the National Government to the side of communal approaches to child rearing and against the family centered approach" (p. 1174-87).

Politicians, however, are not the only source of public reticence toward public policy for children (Cohen and Connery, 1967; Greenblatt, 1977; Kamerman and Kahn, 1978). Many professionals in early childhood education also fear that social action might disrupt the parent-child bond or might infringe on family rights (Sponseller and Fink, 1980). Thus, some educators have a propensity to exhort parents, rather than advocate for societal policies which might conflict with parent practices and the cultural norms. Bettye Caldwell (1977) also has observed that educators sometimes discount studies indicating that children's attachment to parents is not harmed by out- of-home care, while citing authors who point to the dangers in this child care arrangement.

Nevertheless, Americans have not been hesitant to adapt its social ecology around childhood during national emergencies. During the Depression of the 1930's, for example, day care centers were established under the federal government's Works Progress Administration. During World War II, the Lanham Act provided funds for day care and extended school services to facilitate women's participation in war- related industries; these Lanham child care centers were closed at the end of the war (Condry and Lazar, 1982; Steiner, 1976).

The historical record converges to create a society in which it has not been politically feasible nor, in some cases, desirable to develop children's policy. Against this backdrop, child advocates have had difficulty in developing or implementing acceptable public policies targeted to young children.

The non-interventionist tradition in American policy is not absolute. For the most part, however, aside from national emergency, economic disaster or a health crisis, American tradition holds that a family should, and will, care for its own children without public assistance. Although experts differ in their approaches, they share the basic assumption that families, as self-sufficient entities, are responsible for their children's welfare (Keniston et al., 1977).

A variety of child-serving policies have evolved, nonetheless. Government policy consistently has enacted programs or procedures to protect all children from catastrophic and preventable conditions such as polio or blindness. However, in contrast with Presidential oratory on societal commitment to all children, often children and their families must exhibit a dysfunctional range of personal characteristics in order to qualify for public assistance. Indeed, the ecology surrounding program- eligibility is based on a personal deficit model. Child-oriented policies and programs are typically targeted toward those children considered to be "abnormal" by virtue of their social or physical handicaps.

Federal policy which allows for the care of "special needs" children (such as those who have dead, absent or abusive parents) does not, in any fundamental way, threaten the noninterventionist posture of American tradition. Rather, by limiting policy to crises in poor or dysfunctional families, the tradition is preserved (Steiner, 1981). Indeed, public policy as a response to human "deficiencies" has the benefit of appearing indicative of a mature and humane society.

The "normal" development of a child tends to exclude him or her from most federal policy which affects young children. Legislative actions and policies have focused primarily on children identified as needy (Verr, 1973). If individual deficiencies would cease to exist, then so would child and family policy. "If we want less government," stated President Jimmy Carter (1978), "we must have stronger families. For government steps in by necessity when families have failed" (p. 463, 464).

Justifying federal programs as a response to the individual's personal failure has been a vital part of the development of policy aimed at children. Rooted in English Poor Law, America's deficit model of the poor partly reflects the Victorian attitude that poverty is the result of individual handicaps and deficiencies. Steiner (1981) observes that a large part of the interest in family policy would disappear if there were no indigent families requiring assistance. Certainly, proponents of child policies inevitably depend on indicators of inadequate income and dysfunctional behavior as their rationale. Consequently, federal policies aimed at specific groups implicitly or explicitly define the groups as inadequate (Keniston et al., 1977).

This focus on personal deficiencies and abnormalities does not occur without costs. Labelling, stigma, categorization, and contempt of the poor necessarily follow this deficit philosophy (Mandell, 1975). Families which do not attain self- sufficiency are subject to "blame." The public response is to remediate or uplift the family through "parent education," or through "rehabilitation and opportunities" programs, which focus on changing individuals (Bowler, 1974; Keniston et al., 1977).

Despite the legitimate concerns of critics of social programs (Anderson, M., 1978; Koldon, 1971) the deficit assumptions of public assistance overlook the fact that young children are "typical" welfare recipients.

A variety of policies and programs have evolved to address the needs of poor children. These programs provide income support, health care, protection from abuse, nutritional assistance, and child care (see Washington, V., 1985B).

Partly as a result of the proliferation of fragmented programs, the deficit model for public assistance recipients is gradually being replaced by a growing awareness that many of the stresses facing children and families are beyond their control. Rather than being the "cause" of their problems, families are typically subject to broader social and economic forces. The Depression of the 1930's, from which many social programs (including AFDC) emerged, helped to trigger the evolution of the principle that poverty and social catastrophe are not necessarily the result of individual deficiencies

(Moroney, 1976). Indeed, "adequate" families, contrary to the myth of self-sufficiency, are not insulated from outside pressures (Keniston et al., 1977).

It is suggested that policies which focus on deprivation fail to recognize the unmet needs of millions of children who many not be poor or handicapped. For example, Census Bureau figures indicate that almost seven million children have no known source of day care (USDC, 1976). The number of births to unmarried women has been steadily increasing for many years, with about 44 percent of these births being to adolescent women (USDC, 1981C). Many children are in homes lacking the support system and structure which traditional nuclear households are presumed to provide.

Largely as a consequence of these changes in the family lives of the nonpoor, the societal principle of nonintervention for children has been challenged by the women's movement, child development specialists, teachers, and parents' groups. Rather, it is argued that America needs a universal and developmental philosophy of care for children. It is not enough to protect children against abuse, abandonment, abject poverty, or dramatic conditions such as polio and blindness, although these activities should not be forsaken. In addition, the government has a responsibility to insure the development of every child, according to his or her potential (Steiner, 1976, 1981).

Recognizing that government cannot provide services to fill all the needs of all the nation's families, Keniston and his colleagues (1977) concede that, in practice, priority will most often be given to lower-income families. It is suggested that when services are in short supply priority should be given to children with special developmental, emotional, or educational needs.

Priority to needy children is also most likely to receive a favorable consideration by policymakers. President Carter, when attempting to formulate family policy without regard to conditions of poverty and race, did not find it easy to break the traditional focus on the needy. Sensitive to the tradition of family privacy, a focus on deprivation is most likely to receive serious consideration because it addresses identifiable problems (Steiner, 1981).

Social Forces Challenging Poor Families

Even among the poor, however, changes in family structures have altered the ability of many families to achieve or to maintain self-sufficiency. Programs serving low-income families, such as Head Start, are particularly affected by four trends in family life: the feminization of poverty; the rise in adolescent parenting; the increase in employed mothers; and the increasing challenge to attain economic self- sufficiency.

The Feminization of Poverty

In recent years, the ideal concept of the American family was that of a male worker with a homemaker wife and two children. However, only 11 percent of families now fit this form. Indeed, about 20 percent of all children live in female-headed households.

This change in family structure has serious economic implications. Female-headed families are 3 times as likely to be in poverty as two-parent families (Auletta, 1982). In fact, 1 in 3 families headed by women is in poverty, compared with only 1 in 10 headed by men, and only 1 in 19 headed by two parents.

Teenage Parenting

The feminization of poverty has particularly severe consequences for teenage mothers. Even a decade ago, more than one-half of all AFDC assistance was paid to women who were or had been teenage mothers (Auletta, 1982).

A dramatic increase in the incidence of teenage pregnancy has occurred in the last 20 years (Chilman, 1979). In 1979, one in six babies was born to a teenage mother; among blacks, the figure was one in four, and 85 percent of black teenage mothers were unmarried (Auletta, 1982).

Employed Mothers

For the first time in history, more than one-half of all children younger than 18 have an employed mother (Kahn and Kamerman, 1982). Mothers of preschool children constitute the fastest growing segment of the labor force (U.S. Bureau of the Census, 1983A, 1983B, 1982; Burud, Collins, and Divine- Hawkins, 1983; Friedmen, 1983). Mothers with young children are almost as likely to be employed full time as are mothers with older children (Kamerman and Hayes, 1982).

Economic Self-Sufficiency

Many low-income families are rooted in economic distress. As many as 45 percent of these families continue on welfare for at least five out of every seven years. Many individuals mired in poverty are the unemployed who are either discouraged in their efforts to find a job, or who are among the nearly 20 percent unemployed people from ages 16 to 19. Still others trapped in poverty are school dropouts who lack the skills to match the available jobs (see Auletta, 1982).

In the following chapters of this book, each of these four changing family trends is analyzed. This analysis is followed by recommendations which can be implemented in the Head Start program to mitigate against the deleterious effect of these four trends.

In 1983, Zigler and Lang suggested that rather than expand the numbers of Head Start children without regard to program quality, program providers and child development specialists should examine together the changing needs of children in the society at large. They further asserted that the standard Head Start program should be no longer viewed as a panacea required by every child whose family income falls below some arbitrary level. Poor families, like more affluent ones, face a number of stresses and have a variety of needs. Some income-eligible children do not need early intervention such as that provided by Head Start. Other children need alternative types of services -- services which the founders of Head Start did not even envision. Communities and national planners should tailor Head

Start programs, and other programs for children, to the needs of children and their families rather than expecting them to tailor themselves to fit the programs. It is in this context that we now present an analysis of changing family trends with recommendations for Head Start.

CHAPTER 9

THE FEMINIZATION OF POVERTY

The ideal American family is generally perceived as one with both parents living together with their children. Most families, however, do not fit that model of a family. About 11 percent of families fit this form while an astonishing 20 percent of all children live in female-headed households. There are, in fact, about 12.1 million families in America headed by a single parent and almost 63.6 percent of these are headed by women (U.S. Bureau of the Census, 1985).

There has been a constant increase in female- headed households. In 1950, there were 9.4 percent female-headed households and this increased to 15 percent by 1982 (Rodgers, 1986).

Black mothers are far more likely than white mothers to raise their children alone. Whereas 80 percent of white children live in two-parent families, only forty percent of black children do. Today, half of the black children (15 percent of white children) live in female-headed households compared to one- fourth in 1960 (CDF, 1985; see Rodgers, 1986). Two-parent black families are concentrated among middle-class blacks, but it is precisely in these families that the greatest reductions in childbearing are occurring (Darity and Myers, 1984).

Further, black female-headed families are much more likely to stay poor. In female-headed families with older mothers ages 25 to 44, there is a 25 percentage point gap between black and white poverty rates (CDF, 1985).

The increase in families headed by women has serious economic implications. According to Auletta (1982), 1 in 3 families headed by women live in poverty compared with 1 in 10 families headed by men, and 1 in 19 headed by two parents. Put another way, female-headed families are five times as likely to be poor as two-parent families.

It is not surprising, then, that a disproportionate number of families receiving public assistance are female-headed. Four out of five AFDC (Aid to Families with Dependent Children) families are headed by single women. More than one-half of these women on "welfare" have at least one child under the age of six.

Further, these statistics on poor women indicate a startling trend popularly called "the feminization of poverty." A disproportionate number of poor households are headed by mothers, many of whom have young children. Since Project Head Start serves AFDC families with preschool children, the increase in poor families headed by women has a tremendous impact on the delivery of Head Start Services.

The trend toward the feminization of poverty is so pervasive that many policy analysts suggest that attention to poor women and children should be given priority in any government action to reduce poverty. For example, Robert Hill (1979), formerly of the National Urban League, says that if he were forced to choose which group to target for reducing poverty, he would take aim at "female-headed families," which in his view are the main cause of the underclass. Indeed, Auletta (1982) suggests that there appears to be at least two distinct minority communities -- one consisting mainly of female-headed households which slip more deeply into poverty, and another consisting of two-parent families which move forward towards the economic middle class.

Project Head Start represents an already existing mechanism which serves poor parents, primarily mothers and their children. In order to provide a basis for recommendations on how Head Start can respond to the feminization of poverty, this chapter explores the causes and consequences of this trend.

The Feminization of Poverty: Causes

There are several primary causes of the formation of female-headed households: adolescent parenting; increases in out-of-marriage childbearing; divorce; limited paternal support; and labor force discrimination against women, particularly the minority women generally served by Project Head Start. Adolescent pregnancy and childbearing are discussed in Chapter 10. The other causes cited are presented here.

Out-of-Marriage Childbearing

There is an increasing number of single-parent families in America and a large percentage of these are headed by women (Rodgers, 1986). One explanation offered for the increasing number of female-headed households is the fact that women tend to live longer than men, so there are many widows. There are also many young women who are single parents because they never married.

For example, there has been dramatic change in the frequency with which black teens marry. In 1950, only about 18 percent of all black infants born to teenagers were out of wedlock; today that figure is almost ninety percent, about two-and-one-half times the white rate.

Further, in 1982, about 57 percent of *all* births to black women were born out of wedlock. Black children are 12 times more likely than white children to live with a parent who never married. One black child in 4 lives with a parent who has never married compared to one white child in 48.

Importantly, the driving fact in this trend has not been an increase in the number of black infants born to teenage mothers. Rather, it has been a decline in the marriage rate among black women generally (CDF, 1985). According to the Children's Defense Fund, these high levels of out-of-marriage childbearing essentially guarantee the poverty of black children for the foreseeable future.

It is important to recognize that historical factors also account for the structural and functional differences in black and white families. These differences may be an unintended consequence of long-standing economic, educational, and occupational discrimination against black men (Scanzoni, 1971; Steady, 1981; Allen, W. 1979). These differences also reflect the result of large social forces impinging differently upon white and black family systems (Scanzoni, 1977). Further, studies (e.g., Parker and Kleiner, 1969; St. Pierre, 1982) have found the relationship between socioeconomic discrimination and family instability to be direct; problems of instability in the black family often appear to be created and maintained not by a deviant subculture but by the social and psychological consequences of unemployment and discrimination.

Several decades ago, some researchers thought that as blacks migrated to Northern urban areas, family characteristics such as the female-headed family and the unwed birthrate (eight times the white rate in 1940) would decrease (MacIntyre, 1964). Not only did this prediction fail to occur, as Darity and Myers (1984) point out, for blacks the female-headed family has rapidly moved toward becoming the norm as the rate grew from 21 percent in 1960, to 28 percent in 1970, and to 46 percent in 1981.

Contrary to some assertions, the female-headed household is not a legacy of slavery. Rather, between 70 and 90 percent of postbellum black families had two parents (Wolock, 1984).

Darity and Myers (1984) show that the cause of female-headed households has changed from the death of the husband at the turn of the century through the early 1960's; after 1963, desertion and divorce became the primary immediate source of marital disruption; by 1970, more black families were being formed by women who never married (see Wolock, 1984). The marked fall in fertility among husband-wife black families in the 1970's bears statistical responsibility for the growing proportion of black children born out of wedlock (Darity and Myers, 1984).

Divorce

According to Brandwein (1977), divorce is not just a legal action which occurs at one time, but rather, it is a continuing state which evolves into another type of family structure. Female-headed families have become more prevalent in the society today since the increasing rate of divorce suggests that one in every three marriages will dissolve.

Once couples get divorced, there follows a downward economic mobility, especially for women. Weitzman (1980) points out that after divorce men usually have more disposable income than their wives and children. It was found that men lose about 19 percent in real income while divorced women lose almost 29 percent. It was also found that there is a striking change in the standard of living of the two families just one year after divorce. While the standard of living of men improved by about 42 percent, the women experienced a 73 percent loss (Weitzman, 1980: 1251).

These data suggest that divorce can lead women into poverty. They experience not only a sharp decline in income but also a serious drop in their standard of living. These two factors arise, in part, because the wife often assumes most of the cost of caring for the child. Indeed, the most common reason why people seek AFDC assistance is the break-up of a marriage. About 45 percent of AFDC children become eligible due to parental separation or divorce (CDF, 1984).

Limited Paternal Support

Weitzman (1980) contends that the financial burden of women after divorce is further compounded by noncompliance with court-ordered child and spousal support by the fathers. She examined several studies and found that less than half of the fathers fully carried out court orders, many pay irregularly, and some do not pay anything. This irresponsible attitude on the part of fathers can seriously affect the mother and the children. It has been found that about one- third of the divorced and separated women who failed to receive the financial support ordered by the court fell below the poverty line. Of those who received payments only 12 percent lived in poverty (U.S. Bureau of the Census, 1979; also see NCSS, 1977).

One study of child support enforcement found that only about 22 percent of fathers were carrying out their court orders, while about half were not paying anything. It was also found that among some of the AFDC cases, there was no child support agreement to be enforced (Pearce, 1977). Some efforts of the AFDC to increase child support payments have had little effect because the fathers are either not accessible or do not have the resources themselves.

Again, special mention must be made of fathers from minority ethnic groups since Head Start largely serves these families. Research has found that custodial white mothers are twice as likely as custodial black mothers to be awarded, and to actually receive, child support (CDF, 1985). Some scholars (e.g., Stack and Semmel, 1975) point out that black mothers often receive support from the paternal relatives, and that society's punitive attempts to collect from fathers increases family stress without increasing funds to children, particularly for those children receiving public assistance.

Further, Wilson and Neckerman (1985) point out that without jobs, black men cannot support families; while the labor force participation patterns of white men have changed little over the past 40 years, the labor force participation of black men declined substantially from 84 percent in 1940 to 67 percent in 1980. The increasing rate of joblessness among black men merits serious consideration as a major underlying factor in the rise of black single mothers.

Labor Force Discrimination

Because they are single, divorced and/or unable to get full support from the fathers of their children, many poor women seek work out of economic necessity, as well as desire (CDF, 1984). It seems paradoxical that so many female-headed families live in poverty at the same time that women have joined the labor force in large numbers. Not only have more women joined the work force, but they have been filling jobs traditionally done by men (see Chapter 11).

Despite these gains, however, several studies show that unlike many other groups which worked their way up from the bottom, women entered the labor force and were hindered from moving up (e.g., Treiman and Terrell, 1970; Darien, 1976; Sorkin, 1973). Employed women are concentrated in the service sector jobs with low pay and little hope for advancement (Pearce, 1977). Women also receive, on the average, less wages than men. As Pearce (1977) puts it, "the demand for cheap labor and the demand for female labor became synonymous" (also see Knudsen, 1969; Sawhill, 1976; Brandwein, 1977; Willensky, 1961).

Further, employers have taken few steps to accommodate the needs of working mothers. Employed mothers with young children need inexpensive and full- time child care. Women workers pay a premium price for occupational segregation and the failure of employers to consider their needs. Shortridge (1976) reported that in 1970 there were 6 million women who worked full time and earned about $4,000 per year, pretty near the poverty level of $3,700. Similarly, Sawhill (1976) found that if the variables of age, race, education, and residence were controlled, then females who were household heads would earn 36 percent more if they were men. However, when male labor force participation, e.g., hours worked, was added into the equations, the women's wages would increase by only 13 percent.

Since Head Start serves a large proportion of families from ethnic minority groups, many of these families experience labor force discrimination because of both race and sex. Although black women work more years of their lives than do their white counterparts, they have the lowest median level of occupation and earnings, and their unemployment rate is greater (Rodgers-Rose, 1980). Black females also have higher unemployment rates at both the high school and college level (CDF, 1985; also see Gary, 1981). While the reasons for these low attainments has been subject to both research and debate (see Rodgers-Rose, 1980), the racial gap in income is linked more to different reward structures than to worker characteristics (Hanushek, 1982).

The Feminization of Poverty: Consequences

When the mother's sources of income are inadequate, the state and federal governments supplement family support. (Public assistance should clearly be considered as partial support given that official documents indicate that the levels of aid are below the standard of need -- see Washington, V., 1984.) For some black lower-class women, marriage appears to have limited possibilities for acquiring a husband to fill the breadwinner role. A poor woman who decides to marry may be gambling her control over a stable low income against an income that may be even lower and less stable.

Yet, despite assertions to the contrary, Darity and Myers (1984) argue that research fails to demonstrate a statistical link between variations in AFDC payments relative to typical black male income and variations in the proportion of black families headed by women. Further, they concluded that the evidence so far suggests that welfare benefits do not provide an incentive to teenagers to bear children. Research is similarly unable to establish a direct link between welfare and the incidence of out-of- wedlock births. Nevertheless, social transfer programs may have contributed to an environment less conducive to the financial necessity of and support for the traditional two-parent family.

Concerns about the feminization of poverty are likely to continue. For blacks, there was a worsening of living standards during the 1970's and early 1980's particularly in terms of unemployment and income (Willhelm, 1983). This is particularly bad news for black mothers; annual statistical data since 1930 reveal a black underclass characterized by mother-headed families with low income and mobility levels. The children in these families are the poorest in the nation; they are three times more likely to be poor than white children in such families (CDF, 1985).

The fragile living standards of many poor mothers have required a high degree of sharing and cooperation within a network of mothers and the extended family. In child care as well as other areas of life, both fictive and blood "relatives" are integral to the survival of these women. Many scholars have documented the stabilizing influence of the extended family among poor, single mothers. It is likely that the extremely poor black family has not developed along the nuclear pattern because there is a need to provide an alternative system of savings and insurance (see Gary, 1981; Rodgers-Rose, 1980).

Indeed, the monetary assistance that families receive from AFDC is insufficient to help them rise above the poverty level. Further, every time a woman on welfare has another baby after her first child, she digs herself deeper into poverty, according to a study by Population Environment Balance, a nonprofit advocacy group for population stabilization (*The Washington Post*, Saturday, April 19, 1986, p. A10).

Rodgers (1986) shows that in 1983 only 4 percent of all poor families and 35 percent of all poor children receiving AFDC assistance rose above the poverty line on those benefits. Usually about 40 percent of those who leave the program remain below the poverty line and about one-third of all families return to the program at least once (Bane and Elwood, 1983).

Pearce (1977) argues that the welfare system was developed to play a functional role in society. She contends that the system was designed to protect a labor market that was already overcrowded in the era of the Depression. The government had to appear to be taking care of certain people while at the same time keeping them out of the labor force. This served the government's purpose for a while, but by the 1950s the problem became one of too much dependency rather than too many workers. Programs like AFDC did not help their members to become self-sufficient and rise above poverty. Many mothers under the AFDC program remain at home, unemployed and without any particular skill. But there are several studies that show that many women would rather be employed than on welfare (e.g., Pearce, 1977; Rodgers, 1986).

The government's answer to the desire of welfare recipients to work was to force them into certain work training programs like WIN. These programs are still not well organized, and they allow the members to feel that they can offer a lot while in fact, they do not deliver much. For example, in November, 1975, there were 1,175,800 people registered for WIN, but only 6,900 found employment that month and many of these found jobs on their own (Pearce, 1977). Here again, we see sex as an important variable because most of those who do get jobs through WIN are males -- white males.

Poor mothers have survived by means of their high participation in the work force, their participation in helping networks of kin and nonkin, public assistance, and assistance from the fathers of their children. It is important to recognize that a combination of support systems continues to be necessary to sustain a modest or stable living standard. For example, the low wages earned by these women often makes it difficult for them to purchase child care, therefore they must rely on relatives and friends. The level of child support which many fathers can afford makes it necessary to receive public assistance. A picture emerges wherein typical poor mothers are involved in complex family support systems integral to their survival. Nevertheless, despite multiple sources of support, nearly half of all black children continue to live in poverty.

Many authors have asserted that the female-headed household is a self-perpetuating institution. St. Pierre (1982) found that black single-parent females in both the middle- and lower-classes had themselves come from single-parent families and had close relationships with their mothers. Becoming an "adult" in this manner is reinforced by the shortage of young black men who would make suitable marriage partners as a consequence of the black males' shorter life expectancy and higher rates of infant mortality, drug addiction, accidents and homicides, incarceration, and military participation (Darity and Myers, 1984; Gary, 1981).

Thus, many young black men and women come to expect adult life without spouses, even if they desire a traditional family. After a relatively long period of greater incidence of female headship coupled with poverty, cultural elements may emerge that treat the female-headed family as the normal or accepted form (Darity and Myers, 1984).

CHAPTER 10

ADOLESCENT PARENTING

The feminization of poverty has particularly severe consequences for adolescent parents. Even a decade ago, more than one-half of all AFDC assistance -- a key factor in determining Head Start eligibility -- was paid to women who were, or had been, teenaged mothers (Auletta, 1982).

Finally, Burden and Klerman (1984) have identified several factors that lessen the economic/welfare dependence of teenage parents. The factors that lessen the long-term negative economic consequences of early motherhood include deferment of marriage, support from the family of origin, increased education and career motivation, decreased fertility, and comprehensive programs.

Still, the Children's Defense Fund (1985) notes that, whether black or white, young mothers under age 25 heading families are very likely to be poor. The poverty rates in 1983 were over 35 percent for young black female-headed families and over 72 percent for young white female-headed families. This phenomena becomes of particular concern with the increase in the number of teenage mothers under seventeen years of age and even as young as eleven years (also see Nye, 1976).

A dramatic increase in the incidence of adolescent pregnancy has occurred in the last 20 years. Chilman (1979) points out that the number of teenage mothers under 17 increased by as much as 60 percent between 1965 and 1975. In 1979, one in six babies was born to a teenage mother; among blacks the figure was one in four with 85 percent of black teenage mothers unmarried (Auletta, 1982). While there has been a drop in the rate of increase between 1971 and 1980, some writers contend that pregnancy rates among American teenagers are higher than those of many other developed countries (Lincoln, 1983; Westoff, Colott, and Foster, 1983).

Still adolescent parenting has the potential to reach far greater epidemic proportions when one considers that:

1. Black female adolescents are more likely to have more children out-of-wedlock while still teenagers (Ventura, 1969).

2. Children of teenage parents are at greater risk for adolescent pregnancy (Chilman, 1979; also see Ford, 1983; *Hospital and Community Psychiatry*, 1984).

Concern about black adolescent parenting is not new. It was significant to Moynihan (1965) that the gap between the "generation rate" between whites and nonwhites was particularly wide and concentrated among the poor. The teenage pregnancy rate for black teenagers has been 7 to 13 times higher than that for white teenagers since 1955 (Ventura, 1969).

Today, about 30 percent of all births to teenagers are to black females; teenagers account for about 25 percent of all black births and about 12 percent of all white births. Further, almost six out of 10 births to teens under 15 were to blacks. Consequently, black children are twice as likely to be born to a teenage or single-parent family (CDF, 1985).

The proportion of black women who were mothers by the time they are age 20 has increased slightly since 1940, from 40 to 44 percent. However, birth rates for black teens, married and unmarried, have been declining while the birth rate among white unmarried teens has been increasing in recent years (CDF, 1985).

Adolescent Parenting: Causes

Social factors contributing to teenage pregnancy are among those frequently discussed in the literature. Many of these came about as result of the advent of industrialization (Chilman, 1979). As families, and particularly women, began to move to the cities to find jobs, social networks disintegrated, and social control lessened. With both mother and father employed, teenagers often are left unsupervised. With social control being reduced and feelings of anonymity increased, permissiveness often becomes rampant.

Further, it is not difficult to engage in sexual permissiveness when, as Reiss (1967) points out, the society appears to accept sexual liberalism. As teenagers are left more and more on their own, they begin to turn to each other for companionship, and love and affection are shared among them (Sorensen, 1973). As participation in sexual activities increased, so did the feeling among teenagers that it was their right. But as Thornburg (1979) points out, the responsibilities that accompany the right to engage in sex are rarely considered.

The fact that the society accepts childbirth outside of marriage also contributes to the attitude of teenagers towards sexual participation. In many cases, the birth of a child to a teenager is regarded as a mark of achievement into adulthood. So there may be peer pressure on those young people who would rather complete high school than give birth to a child. Research in this area shows that sexual activity is beginning at younger ages and increasing among older age groups (Chilman, 1979).

With this increase in sexual participation there is a surprising lack of knowledge about contraceptive use (Washington, A.C., 1982). While there are contraceptive programs for teenagers, many adolescents are not reached by those programs. It is possible that if many teenagers were really informed of the facts of childbearing and parenthood there may be some increment of change in their attitude towards sexual participation.

There are economic factors closely linked to the attitude of teenagers towards pregnancy. While many teens would rather conceive their children within wedlock, marriage is ruled out because of poverty. A few young girls may even become sexually involved with the hope that some sort of financial gain may arise from the birth of the child if the father of the child is employed. On the other hand, while some commentators (e.g., Placek and Hendershot, 1976) continue to claim that many young mothers use the public assistance program as a means of economic gain, Darity and Myers (1984) found that welfare benefits do not provide an incentive for teenagers to bear children.

According to Kohlberg (1964), some teenagers tend to think of permissive sexual behavior as traditional since their parents before them engaged in the same type of behavior. There are other teenagers who have very young mothers with whom they try to compete (Chilman, 1979).

The increases observed in teenage pregnancy may also be due to certain historical factors. Birth registration is now better than it was a few decades ago, so the Census is taking a better count than it did years ago. Demographers also argue that there has been a dramatic decrease in the infant mortality rate because of the improvement in medical knowledge and technology. The modernization in control and treatment of many diseases and the growing awareness of the harmful effects of drugs and alcohol have all contributed to the decrease in mortality rates. The result is an increase in the number of live births and the number of babies who survive the first year.

Adolescent Parenting: Consequences

The personal, social, and economic consequences of being a teenage parent are usually tragic. The birth of children to a teenaged woman entails a substantial risk for the well-being of both mother and child. Social isolation for the mothers and social and physical maladaptations of children threaten optimal development (Kellam et al., 1982; Washington, V. and Glimps, 1983).

Among the far reaching consequences of adolescent pregnancy and childrearing for mother and child are:

1. Inadequate prenatal and health care;

2. Disruption of education;

3. Marital instability; and

4. Less than optimal parenting skills.

Inadequate Prenatal and Health Care

Early and adequate prenatal care is essential to monitor the health of both the expectant mother and child. Adolescent mothers, however, too often do not have the advantage of prenatal care.

The Children's Defense Fund (1985) reported that mothers under age 20 are much more likely than older mothers to have late or no prenatal care. For black and white teenagers under age 15, about 20 percent received late or no prenatal care (see Table 7; also see Johnson, Rosenbaum, and Simons, 1985; Makinson, 1985; Rosenbaum, 1983).

Pregnancy to a teenage mother may come as a shock, especially if the pressures of sexual participation were never overshadowed by thoughts of parenthood. An unprepared teenager may be momentarily traumatized to learn of a pregnancy. As Bolton (1980) puts it, the pregnancy may be regarded as a crisis and the mother may develop an attitude whereby she refuses to get prenatal care during the pregnancy. Some mothers may develop an attitude of denial in that they psychologically reject the problem by doing nothing about it. Koos (1964) argues that this indifference is not difficult for the teenager to prolong if there is no pain or everyday activities are not disrupted.

The choice of not seeking prenatal care is prevalent among poor mothers (Osofsky, 1968). Generally, persons from this income bracket use medical care as curative rather than preventive. So, many poor teenager mothers would rather wait for the moment when there is a problem with the pregnancy before going for prenatal care.

Bolton (1980) attributes some of the blame for this reluctance by poor mothers to visit prenatal clinics to the clinics themselves. Often, these clinics are provided by the State for the benefit of those who cannot afford the high cost of medical care. Sometimes conditions are poor and much time is wasted in trying to get attention. In effect, some health care delivery systems may inhibit the use of the very service they provide.

This refusal to obtain parental care can be manifested in health risks not only for the child, but also for the mother. One of the damages may be low birth weight which can result in other physical and mental disabilities (Chilman, 1979). Many studies show that the incidence of low birth weight is correlated with lower social class which is itself related to poor nutrition and some degree of ignorance (Menken, 1975; Kovar, 1968). Teenage mothers are more likely to be among those malnourished since they are least likely to pay attention to their diet.

Further, it has been demonstrated that mothers who do not have prenatal care suffer more pregnancy complications and have a higher infant death rate than mothers who do receive prenatal care (Bolton, 1980; Menken, 1975). Teenage mothers -- particularly those who are poor, nonwhite, or unmarried -- are clearly at risk (Herzog and Bernstein, 1964; Pasamanick and Knoblock, 1958).

TABLE 7

PERCENTAGE OF BABIES BORN TO WOMEN WHO RECEIVED LATE OR NO PRENATAL CARE, BY AGE AND RACE, 1982.

Age of Mother	*Black*	*White*	*Total*
Under 15	20.7	21.6	21.4
15-19	13.7	10.2	11.3
20-24	9.7	5.2	6.1
25-29	6.9	2.7	3.4
30-34	6.3	2.4	3.1
35-39	7.5	3.9	4.5
40+	10.3	7.8	8.4
TOTAL	**9.6**	**4.5**	**5.5**

Source: The Children's Defense Fund. *Black and White Children in America: Key Facts*. Washington, D.C.: CDF, 1985, p. 76.

Disruption of Education

In addition to health risks, teenage mothers are less likely to have completed high school than are older mothers. Only about 54 percent of teenagers who gave birth at age 18 or 19 had completed high school, compared to about 77 percent of women who gave birth in their early twenties. Among teenagers ages 15 to 17 years old who gave birth in 1981, less than 10 percent had completed high school (CDF, 1985).

Card and Wise (1978) noted that adolescent mothers are more likely to terminate their studies. It is an unfortunate fact that the mother suffers the most in such situations. The teenage father can go on with his studies while the mother is left to care for the child at the expense of her own education.

In self-reports of the major reasons for dropping out of high school, 40 percent of black females, and 14.5 percent of white females, cite pregnancy (CDF, 1985). White females cite marriage as a reason four times more often than do blacks; blacks give pregnancy as a reason three times more often than do whites (CDF, 1985).

Chilman (1979) was careful to point out that not all teenagers who become pregnant drop out of school. Much of the decision has to do with the ability and motivation of the person. Family encouragement and school support also play a part in the decision process. It was found that many teenage parents who drop out of school were already marginal students (Furstenberg, 1976). Other writers have argued, however, that it makes more sense to examine the role of the school system in the decision to drop out. If there is no policy whereby a drop out can easily return to school, or if there is no support structure within the school system, then the decision to drop- out would have to be made more readily (Bolton, 1980).

The limitations placed on the education of the teenage parent would lead directly to unemployment or underemployment. This places the young family in a situation of dependence, often upon the state and federal governments.

Marital Instability

Given the economic and social pressures faced by adolescent parents, marriage is hardly a panacea. While it may be argued that it is desirable for children to be born in wedlock, studies show that marriage is often not the best solution to the problem, especially among low-income black groups (Chilman, 1979). Teenage marriages were found to be about four times more likely to end in divorce and separation than those who were married in their twenties (Burchinal, 1965; Glick and Mills, 1974). Also, Bolton (1980) found that about two-thirds of adolescent marital relationships end in divorce within five years.

Similarly, Bacon (1974), found that marital stability, particularly among whites, was related to the age at which marriage occurred. He revealed that one-third of the marriages of those who gave birth before 15 ended in divorce or separation; and 10 percent of those who bore their first child after age 22 dissolved.

Apart from age, the other intervening factors that contributed to marital instability were undereducation and poor economic conditions. For these reasons, those families whose incomes were above the poverty level were likely to have more stability in their marriages (Baldwin, 1980).

Less Than Optimal Parenting Skills

Although there is disagreement about whether the quality of care provided by adolescent mothers is less optimal than that of adult mothers, teenage mothers, particularly those under 17, are widely presumed to be less competent in preparing their offspring for school success. For example, Baldwin and Cain (1981) found that children of adolescent mothers appear to experience less optimal cognitive and socioemotional development than children born to mothers who postpone parenthood. Similarly, Yong (1981) found that teen mothers were less likely than adult mothers to favor fostering reciprocal relationships between themselves and their infants. Thorman (1982) found that teen mothers were much less adaptive in their attitudes than were adult parents.

A primary obstacle which these young mothers face is helping their children to develop the language and pre-reading skills which are the basis for school learning. This academic risk is compounded for the black adolescent parent who speaks a linguistically sound, yet socially and academically unacceptable black "dialect" (Troutman and Falk, 1982; Seymour and Seymour, 1981; Fergenbaum, 1970; Houston, 1970; Burling, 1973).

The mother's language has been found to have a significant effect on the language that children speak; the mother's language correlates positively with the child's IQ tests scores (Rogers, 1976). In investigations of mothers' language in teaching children to perform tasks, Hess and Shipman (1965A, 1965B) found that the mothers with a "restricted code" correlated with children's low IQ scores while the "elaborated code" correlated with high IQ scores. Further, the mother's praise and encouragement and the use of questions increased the volume and complexity of children's speech (Hess and Shipman, 1968). Since there are indications that parents' speech influences the way children achieve on tests, it has been suggested that mothers, home adults, and peers stimulate the child's language to higher levels of volume and complexity than teachers (Labov, 1972).

Stevens and Duffield (1986) found that, in general, maternal youth was associated with less verbal responsivity, and with less support for language development, when the mothers were also poor and less well educated. Younger parents with less schooling and lower incomes were less likely to provide language development experiences such as children's books and story reading; the relationship between such experiences and subsequent cognitive development is well documented (Clarke-Stewart, 1977).

In a study of black teen, black adult, and white adult mothers, Stevens (1984) found that knowledge of normative development contributed less to predicting parenting skills than did the mother's awareness of the potency of play materials, of the value of parental teaching, of instructional strategies which promote language development, and of the importance of monitoring infant health. Field (1981) found that after four months of intervention with the teenage mothers of premature infants, the mothers held greater knowledge about child development and more appropriate interactional skill. Experimental studies have found generally that systematic education programs produce concurrent benefits, both in parents' knowledge and in their skill.

In another study, Stevens and Duffield (1986) found that, while maternal youth was a significant predictor of parenting skill even when parity, income, and maternal education are controlled, maternal age appeared to explain only a very small proportion of the total variance in parenting skill. Moreover, the researchers observed a range of parenting skill, with some adolescent mothers being quite adept. The authors concluded that the early onset of parenthood need not have a lasting effect on parent's verbal responsivity, their support for language development, or the effects for cognitive development once the effects of income, education, and experiences in rearing children were removed.

These findings are further evidence to support the importance of parent involvement programs as essential components of Project Head Start, parent- child centers, or other preschool facilities that target poor children. Federal, state, or local education policies which recognize parents as the primary educators of their children should be encouraged. For example, new regulations governing the Chapter 1 compensatory education program published May 19, 1986, contain strengthened provisions requiring parent involvement. While the regulations do not require specific means for involving parents, several activities are recommended such as providing parent training in at-home reinforcement techniques (*CDF Reports*, 1986).

In conjunction with increased efforts to prevent teenage pregnancy and parenting, it is important to face the reality that most black teenagers who become pregnant will keep their children (Ladner, 1985). Rather than assume a trajectory of failure, successful interventions such as Head Start, offering more optimal conditions for the child's development, are possible. The Head Start philosophy challenges the assumption of unresolvable failure and suggests an instructional program that can be a catalyst for change.

Efforts to Prevent Teenage Pregnancy

It seems clear that any effort to help teenagers avoid the problems of early pregnancy is to make available to them the means whereby they can prevent themselves from becoming pregnant. The preferred ways to reduce adolescent pregnancy are influenced significantly by political and religious beliefs. Also, largely due to the high public costs of adolescent childbearing, there have been many legislative attempts to deal with the problem (Gilchrist and Schinke, 1983; Burt and Somerstein, 1985; Maggard, 1986; Mecklenburg and Thompson, 1983; U.S. Congress House Committee on Energy and Commerce, 1985; U.S. Congress House Committee on Ways and Means, 1985; U.S. Congress House Select Committee on Children, Youth, and Families, 1983, 1986; U.S. Congress Senate Committee on Labor and Human Resources, 1984; Moore, K. and Wertheimer, 1984; Burt, 1986; Moore, K. and Burt, 1982).

Discussion about what can or should be done about teenage pregnancy has increased in recent years (Barret and Robinson, 1982; Dash, 1986; Height, 1985; Wallis, 1985; Stengel, 1985). It is generally agreed that education in preparation for adulthood is of primary importance. However, educational efforts vary from efforts to help teens "just say no" to providing explicit information about sexuality and birth control.

Promoting self-esteem and independent thinking among adolescents may also be a useful component of pregnancy prevention (Chilman, 1979). Facilitating racial justice and equal opportunity may also assist prevention efforts: Racial divergences in family planning may be due to the fact that blacks (males especially) have been systematically denied equal access to educational and occupational opportunity structures in which individualistic aspirations are most generally carried out (Scanzoni, 1975). Thus, for several decades, higher income, better educated blacks have had fewer children than lower-class blacks have had. Poor and minority teens must be provided opportunities which will confirm that they can contribute more to the society than helping to increase the population. They should be able to assess the opportunities open to them and to determine how their own skills and interests can be tailored to master all possibilities (Chilman, 1979).

The government and other agencies have recognized the need to educate teenagers and also the wider community about adolescent pregnancy. The Select Committee on Children, Youth, and Families reported that in 1985 thirty-one states formulated programs which fell into the categories of "community education, public awareness of educational interventions in schools." The Children's Defense Fund (1986) developed programs through which teenagers build self-esteem, such as after-school programs in community volunteer work, educational and recreational activities, and counseling services. Other programs include general health and reproductive health care, (both school-based and hospital-based), sexuality and decision-making, and family-centered programs.

The provision of information about contraceptives for both males and females also has an important role in efforts to prevent teenage pregnancy. The tragedy so far has been that few pregnant teenagers had knowledge of birth control from their parents (Furstenburg, 1976), aside from "warnings" not to do something they may later regret. DeAnda (1982) also found an inadequate use of birth control among sexually active teenagers; 42 percent of the subjects claim not to have taken birth control measures before becoming pregnant. Many who did use contraceptives did so ineffectively.

School-based health clinics have been presented as one approach to preventing adolescent pregnancy (Dryfoos, 1985). Yet, several studies (e.g., Herold and Goodwin, 1981; Herold 1983; Zabin and Clark, 1983) point to the fact that some teenagers tend to be against having to plan their sexual activities. While some feel embarrassment at purchasing contraceptives, others fear the taunt of their peers or the anger of their parents if it is discovered that they use contraceptives. There are other cases where teenagers are not regular participants in sexual intercourse because of the ebb and flow of relationships. This may result in an unintentional neglect of birth control measures.

Marsiglio (1985) has proposed another approach to the task of education on birth control methods. He suggests a theory of social marketing which can be used to augment family planning services. Social marketers will be expected to come up with the best possible ways of making teenagers aware of the dangers of an unplanned pregnancy and the variety of methods by which this can be avoided. Much of this depends, of course, on government support and resources.

CHAPTER 11

MATERNAL EMPLOYMENT ISSUES

As indicated earlier, many poor mothers, teenage and adult, work out of economic necessity. Many of these women work in addition to receiving AFDC benefits.

Since over 90 percent of Head Start families are poor, they are qualified to receive AFDC. AFDC is the only federally-sponsored program that provides cash assistance to poor children and their families. Designed in 1935, AFDC largely assumed that poor children were in single parent households with a mother who was widowed, divorced, or deserted by the child's father. Given the prevailing customs on the role of women, AFDC guidelines generally accepted that these mothers would devote a full-time effort to child care and family responsibilities rather than participate in the work force.

The notion that nonemployment was a "right" of poor mothers consistent with American lifestyles and values was soon entrenched in the minds of many recipients and their supporters. Indeed, one of the strongest criticisms of President Richard Nixon's welfare reform strategy was that it would "force" poor women into the paid labor force (see Washington, V. 1985B).

Consistent with AFDC policies, Head Start program planning presumed that the mothers were not employed. As we shall see, even in the 1960's this assumption may have been false for large numbers of poor families who were eligible for Head Start services. The assumption is perhaps even more incredible today as large numbers of poor as well as middle-class women have joined the work force. The fact of maternal employment has serious structural and content implications for Project Head

Start: Head Start as a child care arrangement, in addition to its value as an enrichment experience, is the current reality for many families.

In this chapter, we examine maternal employment, including a case study of poor black mothers in the labor force. We also outline changes in the workplace that impact poor women: workfare and employer- sponsored child care.

Maternal Employment: An American Revolution

Perhaps the most significant change in the family has been the dramatic increase in the participation of wives and mothers in the work force. For the first time in history, more than half of all children under age eighteen have a working mother (Kahn and Kamerman, 1983). There has also been a large increase in the labor force among the group of women least likely to work outside the home: married women with preschool children (U.S. Bureau of the Census, 1982, 1983B).

Mothers with young children are almost as likely to be employed full time as are mothers with older children (Kamerman and Hayes, 1982). In 1950, only 12 percent of mothers with children under age six worked; by 1982, 50 percent were in the labor force (*Children Today*, 1983). In 1974, 34 percent of mothers with children under age three worked compared to 46 percent in 1982 (Friedman, 1983). Among children under age one, one-third of the married mothers and 40 percent of single mothers work (*Children Today*, 1983). Mothers of preschool children constitute the fastest growing segment of the labor force. These mothers are often the primary or sole earners for their families. Forty-three percent of working women are single, widowed, divorced, or separated (U.S. Department of Labor, 1977).

These changing conditions in the family have created unprecedented demands for child care. Many observers agree that these dramatic changes are neither short term nor likely to be reversed (Cherlin, 1981).

Poor Black Mothers: A Case Study

Since a significant minority of Head Start-eligible families is black, the labor force participation of poor black mothers is illustrative of trends which should be noted by program planners.

Primary among the black mothers' means of support is their own employment. The weight of evidence suggests that labor force participation is an enculturated aspect of black women's sex-role identity and of black community life. Since the abolishment of slavery, black women have been employed in disproportionate numbers to white women (Wolock, 1984; Moynihan, 1965B; CPR, 1965). Thus, while the labor force participation rates of white women have catapulted during the past quarter-century, black women's rates have been fairly constant during this period (Engram, 1980). Consequently, female employment has become much more institutionalized and normative among black families (Scanzoni, 1977). Moreover, history has had a strong bearing on intergenerational labor force activity (Engram, 1980; McCray, 1980), thereby strengthening cultural imperatives which transcend major social and economic trends in American society.

The high rates of labor force participation among black women have also been less sensitive to the effects of assuming maternal roles (Engram, 1980). Compared to white mothers, black mothers enter or return to the labor force when their children are younger, and they are more likely to work full time. As a result, four out of five black mothers with children in the age group served by Head Start work, compared to three out of five white mothers (CDF, 1985).

The prevalence of work among black mothers holds true regardless of family types. For example, young black children in two-parent families are more likely than white children to have working mothers (CDF, 1985). Further, the high employment rates among black mothers, especially those in the upper income brackets, demonstrate their importance as wage earners; black women are more likely to work whether or not it is necessary than their white counterparts (Beckett, 1976; CDF, 1985).

Whereas for many white women the decision to pursue a career is optional, black girls are reared with the expectation that whether or not they marry, whether or not they have children, they will work most of their adult lives; "work to them, unlike to white women, is not a liberating goal, but rather an *imposed* lifelong necessity" (Lerner, 1978). Working has become less of an option and more of a right for many black women (Scanzoni, 1978). Now many younger white women are coming to define work in the way that has characterized black women for some time (Scanzoni, 1978). While black women may actually desire homemaking roles, they have been denied the freedom to choose between work or family (Engram, 1980).

The Working Poor and Workfare Policies

Historical trends in the work patterns of black mothers are becoming the contemporary norm for poor mothers of all ethnic groups. It must be pointed out that it is very likely that uneducated, unskilled women can work in jobs paying the minimum wage while earning incomes that leave them well below the official poverty level.

Despite the assumption that women in female-headed households are dependent upon public assistance, in 1946 50 percent of the black women, and 39 percent of the white women, with no husband present were in the labor force (CPR, 1965). Citing Census data, Robert Hill (1971) found that three-fifths of female heads of household worked, most of them full time. Conversely, recent data suggests that young black children in female-headed families are less likely than white children in these families to have mothers in the labor force (CDF, 1985).

Many low-income mothers are already employed or seeking employment. Of every 10 mothers on AFDC, four are caring for preschool children; three are employed, seeking employment or in training; one is disabled; and two are not currently seeking employment. Of this latter group, more than half are either older than 45 or have never been employed (CDF, 1984). Only about one percent of AFDC recipients are adult male fathers who are incapacitated or unemployed and job hunting (CRS, 1981). Despite impressions to the contrary, AFDC does not support large numbers of employable adults.

Yet, recent federal public assistance policies, which impact directly on Head Start eligible families, are based on the assumption that poor mothers must be coerced or forced to work. One major change wrought by 1981 AFDC amendments was a conceptual one: Employable AFDC mothers whose children are three years of age or over may be required to participate in "workfare" programs if adequate child care is available. (Previously, mothers with children under six years old were not required to work.) These women with young children were told that they must register for employment and accept a job if one is offered (CRS, 1982).

Bernstein (1982) has suggested that this provision makes it possible to avoid long-term dependency that is likely to occur if one waits until the youngest child reaches age of six. However, unless efforts are focused on younger women with only one or two children, the limited resources available to the workfare program are likely to be dissipated as they have been in the past.

According to the General Accounting Office (GAO, 1983) several states already had workfare programs for recipients of their state-funded General Assistance programs. The Food Stamp Act of 1977 authorized workfare demonstration projects for Food Stamp recipients. However, it was not until the Omnibus Reconciliation Act of 1981 that all states were given the option of establishing a form of workfare for AFDC called CWEP (Community Work Experience Program) demonstrations.

By October 1982, eleven states had established CWEPs which were intended to "provide work experience and training for individuals not otherwise able to obtain employment, in order to assist them to move into regular employment" (P.L. 97-35, Sec. 2307 (a)). CWEPs are intended to increase the number of AFDC recipients who obtain unsubsidized jobs after participating in CWEP, thus reducing the cost of AFDC programs. Requiring AFDC recipients to participate in CWEP has been proposed because "the American public is not willing to bear the burden of supporting people who can work" (U.S. Congress, 1981, p.11).

Workfare programs are controversial partly because of the lack of solid information about their effectiveness (GAO, 1983). Whatever the final policy structures of work experiments, the pressures for workfare coupled with current trends for maternal employment have specific and direct implications for the delivery of Head Start services, particularly the parent involvement component:

1. Working parents are likely to have less time to volunteer to assist in Head Start classrooms or to participate in special programs;

2. Working parents are likely to perceive Head Start as a child day care arrangement in addition to other perceptions; and

3. Working parents are less likely to be able to participate in increasing numbers of program options such as variations in center attendance, double sessions, and home-based models.

In order for workfare to be implemented effectively and realistically with participants in Project Head Start, consideration must be given to child care arrangements and to parent needs relative to program goals. For example, CWEP demonstration projects have exempted individuals from the work requirement because of the age of their children. However, a state may require the parent of a child three years old or older to participate in CWEP if child care is available. Michigan and Oklahoma had obtained waivers to require participation by parents of children younger than three (GAO, 1983).

The Working Poor and the Changing Workplace

Any responses and accommodations that Head Start would make for its employed parents would be consistent with general efforts to alleviate the work-family strain. Indeed, the changes that have occurred within American families influence the workplace. While the "myth of separate worlds" of home and work still exists, work and family are increasingly recognized as related spheres (Kanter, 1977). Dana Friedman (1983) has analyzed both the internal and external pressures that influence corporate concern about the intersection of work and the family. External pressures include the needs of working parents, requests by community agencies for private- sector support, and increasing appeals for "corporate social responsibility."

Internal pressures also influence corporate concern (Friedman, 1983). First, employers today must face "new values workers" who are increasingly interested in the quality of their lives (Katzell and Yankelovitch, 1975). Second, as the baby boom generation matures, workers caught in the "pyramid squeeze" will require benefits and rewards as compensation in lieu of promotions. Third, humanistic management, including concern for family needs, is a growing response to declining productivity. Fourth, as a result of labor shortages related to movement from an industrial to a technological society, women will play a vital role in management competition to recruit and retain a productive work force.

These internal and external pressures suggest that policies and practices developed in response to a predominately male work force are less viable. Indeed, if the corporate community ignores the family concerns of its work force, it will be ignoring the predominant concerns of an increasingly large portion of its labor pool (Friedman, 1983).

Employer-sponsored child care seems to provide a variety of benefits to employers (Balsey, 1983; Romaine, 1983; Friedman, 1983; U.S. Department of Labor, 1982). These benefits include reduced tardiness, training costs, job turnover, absenteeism, and the need for overtime or temporary help; they also increase affirmative action and productivity. Other benefits were improved employee attitude toward the employer, morale, and scheduling flexibility.

There are also disadvantages in employer- sponsored child care, particularly on-site child care centers. The adverse effects of worksite child care include disrupting a child care arrangement if parents wish to change jobs, transporting children long distances during peak commuter hours; the lack of neighborhood friends when a child's relationships are limited to the children of other employees; and parental preferences for neighborhood-based care (Kamerman and Kingston, 1982).

Because cost is an important factor in employer- sponsored child care, government support of private- sector initiatives is evolving, perhaps in lieu of increased publically-sponsored care, such as Head Start. Although the federal government has not established minimum national standards for private day care facilities as it has for hospitals and nursing homes (Crittenden, 1984), there are several government initiatives to support employer-sponsored child care (see Friedman, 1983; Plave, 1983; Malone, 1981; Burud, Collins, and Divine-Hawkins, 1983). For example, as a "model employer," the federal government provides eighteen on-site child care centers at government agencies across the country.

The President's Task Force on Private Sector Initiatives initiated ten forums on family and work issues for local employers. The Women's Bureau has published reports and provided seed money for conferences, brochures, and seminars. Funds from the Appalachian Regional Commission have been used to conduct feasibility studies of the prospects of employer-sponsored child care in Appalachia.

The Administration for Children, Youth, and Families (ACYF) funded Child Care Dallas to coordinate a family day-care home system for corporations. ACYF sponsored the National Employer-Supported Child Care Project. A Task Force on Child Care was sponsored by Senator David Durenburger. The Senate Labor and Human Resources Committee had hearings on November 15, 1983, which covered employer-sponsored child care.

The Internal Revenue Code allows several tax deductions and credits that encourage employer support of child care including the Dependent Care Assistance Plan.

Despite the rapid growth of employer-sponsored child care, it is still limited in absolute terms. It accounts for less than one percent of all children in day care (Kamerman and Hayes, 1982). The number of industry-sponsored centers has actually declined since 1970 (U.S. Labor Department, 1982). Yet, employer- sponsored child care is the fastest growing area of child care today and is expected to increase dramatically in the future.

For this reason, the involvement of government in stimulating private sector provisions for child care has direct implications for poor Head Start families. In an era of massive budget cuts in response to the federal government's financial deficits, there is legitimate concern that dollars are being shifted from the poor to the middle-class.

For one thing, corporate benefits tend to be unequally distributed as the unskilled, racial minorities and women are concentrated in sectors of the economy that offer poor benefits (Kamerman and Kingston, 1982).

The unequal distribution of benefits leads to concern about the use of tax incentives for businesses. The loss of government revenues may decrease the amount available for direct subsidies to parents and programs. The net effect may not be a real increase in the total amount of revenues available for family support, but rather, there may be a shift in the decision-making responsibility for the expenditures of available resources from the public to the private sector (Friedman, 1983).

Head Start Initiatives for Working Parents

Government initiatives to promote employer- sponsored child care and to recognize changing family trends such as maternal employment recognize an important reality as we approach the twenty-first century: New ways to deliver services to families must be developed. These new service delivery strategies must forge new institutional relationships and examine alternative funding mechanisms, curriculum additions, and training needs.

Project Head Start officials have recognized the need to address the needs of their working parents. For example, ABT Associates, Inc., prepared a discussion paper designed to help the Administration for Children, Youth, and Families (ACYF) develop an initiative for working papers. On the occasion of Head Start's 15th anniversary President Jimmy Carter requested an analysis of Project Head Start and included the recommendation for more assistance to children of working parents (Muenchow and Shays, 1980). Both of these reports highlighted statistics on the growing labor force participation of poor mothers and the inadequacies of Head Start services in meeting these changing parental needs.

While the precise number of employed Head Start parents is not known, available data for low-income women, black women, and AFDC recipients suggest that at least half of these parents are working. Thus, in 1986, about 226,000 children needed more care than Head Start services could provide.

As Muenchow and Shays (1980) point out, the relationship between Head Start and day care has always been problematic: While over 200,000 Head Start eligible families need full-day care for their children, the current budget is insufficient to provide this care. Indeed, full-day Head Start programs have declined from about one-third of the grantees to only 15 percent since 1972. Further, Head Start centers operate for an average of 34 weeks each year, whereas most employees work 48 to 50 weeks.

As a result, many Head Start eligible families are unable to enroll their children in the conventional program due to the inconvenience and difficulty of making additional child care arrangements. ABT Associates, Inc., found that most Head Start programs offer a three-hour morning or afternoon program or an extended day from about 9:00 a.m. to 2:00 p.m. Under this arrangement, working parents are required to leave work to transfer their child to another facility or to arrange for a parental designate to make this transfer. This burden may be compounded if the parent must leave for work before the Head Start program begins and if there are siblings with different day care arrangements. Consequently, conventional programs had trouble meeting their enrollment goals, whereas full- and extended-day programs were fully enrolled. ABT also found that parents were sometimes persuaded to enroll children in half-day programs with a promise of the first available slot in the full-day programs (Abt Associates, 1979).

Working parents who prefer Head Start's comprehensive child development program may find it necessary to choose a more convenient and inexpensive arrangement for their children. Other child care arrangements are available through AFDC and other workfare programs.

As the numbers of poor women in the workplace continues to grow, these concerns about Head Start services will escalate. The present circumstances in service delivery and public policy do not promote continuity of care for children (see Phillips, 1983), an important variable for maximizing child development.

Several possible solutions have been offered. ABT Associates, Inc., and Muenchow and Shays (1980) suggest:

1. Conducting a needs assessment to acquire a more complete understanding of the kinds of day care arrangements made by Head Start- eligible working parents who are not enrolled in the program.

2. Studying the current population of Head Start's working parents.

3. Providing information and referral services to facilitate parents' search for additional hours of child care without actually providing that care.

4. Enlisting a group of satellite family day care homes which could provide care to Head Start children before and after the program hours, as well as to their younger and older siblings.

5. Offering or coordinating a day care program, funded through Title XX and other sources, before and after the Head Start program. In some areas, Head Start has established linkages with other child care programs.

6. Providing a full-day Head Start program. The additional cost is estimated at $300 to $500 per child per year.

Muenchow and Shays stress that there is no single mechanism for increasing access to full-day care for all the Head Start families who need it. However, Head Start can seek to ensure that children receive as much continuity of care as possible. Towards that end, bureaucratic obstacles to mixing Title XX and Head Start funds should be removed. "Public programs should be shaped to suit people, not people to suit programs."

PART D:

THE INCREASING CHALLENGE OF ECONOMIC SELF-SUFFICIENCY FOR POOR FAMILIES: HEAD START MUST RESPOND

These rapid changes in American families -- female-headed households, teenage parenting, and employed mothers -- are having a profound impact on poor people. As a result of these changing family trends, many low-income families are rooted in economic distress. As many as 45 percent of these families continue on welfare for at least 5 out of every 7 years. Many individuals mired in poverty are the unemployed who are either discouraged in their efforts to find a job, or who are among the nearly 20 percent unemployed people from ages 16 to 19. Still others trapped in poverty are school dropouts who lack the skills to match the available jobs (see Auletta, 1982). The Perry Preschool project found that 11 years after the various stages of their project, two out of five families had no parent employed -- as was the case in the original survey (Berrueta-Clement et al., 1984).

In explaining long-term poverty, Bernstein (1982) argues that welfare has fostered dependency instead of reducing it, has encouraged the break up of families, has weakened the sense of family responsibility, has led to a rejection of the work ethic, and has caused children raised in welfare-dependent homes to become dependent, to lack a work ethic, to fail to take responsibility for their own children, and to engage in antisocial behavior.

Challenging this "welfare dependence theory," Hill and Ponza (1983) found that children from low- income homes exhibit substantial income mobility: 57 percent were not impoverished as young adults. Further, Levy (1980) found that about four out of five new households formed by people from low-income families had incomes well above the poverty line.

We contend that low-income people may fail to achieve due to barriers usually manifested in the form of racial and sexual discrimination, particularly in the job market. Moreover, behaviors such as poor work habits or low self-confidence may be an effect of poverty rather than a cause.

The continuing role of racial discrimination cannot be overlooked. Indeed, the comparably weak economic status of black mothers holds true regardless of whether they are in two-parent or female-headed households. Black children in two-parent families are twice as likely as white children in two-parent families to live below the poverty level. Further, the median income for all black families is less than 60 percent of that of white families, an increasing gap between 1970 and 1983 (CDF, 1985).

Nevertheless, changing conditions in American families create new demands on individuals and on the programs that serve them. Many observers agree that these dramatic changes are neither short term nor likely to be reversed (Cherlin, 1981). New family structures and roles are not automatically accommodated in federal programs, but the implications of these changes for Head Start must be explored by all professionals who are concerned about this nation's children. It is imperative that we consider possible changes because of Head Start's "recognition of the importance of the family, rather than the school, as the ultimate source of a child's values and behavior" (Zigler and Anderson, 1979, p.14).

One of the initially stated purposes of Head Start was to marshal and coordinate federal, state, and local resources to involve low-income families in the process of finding solutions to their own problems (Office of Economic Opportunity, 1967). Head Start jobs and services contribute to the economic vitality of communities and encourage the coordination of community social services (Hubbell, 1983).

From the beginning of Head Start, there has been controversy over whether Head Start sought to empower low-income people politically and economically or to simply provide services (Shriver, 1979).

Based on our belief that both of these goals are possible, we present these recommendations for Head Start as the program:

1. Addresses the feminization of poverty,
2. Works with adolescent parents, and
3. Serves employed mothers.

The Feminization of Poverty

Clearly, the families served by Head Start are likely to be headed by women and even more likely to be headed by minority women. The only income support program for low-income families, AFDC, once presumed that mothers of young children would be homemakers. On the other hand, Head Start's comprehensive design has historically included parent involvement and career development for adults. How can Head Start build on this approach?

1. Head Start must strengthen its focus on parental employability and preparation to enter the workforce to help women and their children emerge from poverty.

2. Head Start can present both boys and girls with positive male images through curriculum, staffing patterns, and involvement in community activities since the feminization of poverty infers an absence of male role models in the home.

3. Head Start can promote positive family relationships through workshops and seminars. Indeed, the philosophical basis of Head Start emphasizes the role of family and community (Harmon and Hanley, 1979). Head Start has already been shown to have a positive effect on parent attitudes toward, and interactions with, their children (Mann, Harrell, and Hurt, 1977). These efforts can be increased.

4. In addition, Head Start programs should focus on adult male-female relationships. There should be renewed emphasis on strengthening family structures and functions through improved marital interaction with a view toward reduction of the divorce rate and hence the number of female-headed households. Head Start programs can also help individuals understand the stresses which impinge upon

family life such as the disproportionate number of black females to black males and the high unemployment or underemployment of black males.

Adolescent Parenting

The social and economic consequences of teenage parenting lead to the poverty cycle that Head Start was designed to address. Since the Head Start- eligible population consists primarily of AFDC families, it can be projected that at least 50 percent of the Head Start families would include, or be at risk for, teenage parenting. Thus, the primary focuses of the parent component of Head Start should be

A. To prevent adolescent pregnancy, and

B. To realize that Head Start is likely to provide services to young mothers.

5. Effective sex education models can be adapted to the Head Start parent involvement program. Several studies have focused on causes, treatment, and prevention of teenage pregnancy in the black community (Washington, A, 1982; Westney, et al., 1983; Oyemade, et al., 1983). Some of the strategies suggested to reduce the incidence of teenage pregnancies have included sex education with an emphasis on traditional morality which discourages teenage pregnancy, and involvement of all the teenager's network (family, neighbors, peers, and schoolmates) in programs of pregnancy prevention.

6. Head Start could influence the quality of social services through its social change and community action model that has traditionally been a part of the parent involvement program. In this way, Head Start could change findings such as the fact that black teenagers may fail to take advantage of contraceptive services because of the clash in values between the black clients and social agencies (Washington, A., 1982).

7. Head Start programs can seek to increase parental knowledge about childrearing and parenting skills. As programs work intensively with teenage parents and their children, it is likely that fewer of these children will be at risk developmentally or educationally (Washington and Glimps, 1983).

8. Head Start must continue to develop leadership potential among low-income families. Zigler (1979) contends that this effort in Head Start can be an important factor in helping parents recognize that they influence their own destiny. Based on social-learning theory, children, too, would develop similar attitudes about control over their lives.

Maternal Employment

9. Head Start must extend hours and services that accommodate the need for full-day care for infants, toddlers, preschool, and school-age children. The increase in the employment of mothers of young children, coupled with the rise in single-parent households, has created unprecedented demands for all-day child care. Head Start has always had a full-day feature for prekindergarten, but the need for infant- and after-school care has been given less priority.

   In a step that further ignores the needs of employed mothers, many Head Start programs are moving toward split sessions or variations-in-center attendance models. Parents who work full time may not be able to take advantage of a part-time Head Start program.

10. Head Start mothers who are employed may require increased support for their children's transportation to the program.

11. The parent involvement component of Head Start must be restructured to accommodate the schedules of working parents.

12. Head Start should increase its focus on the affective and social development of children due to the rise in the number of employed and/or single parents. Programs can foster skills in independence, self-care, and interpersonal relations to help these children cope with the demands necessitated by the life-style of the low-income employed parents.

13. Greater emphasis should be placed on maintaining a stable staff in an effort to enhance the feelings of security and attachment in the Head Start child.

14. Ensure that parent-teacher conferences, policy councils, or program meetings are held at a time when the parent will not have to leave work.

15. Provide child care during parent-teacher conferences, programs, or policy council meetings.

16. Provide courses or workshops specifically for single parents.

17. Arrange for inservice training for staff on how to be more effective working with single parents and children from single parent families.

18. Ensure that Head Start's curriculum includes various family structures including working mothers and single parents.

19. Have an "extended day" program or hours of service which accommodate the needs for before- and after-school care.

20. Provide transportation for parents and children for after-school activities.

21. Watch out for negative expectations based on family structure. Do not assume that any problem a child has (emotional, behavioral, or achievement) is related to parental employment or marital status.

22. Eliminate the use of language which denigrates the single parent or working mother (e.g., "broken home"). Using this terminology perpetuates the mind-set that nontraditional family forms are incomplete or inadequate.

Recommendations from the National Head Start Parent Involvement Task Force

In an effort to see parent involvement increased in Head Start programs nationwide, Dodie Livingston, Commissioner of ACYF, created a national task force in April 1985. Richard H. Johnson, Chief of the Social Services and Parent Involvement Branch of the Head Start Bureau, served as chairperson of the task force. The members of the task force were representatives from the National Head Start Association's four affiliate associations.

The task force deliberations resulted in nine major recommendations to the ACYF Head Start Bureau (see Johnson, R., 1986: pp.15-16). The task force recommends that ACYF's Head Start Bureau:

1. Assure that the parent involvement performance standards and all policies relating to parent involvement are consistently interpreted and enforced across all ACYF Regional Offices, including the American Indian Branch and the Migrant Branch;

2. Develop a policy for Head Start grantees which specifies minimal measurable requirements for involving parents in Head Start programs, and a policy which requires parents to be actively involved in Head Start programs without penalty to the enrolled child or parent;

3. Assure that all policies, whether existing or new, support and reinforce parent involvement in Head Start;

4. Assure that transmittal notices and other communications to the field, pertaining to parent involvement, be thorough, current, simply written, and concise;

5. Use "grass roots" input to help establish national parent involvement priorities and directions;

6. Create a national clearinghouse to disseminate parent involvement information to all Head Start programs;

7. Assure that local Head Start programs establish and maintain parent activity funds consistent with USDHHS policies without programs imposing unnecessary restrictions on their use;

8. Assume leadership and coordinating responsibility to increase interagency cooperation and understanding between Head Start and the school system, assuring ongoing parent involvement in this process; and

9. Require local Head Start programs to increase communication and coordination with local education institutions in order to support the orderly transition of Head Start children to the schools.

Conclusion

The critical point is that Head Start must adapt to changes in families that have occurred since the inception of the Project. At the same time, Head Start staff should continue to recognize that each child and each family must be viewed individually with strengths and weaknesses similar to and different from others.

To accomplish these objectives, Head Start must strengthen its resolve to be a comprehensive program. While Head Start has not suffered direct budget cuts in support services, the program still serves fewer than one out of five eligible children. Efforts should be increased to expand the program and ensure that administrative changes do not dilute parent participation or communication across services.

Also, the parent involvement component of Head Start should:

A. Focus on presenting positive male role models to children;

B. Heighten understanding of adult male-female relationships;

C. Promote positive family relationships;

D. Develop strategies to prevent teenage pregnancy; and

E. Address the concerns of employed mothers.

Head Start planners should also reconsider changes in program models and transportation to determine whether there might be better ways to serve employed parents.

Economic self-sufficiency projects can be implemented through Head Start to prepare adults for work and to coordinate opportunities for skill development and employment beyond Head Start programs.

Family needs assessments should be conducted periodically by Head Start programs to stay attuned to changing trends in family life and to identity new areas for emphasis. Successful learning experiences for children have accounted for much of Head Start's popularity. However, the family focus of the program must be retained because children's futures are clearly tied to the strength and resiliency of their families.

Head Start advocates can capitalize upon the momentum of support for the program, and ensure the adequacy of America's most successful "social safety net," by informing members of Congress of these and other recommendations which realistically respond to family trends.

TABLE 8

STEPS HEAD START CAN TAKE TO ADDRESS THE CHANGING NEEDS OF AMERICAN FAMILIES

1. Strengthen its resolve to be a comprehensive program.
2. Broaden the parent involvement component.
3. Reconsider changes in program models and transportation.
4. Implement new economic self-sufficiency projects.
5. Conduct periodic family needs assessments.

Overall, we agree with the recommendations of the 15th Anniversary Head Start Committee (Muenchow and Shays, 1980) that Head Start should

1. Provide economic counseling, and

2. Introduce a self-help group component.

Many Head Start parents need assistance in the day-to-day tasks of providing for a family. Economic counseling should be included as one of Head Start's comprehensive services (Muenchow and Shays, 1980). Since Head Start has always functioned as a catalyst for individual and social change (Kirschner, 1970), self-help groups and economic self-sufficiency services represent a logical extension of Head Start programs.

Clearly the rise in single-parent households, high rates of adolescent parenting, and consequent overrepresentation of children among the poor are serious causes for concern. These issues reopened discussion of family life among political and ethnic-group leaders; a sensitive, volatile issue arrested significantly by fallout from the "The Moynihan Report." Now, some blacks concede that "Moynihan was right" since he predicted accurately the increasing deterioration of black family structure. Others regret that Moynihan's recommendations for strengthening the family were overlooked as a result of reaction to his thesis.

An observer of social trends, Daniel P. Moynihan, a senator from New York since 1977, has again turned his attention to the status of American family life (Moynihan, 1986). In his 1985 Godkin lectures at Harvard University, Moynihan examined the relationship between the growing erosion of "traditional" family structure and child poverty. In 1965 he said that "the Negro family" was less stable than the white family. Moving from the extreme implication that race and culture were a significant cause of family dysfunction, Moynihan now asserts that the problem of family disorganization is no longer racial.

While we appreciate Moynihan's universal approach, a realistic attack on family crises and poverty must emphasize the fact that there are commonalities and differences in the family experiences of black and white families or poor and middle-class families. However, we agree wholeheartedly with Senator Moynihan that these issues cannot continue to be ignored.

Policymakers must realize that attempts to eradicate poverty require explicit attention to poor mothers, particularly those in female-headed households. It is important to bear in mind that family structure does not *cause* poverty or developmental dysfunction. Also, the degree to which society supports poor mothers through the community and family determines the extent to which they will function adequately. Instead of offering these mothers tears and damnation, training and development should be provided. In this way, poor, single mothers can be prepared to move themselves and their families from public dependency to self-sufficient heads of households. The ultimate solution to these mothers' general poverty is racial and gender equality, allowing access to educational and employment opportunities for poor women and poor men.

As we approach the twenty-first century, the experience for families will be widely divergent. Those families who have highly skilled members will see their incomes increase and their children prosper. On the other hand, poor, single-parent or adolescent families are likely to become increasingly alienated and distant from mainstream American life.

This review of the status of poor families reminds us that not all of them are able to handle the multiple, insidious pressures of economic deprivation with work and family demands. Yes, many poor families and their children have survived -- indeed some have prospered. Yet, this survival has been with a great cost unworthy of either favorable or disparaging mythology.

In addressing these issues, much of today's debate is whether the poor should continue to emphasize the need for government action or to target their energies on self-help. While a combination of government and community initiative is essential, many advocates for children and the poor are now focusing on what can be done using their own resources. For example, since almost half of black females in America become mothers while they are teenagers, the predominant, radical cries that birth control is genocide have given way to a declaration of war against adolescent pregnancy by many black organizations. Amid the correct demands that society fulfill the promises of the Constitution, there is a persistent call for self-reliance. By promoting and extending values and traditions, it is certain that the dilemmas facing poor families and their children will be resolved.

PART E:

REFERENCES AND ANNOTATED BIBLIOGRAPHY

NOTE: An asterisk (*) preceding a reference indicates that the reference was cited in the text.

.belson, W.D., E. Zigler, and C.L. DeBlasi. "Effects Of A Four-Year Follow Through Program On Economically Disadvantaged Children." *Journal of Educational Psychology* 66 (1974): 756-771.

Compared IQ, achievement, and socio- emotional test scores for poor children who attended the full four years of the follow- through program and non-follow-through children. At the end of third grade it was found that follow-through children were superior on all three measures. Nevertheless, the follow-through program did not result in the poor children attaining the level of intellectual achievement shown by nondisadvantaged children.

›t Associates. *Home Start Evaluation Study-Interim Reports 5 and 6.* Cambridge, MA.: Abt Associates, 1974 and 1975 (ED107380).

.bt Associates. *The Rationale for and Development of a Head Start Initiative for Working Parents.* Cambridge, MA.: Abt Associates, 1979.

Presents data on the prevalence of working mothers and discusses the extent to which Head Start has responded or could respond to these issues.

ken, Devon. *Coordinating Human Services.* Chicago, Illinois: The University of Chicago Press, 1966.

Discusses a variety of service delivery systems designed to meet the needs of the mentally retarded in five urban areas. A study was conducted to analyze how various organizations responded to and administered the five federal Vocational Rehabilitation Administration Research and Demonstration grants between 1963 and 1965. Conclusions were drawn as to the most effective model to coordinate new and existing services.

e Alan Guttmacher Institute. *Teenage Pregnancy: The Problem That Hasn't Gone Away.* New York: The Alan Guttmacher Institute, 1981.

exander S., C. Williams, and J. Forbush. *Overview of State Policies Related to Adolescent Parenthood: A Report of the Adolescent Parenthood Project.* Washington, D.C.: National Association of State Boards of Education, 1980.

*Allen, Vernon L. (Ed.) *Psychological Factors in Poverty.* Chicago: Markham Publishing Company, 1970A.

*Allen, Vernon L. "Theoretical Issues in Poverty Research." *Journal of Social Issues* 26 (1970B): 149-165.

*Allen, Walter R. "The Search for Applicable Theories of Black Family Life." *Journal of Marriage and The Family* 40 (1976): 117-129.

*Allen, Walter. "Family Roles, Occupational Statuses, and Achievement Among Black Women in the United States." *Signs: Journal of Women in Culture and Society.* 4(4) (1979): 670-686.

*Allen, Walter R. "Race, Income and Family Dynamics: A Study of Adolescent Male Socialization Processes and Outcomes." *Beginnings: The Social and Affective Development of Black Children.* Edited by M.B. Spencer, G.K. Brookins, and W.R. Allen. Hillsdale, N.J.: Lawrence Erlbaum Associates, 1985, pp.273-292.

Looks at socializaiton processes and outcomes in a biracial sample of families, particularly for adolescent males in middle- income, two-parent families. Found that black mothers occupy more central positions in their families and that many of the socialization patterns were culture-specific.

Alternative Lifestyles 2 (August 1979): Entire Issue.

Looks at changing patterns in marriage, family and intimacy. Among the contents are articles by J. Greenberg, "Single-parenting and intimacy: a comparison of mothers and fathers"; N. Cazenave, "Social Structure and personal choice: effects on intimacy, marriage and the family alternative life-style research"; and J. Scott, "Single rural elders: A comparison of dimensions of life satisfaction."

Alvarez, William F. "The Meaning of Maternal Employment for Mothers and Their Perceptions of Their Three-year-Old Children." *Child Development* 56 (April 1985): 350-360.

Investigates the relationship between features of the maternal employment situation and mother's positive description of their 3-year old children in a sample of 152 white, two-parent families. Employed mothers' positive motivation for working, low role conflict, and gains in self-worth are all associated with mother's favorable descriptions of their children. The study also found that although the socioeconomic characteristics of mothers and their families significantly predicted maternal employment status, these demographic differences do not account for variations in mother's positive perceptions of their children.

American Public Welfare Association. *Memorandum W-5. The FY83 Budget Proposals for Aid to Families with Dependent Children.* Washington, D.C.: APWA, February 1982.

Anderson, Kristin. *Exploring Corporate Initiatives for Working Parents: An Industry by Industry Review.* New York: Center for Public Advocacy Research, 1983.

Anderson, M. *Welfare: The Political Economy of Welfare Reform in the United States.* Stanford, CA.: Hoover Institution Press, 1978.

Anderson, Scarvia, et al. *Priorities and Directions for Research and Development Related to Measurement of Young Children: Report on Task 2.* Princeton, N.J.: Educational Testing Service, 1972.

Presents recommendations from a panel of 15 child development/early childhood education/measurement experts. Key issues were: 1. the special statistical and methodological problems of measuring the behavior of young children and the impact of their environments; 2. the considerations of construct-based measurement, particularly the problems of population and ecological validity; and 3. the dependency of the advancement of measurement research and development on appropriate policy decisions, and the availability and training of staff.

*Anderson, Scarvia, and Samuel Messick. *Social Competency in Young Children.* Educational Testing Service: Princeton, N.J., 1973.

Reports the results of a panel discussion on the meaning of social competency in children. Identifies approaches to defining goals and discusses the role of values, culture, and stage of development in assessing competence.

Andrews, Susan Ring, Janet Berstein Blumenthal, Dale L. Johnson, Alfred J. Kahn, Carol J. Ferguson, Thomas M. Lasater, Paul E. Malone, and Doris B. Wallace. "The Skills of Mothering: A Study of Parent Child Development Centers." *Monographis of the Society for Research in Child Development.* 47 (6 Serial No. 198) (1982).

Reports the results of the PCDC experiment from 1970 - 1975 in Birmingham, Houston, and New Orleans. Significant differences were found between program and control groups in maternal behavior and Stanford-Binet scores. The limitations and strengths of the projects are discussed in the framework of the program goals. Implications for parent education, future research, and social policy are examined.

Applied Management Sciences. *Evaluation of the Process of Mainstreaming Handicapped Children into Project Head Start, Phase I Executive Summary.* Silver Spring, Maryland, April 28, 1978A (Contract No. HEW 105-76-1113).

Applied Management Sciences. *Evaluation of the Process of Mainstreaming Handicapped Children into Project Head Start, Phase II Executive Summary.* Silver Spring, Maryland, December 15, 1978B (Contract No. HEW 105-76-1113).

Asbury, C.A. "Cognitive Factors Related to Discrepant Arithmetic Achievement of White and Black First Graders." *Journal of Negro Education* 67 (Fall, 1978): 337-342.

Clarifies existing research relating to relevant cognitive factors to the discrepant school achievement of white and black economically deprived, first-grade children. Finds that overachievers are superior to underachievers in numerical concept activation and sensory concept activation; girls are superior to boys on associative vocabulary and perceptual ability; and whites are superior to blacks on all cognitive variables except perceptual ability.

*Auletta, Kenneth. *The Underclass.* New York: Random House, 1982.

Examines poverty among different ethnic groups and in different geographical areas in an effort to find out if there was a distinct underclass. Concludes that there is a black and white underclass that feels excluded from society, rejects societal norms, and suffers from behavioral and income deficiencies.

Axelson, Leland, Jr. "The Working Wife: Differences in Perception among Negro and White Males." *Journal of Marriage and the Family* 3 (1970): 457-464.

Found that the differences which exist between black and white males in their perceptions of working wives hold even when the variables of socioeconomic status and age are controlled. The perceived differences relate to both the working wife's relationship to her husband and the working wife's relationship to her husband's career. The majority of black and white husbands thought that a wife who earned more money than her husband was undesirable. All respondents agreed that a wife's employment should not conflict with that of the husband.

Bacon, L. "Early Motherhood: Accelerated Role Transition and Social Pathologies." *Social Forces* 52(3) A74: (1974): 333-341.

Finds from an analysis of national data that early motherhood, a form of accelerated role transition, is closely associated with high incidence of marital disolution, poverty and low educational levels.

*Baden, C. *Work and Family: An Annotated Bibliography 1978 - 1980*. Boston, MA.: Whellock College Center for Parenting Studies, 1981.

*Baden, R.K., A. Genser, J.A. Levine, and M. Seltzer. *School-Age Child Care: An Action Manual*. Boston: Auburn Publishing Co., Inc., 1982.

Estimates that in 1981 there were 16 million children between ages five and thirteen whose mothers worked.

Baldwin, W. "Adolescent Pregnancy and Childbearing- Growing Concerns for Americans." *Population Bulletin* 31: (1976): 3-21.

Examines the negative impact of teenage pregnancy on the society and identifies barriers to the effective use of contraceptives.

*Baldwin, W., and V. Cain. "The Children of Teenage Parents." *Teenage Sexuality, Pregnancy, and Childbearing*. Edited by F. Furstenberg, R. Lincoln, and J. Menken. Philadelphia: University of Pennsylvania Press, 1981, pp. 265- 279.

*Balsey, W.M. *Testimony on Behalf of the First Atlanta Corporation Before the Committee on Labor and Human Resources*. U.S. Senate, 16 November 1983.

Bane, M.J., and D.T. Elwood. *The Dynamics of Dependency: The Routes to Self-Sufficiency*. Cambridge, MA.: Urban Systems Research and Engineering, 1983.

Banks, J.A. *Teaching Strategies for Ethnic Studies*. 3rd Ed. Newton, MA: Allyn and Bacon, Inc., 1983.

Presents a rationale for teaching comparative ethnic studies. Discusses the problems of goals in ethnic studies and key concepts for ethnic studies lessons. Presents an overview of major ethnic groups in the U.S.

*Baratz, J. "Language Development In The Economically Disadvantaged Child: A Perspective." *American Speech and Hearing Association* (April, 1968): 143-145.

Claims that the goals of intervention programs are unrealistic if the existing cultures of poor blacks are not recognize and used. The paper illustrates that social scientists hold an ethnocentric view of the black community.

*Baratz, Stephen S., and Joan C. Baratz. "Early Childhood Intervention: The Social Science Base of Institutional Racism." *Harvard Educational Review* 40 (Winter 1970): 29-50.

Barclay, Lisa K. "Using Spanish As The Language Of Instruction With Mexican-American Head Start Children: A Re-evaluation Using Meta-analysis." *Perceptual and Motor Skills* 56 (1983): 359-366.

Found that the use of Spanish as the language of instruction resulted in larger effect sizes than did the use of English, both languages, or a control treatment using arts, crafts, and music activities. Recently expressed doubts about the efficacy of beginning instruction in non-English speakers' native languages are questioned.

Barnes, Howard L., and David H. Olson. "Parent- Adolescent Communication and the Circumplex Model." *Child Development* 56 (April 1985): 438-447.

Tested the relationship between parent- adolescent communication and the Circumplex Model of Marital and Family Systems.

Barnow, B.S. "The Effects of Head Start and Socioeconomic Status on Cognitive Development of Disadvantaged Children." Ph.D. Dissertation. University of Wisconsin, 1973.

Reviews the controversy surrounding the Westinghouse report, particularly the statistical problems involved in Head Start evaluations, and reanalyzes the data using individual, rather than grouped, data. Barnow's reanalysis also includes more socioeconomic and demographic variables than does the Westinghouse study.

Barret, Robert L., and Bryan E. Robinson. "A Descriptive Study of Teenage Expectant Fathers." *Family Relations* 31 (1982A): 349-352.

Reports demographic data on a sample of 26 adolescent expectant fathers and their relationships with the expectant mothers and their families. The study finds that the fathers maintained positive relationships with the young woman's family and wanted to participate with the child.

Barret, Robert L., and Bryan E. Robinson. "Teenage Fathers: Neglected Too Long." *Social Work* 27 (Nov. 1982B): 484-488.

Reviews the literature on adolescent fathers and offers recommenations for improving services to unwed adolescent parents.

Bates, B.D. *Project Head Start 1965-1967: A Descriptive Report on Programs and Participants*. Washington, D.C.: Office of Child Development, 1970 (ED047816).

Bates, B.D. *Project Head Start: The Development of a Program.* Washington, D.C.: Office of Child Development, 1972 (ED072858).

Beasley, J.O., et al. "Attitudes and Knowledge Relevant to Family Planning Among New Orleans Negro Families." *American Journal of Public Health* 56 (1970): 1847-1857.

*Becker, W.C. "Project Head Start: A Legacy of the War on Poverty." *Merrill Palmer Quarterly* (1981):

*Beckett, J. "Working Wives: A Racial Comparison." *Social Work* (November 1976): 463-471.

*Bee, H., L. Van Egeren, A. Streissguth, B. Nymon, and M. Leckie. "Social Class Differences in Maternal Teaching Strategies and Speech Patterns." *Developmental Psychology* 1 (1969): 726-734.

Explores social class differences in maternal behavior with a sample of 76 lower-class mothers and 38 middle-class mothers. Compared to middle-class mothers, lower-class mothers were more disapproving and controlling; more intrusive in the child's problem solving; used relatively higher rates of negative feedback; used more specific concrete suggestions in the child's problem solving; and used shorter and less complex sentences, relatively fewer adjectives, and more personal references.

Beneville, Marcia, and Susan Bromfield. "Integrated Educational Opportunities for Head Start Children With Special Needs." *Dissertation Abstracts International* 5 (1979): 2586-A.

Assesses the integration of handicapped children into Head Start programs via the observation of 66 Head Start programs in 1973 and 1974. Three dimensions of integration were formulated: adult initiated opportunities for integration, labeled child initiations, and nonlabeled child initiations. Greater degrees of integration were more likely to be associated with a social emotional emphasis in the curriculum, with greater parental involvement, and with relatively positive staff and parental attitudes.

Bereiter, C., and S. Englemann. *Teaching Disadvantaged Children in the Preschool.* Englewood Cliffs, N.J.: Prentice-Hall, 1966.

*Bernstein, Blanche. *The Politics of Welfare: The New York City Experience.* Cambridge, MA.: Abt Books, 1982.

*Berrueta-Clement, John R., L.J. Schweinhart, W.S. Barnett, A.S. Epstein, and D.P. Weikart. *Changed Lives - The Effects of the Perry Preschool Program on Youths Through Age 19.* Ypsilanti, MI.: The High/Scope Educational Research Foundation, 1984.

Reports the results of a longitudinal study which seeks to demonstrate whether or not preschool education of high quality could alter the lives of children living in poverty. The study demonstrated that high quality preschool intervention can prevent developmental attrition and can make a positive impact on the future lives of its participants.

Blechman, Elaine A., and Michael J. McEnroe. "Effective Family Problem Solving." *Child Development* 56 (April 1985): 429-437.

Looks at effective family problem solving techniques. Group interaction appeared to be more valid than definitions that rely primarily on family characteristics.

Bloom, B. *Stability and Change in Human Characteristics.* New York: Wiley and Sons, 1964.

Boger, Robert P. "Sub-Cultural Group Membership and Attitudes of Head Start Teachers." *Dissertation Abstracts International* 27 (1966): 2062.

Seeks to determine whether or not potential Head Start staff from different ethnic subcultural backgrounds varied in attitudes reflecting acceptance of, desirability of, and concern about behaviors of children similar to those they would be teaching in Project Head Start.

Bolliger, Linda K. "Superstar," *Reporter* 6(1981): 13-15.

Calls Head Start a superstar of social programs, because of its popularity and success. Highlights of Head Start's history are presented.

*Bolton, Frank, G., Jr. *The Pregnant Adolescent - Problems of Premature Parenthood.* Beverly Hills, CA.: Sage Publications, 1980.

Presents a developmental record of the adolescent pregnancy-child maltreatment dyad. It also provides some suggestions for the interruption of this dysfunctional development.

Boone, Young and Associates. *Evaluation of Head Start/EPSDT Collaboration.* Washington, D.C.: USDHEW/OCD, 1977.

Booz, Allen. *Retrospective Study of Employee Mobility in Head Start Programs.* Washington, D.C.: May 18, 1973 (ED095265).

Booz, Allen. *Prospective Study of Employee Mobility in Head Start Programs.* Washington, D.C.: February 14, 1974 (ED095264).

*Bowler, M.K. *The Nixon Guaranteed Income Proposal.* Cambridge, MA.: Ballinger, 1974.

Boykin, A.W. "Experimental Psychology from a Black Perspective: Issues and Examples." *Journal of Black Psychology* 3 (February 1977): 29-49.

Discusses experimental psychology as it relates to the psycho-educational needs of Afro- American children. Identifies at least three conceptually separate psychological and behavioral dimensions for which we can specify qualitative uniqueness or salience for the black child, and that may have implications for maximally facilitating academic and task performance.

Boykin, A.W. "Task Variability and the Performance of Black and White School Children: Vervistic Explorations." *The Journal of Black Studies* 12 (1982): 471-485.

Tests the influence of variability in task- presentation format on consequent task performance, and the prediction that the homes of black children, on average, provide a higher level of stimulation affordance than those of white children. Finds that: 1. the home environment of black working-class children provides the highest level of stimulation; and 2. that black working-class and white middle-class children display differential responsivenesss to variability in task presentation format.

Boykin, A.W., A.J. Franklin, and J.F. Yates. (Eds.) *Research Directions of Black Psychologists*. New York: Russell Sage, 1979.

Presents a collection of revised and edited papers from the first two conferences on Empirical Research in Black Psychology.

*Brandwein, Ruth A. "After Divorce - A Focus on Single Parent Families." *The Urban and Social Change Review* 10 (1977): 21-25.

Looks at the rise in single parent families due to divorce and examines the effect of divorce on children. Discusses implications for public policy.

*Bridgman, A. "Head Start's Benefits are Short-Lived, a Three Year Federal Study Concludes." *Education Week* (September 11, 1985): 1,15.

Bromley, David G., and Charles F. Longino, Jr., Editors. *White Racism and Black Americans*. Cambridge, MA.: Schenkman Publishing Co., Inc., 1972.

Presents articles which relate to systematic aspects of racism. The book is thematically arranged according to units of sociological analysis: social processes, social institutions, and culture. In Part I, articles dealing with the social processes of socialization, deviance, and ecology are presented. Part II contains articles on the social institutions through which societies maintain themselves over a period of time--the family, education, economics, politics, religion, and health. The articles in Part III deal with those elements of culture by which a people define themselves.

*Bronfenbrenner, Urie. *A Report on Longitudinal Evaluations of Preschool Programs. Vol. 2.* Washington, D.C.: USDHEW Office of Child Development, 1974 Publication #OHD30025.

*Bronfenbrenner, Urie (Editor). *Influences on Human Development.* Hillsdale, Illinois: The Dryden Press, 1975A.

Fifty-seven readings, primarily research findings, in a variety of disciplines are presented. The book is divided into five sections: the first two deal with the scientific method in the study of human behavior. The last three sections are related to children's developmental stages: infancy, early childhood, middle childhood and adolescence.

*Brofenbrenner, Urie. "Is Early Intervention Effective?" *Handbook of Evaluation Research, Vol. 2.* Edited by M. Guttentag and E. Struning. Beverly Hills, California: Sage Publications, 1975B, pp. 519-604.

*Bronfenbrenner, Urie. "Head Start, a Retrospective View: The Founders." *Project Head Start.* Edited by Edward Zigler and Jeanette Valentine. New York: Free Press, 1979, pp. 77-88.

Bronfenbrenner, Urie. "Children and Families: 1984?" *Society* 18 (Jan.-Feb. 1981): 38-41.

Examines the forces that can destroy the human ecology--"the social fabric that nurtures and sustains our capacity to live and work together effectively and to raise our children to become competent and compassionate members of society"--concentrating on how and why the structure is breaking down and what can be done to retard or reverse the process.

*Brown, Bernard. *How Social Research Changed Public Policy: A History of the Debate on Head Start.* Washington, D.C.: USDHHS/ACYF, 1979.

Brown, Bernard, and Edith H. Grotberg. "Head Start: A Successful Experiment." *Courrier* 30 (1980): 334-345.

Describes two studies which indicate that Head Start has a positive impact on children.

*Burchinal, Lee. "Trends and Prospects for Young Marriages in the U.S." *Journal of Marriage and the Family* 27 (1965): 243-254.

Examines factors that influence satisfaction among young marriages and suggests ways in which rates and outcomes of youthful marriages can be positively influenced.

*Burden, Diane S., and Lorraine V. Klerman. "Teenage Parenthood: Factors that Lessen Economic Dependence." *Social Work* 29 (Jan.-Feb. 1984): 11-16.

Argues that teenage mothers have high rates of welfare dependence. Factors that lessen the long-term negative economic consequences of early motherhood include deferment of marriage, support from the family of origin, increased education and career motivation, decreased fertility, and comprehensive programs for teenage mothers.

*Burling, R. *English in Black and White*. New York: Rinehard and Winston, Inc., 1973.

*Burt, Martha R. *Public Costs for Teenage Childbearing*. Washington, D.C.: Center for Population Options, 1986.

*Burt, Martha R., and Freya L. Somerstein. "Planning Programs for Pregnant Teenagers: First You Define the Problem." *Public Welfare* 43 (Spring 1985): 28-47.

Evaluates the cost effectiveness of 21 federally-funded programs for pregnant and parenting adolescents.

*Burud, Sandra L., Pamela R. Aschbacher, and Jacquelyn McCroskey. *Employer-Supported Child Care. Investing in Human Resources*. Boston, MA: Auburn House Publishing Company, 1984.

Designed to guide employers from the initial stages of establishing child care options for employees to the actual establishment of programs. The major source of information for the book was a study conducted by the National Employer Supported Child Care Project in 1982. That project identified and surveyed 415 active employer-supported child care programs in the United States. A growth rate of 395 percent was noted between 1978 and 1982 (see Perry, 1980B).

urud, S.L., R.C. Collins, and P. Divine-Hawkins. "Employer Sponsored Child Care: Everybody Benefits." *Children Today* 12(3) (1983): 2-7.

Synthesizes the results of a 1982 survey of employers who provided child care support (also see Burud, Aschbacher, and McCroskey). The findings revealed that: 1. two-thirds of the employers attribute reduction in turnover to child care programs; 2. eighty percent report improved recruiting; 3. half report reduced absenteeism and improved productivity; and 4. ninety percent indicate improved public relations and corporate image. In this survey, virtually none of the companies report adverse effects. Some employers indicate that the effects of employer-sponsored child care were not known due to the newness of programs or based on insufficient data. One-fifth of firms indicate that child care support had no effect.

ldwell, Bettye M. "A Decade of Early Intervention Programs: What We have Learned?" *American Journal of Othopsychiatry* 44 (1974): 491-496.

Highlights developments in early childhood intervention programs over a ten-year period, including evaluation designs, measurements strategies and the lessons learned.

'aldwell, Bettye M. "Child Development and Social Policy." *Current Issues in Child Development*. Edited by M. Scott and S. Grimmett. Washington, D.C.: National Association For the Education of Young Children, 1977, pp. 61-88.

Calhoun, John A., and Raymond C. Collins. "From One Decade to Another: A Positive View of Early Childhood Programs." *Theory into Practice* 20(1981): 135-140.

Describes research and evaluation efforts in Head Start, preschool education and day care.

*Calhoun, Ura Jean. "Standardization and Quantification of the Incomplete Man Test on New Orleans School Children." Masters Thesis. Tulane University, 1967.

*Caliguri, J. "Will Parents Take Over Head Start Programs?" *Urban Education* 5(1970): 54.

*Campbell, Donald T., and Albert Erlebacher. "How Regression Artifacts in Quasi-Experimental Evaluation Can Mistakenly Make Compensatory Education Look Harmful." *Disadvantaged Child Volume III: Compensatory Education: A National Debate.* Edited by Jerome Hellmuch. New York: Brunner/Mazel, 1970A, pp. 185-210.

Critiques matching and analysis of co-variance and partial correlation; they produce regression artifacts that make compensatory programs look deleterious. Other inadequacies of social science methodology, such as that used in the Westinghouse Report, are cited. Randomization experiments are suggested as a better alternative.

*Campbell, Donald T., and Albert Erlebacher. "Reply to the Replies." *Disadvantaged Child Volume III: Compensatory Education: A National Debate.* Edited by Jerome Hellmuch. New York: Brunner/Mazel, 1970B, pp. 221-225.

Point-by-point comments are made in this reply to Cicirelli, Evans, and Schiller in the debate on the bias of the Westinghouse/Report. While Cicirelli, Evans, and Schiller argue that the magnitude of bias was minimal, Campbell and Erlebacher emphasize their opinion that the degree is unascertainable for two reasons: first, the lack of information on the characteristics of the populations from which matches were chosen prior to matching; second, lack of information on the factorial composition of the co-variates.

Card, J.J. *Long Term Consequences for Children Born to Adolescent Parents. Final Report.* Palo Alto, California: American Institute for Research, 1978.

Card, J.J., and L.L. Wise, "Teenage Mothers and Teenage Fathers: The Impact of Early Childbearing on the Parents' Personal and Professional Lives." *Family Planning Perspective* 10 (1978): 199.

Carnevale, Anthony P., and Harold Goldstein. *Employee Training: It's Changing Role and An Analysis of New Data.* Washington, D.C.: Society for Training and Development, 1983.

Carter, J. "A Statement in New Hampshire." *The Presidential Campaign, 1976. (Vol.1).* Washington, D.C.: Government Printing Office, 1978.

Carter, K.K. *Workfare. Point -- Counterpoint.* Washington, D.C.: National Urban League, June 1982.

Caruso, David R., and Douglas K. Detterman. "Intelligence Research and Social Policy." *Phi Delta Kappan* 63 (November 1981): 183-186.

Concludes that social science research has minimal effect on social policy: Research which casts doubt on Head Start's effectiveness has not affected negatively federal funding for the program.

Catalyst. *Corporations and Two-Career Families: Directions for the Future.* New York: Catalyst, 1981A.

Suggests that dual-career families in private corporations make heavier use of center- based child care than does the general population.

Catalyst. *Two Career Families: A Bilbiography of Relevant Readings*. New York: Catalyst, 1981B.

**CDF Reports*. "Parents Gain in New Chapter 1 Rules." Washington, D.C.: CDF, July 1986, pp.6.

Discusses the new regulations governing the Chapter 1 compensatory education program published May 19, 1986. These regulations contain strengthened provisions requiring parent involvement and requiring that Chapter 1 funds be targeted more closely to schools serving large numbers of children from low-income families.

*Cherlin, A.J. *Marriage, Divorce, Remarriage*. Cambridge: Howard University Press, 1981.

**The Child and Family Resource Program: Guidelines, February 7, 1973*. Washington, D.C.: USDHEW/OCD- 73-1051, 1973.

**The Child and Family Resource Program: An Overview*. Washington, D.C.: USDHEW/OCD, 1975.

**Children Today*. 12(3) May-June 1983. Entire issue.

Looks at employer supported child care. Includes articles which describe how "everybody benefits" from employer supported child care; how child care services are "a boon to a textile plant"; and how the information base for planning child care services can be improved.

*Children's Defense Fund. *Portrait of Inequality*. Washington, D.C.: CDF, 1980.

*Children's Defense Fund. *America's Children and Their Families: Key Facts*. Washington, D.C.: CDF, 1982A.

Provides tables, charts, and statistics from government sources on the numbers of children and families; income and poverty levels; working parents; vital statistics such as births, marriages, and divorces; child care arrangements; maternal and child health; education; housing; juvenile justice; food and nutrition; and youth employment.

*Children's Defense Fund. *Employed Parents and Their Children: A Data Book.* Washington, D.C.: Children's Defense Fund, 1982B.

Serves as a reference book which advocates working for public and private sector policies that will meet the needs of employed parents and their children.

Children's Defense Fund. *Children and Federal Child Care Cuts.* Washington, D.C.: CDF, 1983A.

Surveys all 50 states and finds that 32 of them are providing Title XX child care to fewer children in 1983 than in 1981 as a result of budget cuts. 33 states lowered child care standards.

Children's Defense Fund. *A Children's Defense Budget: An Analysis of the President's FY 1984 Budget and Children.* Washington, D.C.: CDF, 1983B.

Children's Defense Fund. *A Corporate Reader. Work and Family Life in the 1980's.* Washington, D.C. CDF, May 1983C.

Anthology of brief articles which attempt to identify connections among the many demographic, economic, and social factors underlying the growth of mothers in the work force.

Children's Defense Fund. *Give More Children a Head Start. It Pays.* Washington, D.C.: Children's Defense Fund, 1983D.

Provides a brief overview of Head Start's history, benefits and accomplishments. Enrollments and appropriations are presented from 1965 through 1983. Six Head Start programs are examined to show what a difference the program means for individuals from diverse backgrounds in diverse settings.

*Children's Defense Fund. *A Children's Defense Budget: An Analysis of the President's FY 1985 Budget and Children.* Washington, D.C.: CDF, 1984.

Fourth annual analysis of the President's budget and its effects on a variety of children's programs in the areas of child care, education, maternal and child health, child welfare, child nutrition, AFDC, youth employment, and others.

*Children's Defense Fund. *Black and White Children in America: Key Facts.* Washington, D.C.: Children's Defense Fund, 1985.

Provides overall and comparative data on the status of black and white children in the United States in several areas: child welfare; adolescent pregnancy; income and poverty; employment and unemployment; maternal employment and child care; and child health and education.

*Children's Defense Fund. *Programs that Help Prevent Adolescent Pregnancy and Build Youth Self- Sufficiency.* Washington, D.C.: CDF, April, 1986.

Documents some of the available programs that help families cope with the basic needs of children as they prepare for adulthood.

Children's Policy Research Project. *The State of the Child.* Chicago, Ill.: The School of Social Service Administration, Univ. of Chicago, 1980.

Children's Policy Research Project. *Children of the State.* Chicago, Ill.: The School of Social Service Administration, Univ. of Chicago, 1983.

*Chilman, Catherine, S. *Adolescent Sexuality in a Changing American Society - Social and Psychological Perspectives.* Washington, D.C.: USDHEW, Public Health Service, National Institutes of Health. USDHEW Publication No. 79- 1426, 1979.

Presents a socio-psychological view of adolescent sexuality in American society. Examines some of the consequences of teenage pregnancy and makes suggestions which may help policy formation.

Chinn, P.C. "Exceptional Minority Children: Issues and Some Answers." *Exceptional Children* 45 (April 1979): 532-536.

Discusses the relationship of cultural diversity to exceptionality as it relates to minority children. Specific ways of identifying the exceptional minority child and identifies ways in which the educational process of the exceptional minority child can be facilitated.

Cicirelli, Victor G. "The Relevance of the Regression Artifact Problem to the Westinghouse-Ohio Evaluation of Head Start: A Reply to Campbell and Erlebacher." *Disadvantaged Child Volume III: Compensatory Education: A National Debate*. Edited by Jerome Hellmuth. New York: Brunner/Mazel, 1970, pp. 211-215.

Replies to a paper by Campbell and Erlebacher on the biasing effects of matching or co-variance techniques in ex post facto or quasi-experimental evaluations of compensatory education programs. The author defends the analyses of the 1969 Westinghouse/Ohio study of Head Start. The feasibility of true experiments, as proposed by Campbell and Erlebacher, is questioned.

Cicirelli, Victor G., et al. "The Impact of Head Start: A Reply to the Report Analysis." *Harvard Educational Review* 40 (1970): 105-129.

Reponds to an article by Smith and Bissell on the impact of Head Start in which the authors dispute both the criticisms of the Westinghouse methodology and the re-analysis of the data.

Clarizio, Harvey E. "Maternal Attitude Differences Associated with Involvement in Project Head Start." *Dissertation Abstracts International* 27(7-A): (1966): 2063.

Investigates the influence of school-home programs for the deprived on attitudes toward education and the school.

Clark, Kenneth B. *Dark Ghetto: Dilemmas of Social Power*. New York and Evanston, Ill.: Harper and Row, 1965.

Using materials obtained from an antipoverty program HARYOU (Harlem Youth Opportunities Unlimited), surveys, and participant-observation of Harlem, an exploration of the political, psychological, and social problems of an urban ghetto is provided within this text. The black family is discussed in the context of the psychological forces operative in the ghetto.

Clark, R.M. *Family Life and School Achievement: Why Poor Black Children Succeed or Fail*. Chicago: University of Chicago Press, 1983.

Identifies those aspects of family life in one particular cultural niche that have important influences on children's school success. Discusses a specification of the attitudes, knowledge, skills and behaviors that students must develop if they are to succeed in school. Describes in detail the types of activities, interaction styles and support systems that are found in the homes of successful students and contrasts these with the homes of unsuccessful students.

Clark, Ruth, and Greg Martire. "Americans, Still in a Family Way." *Public Opinion* 2 (Oct.-Nov. 1979): 16-19.

Data from various surveys indicate that although the American family no longer fits the traditional mold of the past, it remains today, and will remain tomorrow, the basic institution of our society.

*Clark, Vernon L., and Frank P. Graham. "The Case of Black College Sponsorship of Head Start Programs." *Journal of Negro Education* 44 (1975): 476-481.

Asserts that black institutions of higher learning should champion the cause of black education. The presence of a Head Start population on black college campuses would stimulate more substantive research on basic educational issues of relevance to blacks and educators; would have a positive effect on the developing self-concept of the children; would provide an asset to teacher education programs and could offer to Head Start staff and children the resources of the college's faculty and facilities, as well as maintain relationships with the community the school serves.

Clarke-Stewart, A.K. *Child Care In The Family*. New York: Academic Press, 1977.

*Cohen, N.E., and M.F. Connery. "Government Policy and the Family." *Journal of Marriage and the Family* 29(1967): 6-17.

*Cole, Michael, and J. Brunner. "Cultural Differences and Inferences About Psychological Process." *American Psychologist* 26 (1971): 867-876.

*Cole, Michael, and Sylvia Scribner. *Culture and Thought*. New York: Wiley and Sons, 1974.

Presents the influential works of Spencer and others placed European culture, especially Northern and Western European culture, at the top of the culture hierarchy.

Cole, O. Jackson, and Valora Washington. "A Critical Analysis of the Effects of Head Start on Minority Children." *Journal of Negro Education* 55 (1986): 91-106.

Critiques Head Start research with emphasis on determining its effects on minority children. Urges more involvement by minority scholars in Head Start research.

Collins, Raymond C. "Home Start and Its Implications for Family Policy." *Children Today* 9 (1980): 12-16.

Presents the goals and objectives of the Home Start program; a description of the program; evaluation results; dissemination and replication outcomes; and results of a longitudinal research study of Home Start. The article concludes with implications for family policy as inferred from findings regarding Home Start.

Collins, Raymond C. "Children and Society: Child Development and Public Policy." Ph.D. Dissertation. Princeton University, 1981.

Explores the role of science in the formulation of public policy for children. The author asserts that theoretical understandings of how children learn and develop and scientific evidence on what programs work and why should play a more important role in the formulation of public policy for children. This study examines the research and evaluation data concerning Head Start, Follow Through and day care in order to determine what existing scientific evidence reveals about successes and failures. Social competence rather than superior performance IQ tests is viewed as the goal of child development and early education programs.

*Collins, Raymond C. *Head Start: Foundation for Excellence.* Washington, D.C.: USDHHS/ACYF, 1983B.

*Collins, Raymond C., and Dennis Deloria. "Head Start Research: A New Chapter." *Children Today* 12 (July-August 1983): 15-19.

Discusses the Head Start Synthesis, Evaluation, and Utilization Project, conducted by CSR Incorporated, which involves a review of Head Start literature from 1965 to the present. Findings of the study reveal: Head Start produces substantial gains in children's cognitive and language development; Head Start has grown more effective over the years; and the most needy children appear to benefit from the program. It was also found that Head Start favorably affected social development, task orientation, curiosity, and socialization of handicapped children. The positive effect of Head Start on children's health, families, and the community are also discussed.

*Condry, S.M., and I. Lazar. "American Values and Social Policy for Children." *Young Children and Social Policy.* Edited by W.M. Bridgeland and E.A. Duane. Beverly Hills, CA.: Sage, 1982, pp. 21-31.

Argues that a research study is likely to impact social policy if: 1. it uses direct outcome measures so that nonscientists can understand the results; 2. it addresses the economic implications of the proposed policy, consistent with contemporary political values; and 3. it is communicated directly to political professionals.

Congressional Research Service. *Need and Payment Levels in the Program of Aid to Families with Dependent Children (AFDC): Legislative History and Current State Practices. Report Number 81- 149 EPW.* Washington, D.C.: CRS, September 1981.

Congressional Research Service. *AFDC Fiscal Year 1982 Budget Cuts. Issue Brief IB81051.* Washington, D.C.: Congressional Research Service, March 18, 1982.

Congressional Quarterly. "Changing American Family." Entire Issue.

Discusses violence in the family, teeenage pregnancy, women in the work force, college tuition costs, housing, and mandatory retirement.

Consortium for Longitudinal Studies. *As the Twig Is Bent... Lasting Effects of Preschool Programs.* Hillsdale, NJ: Lawrence Erlbaum Associates, 1983.

Contracting Corporation of America. *Bilingual/ Bicultural Preschool Projects Conference: Conference Proceedings.* Denver, Colorado: Author, 1977.

Presents a number of articles on different aspects of the Head Start Strategy for Spanish- Speaking Children written by participants in that effort. The first section describes Bilingual- Bicultural Curriculum Development and Evaluation projects and includes descriptions of four curriculum development projects and an evaluation of the initial phase of the Head Start curriculum development project. The second section focuses on the Bilingual-Bicultural Child Development Associates (CDA) Training

Program. The third section briefly reports the operation of a network of human and material resources for Head Start programs in six Western states. Section 4 presents some recent research on bilingual- bicultural preschool child development. Section 5 provides information about a graduate fellowship program initiated to promote research on the early childhood development of the Spanish-speaking child. In the final section, suggestions are made for disseminating the results of the Head Start programs.

Cook, Richard A., et al. "Nutritional Status of Head Start and Nursery School Children Part 1: Food Intake and Anthropometric Measurements." *Journal of the American Dietetic Association* 68(1976A): 120-126.

Determines the nutritional status of preschool children enrolled in a Head Start program in Maine. The children were from families receiving food from the USDA Commodities Distribution Program.

Cook, Richard A. "Nutritional Status of Head Start and Nursery School Children. II. Biochemical Measurements." *Journal of the American Dietetic Association* 68(1976B): 127-132.

Determines the nutritional status of a group of Maine preschool children of low socio-economic status attending a Head Start program and a group of high socioeconomic status attending a university nursery school. At the beginning of the Head Start and nursery school programs in the fall, nursery school children had significantly higher hemoglobin and hemotrocrit levels and mean corpuscular/volume than Head Start children. By the spring, the disparity between the two groups had decreased.

Cooke, R.E. "Introduction." *Project Head Start.* Edited by Edward Zigler and Jeanette Valentine. New York: Free Press, 1979, pp. xxiii-xxvi.

Copeland, Margaret Leitch. "The Impact of Participation in Head Start's Exploring Parenting Program on Low SES Mothers' Parent Attitude." *Dissertation Abstracts International* 42(2) (1981): Section A. 537.

Measures the impact of the "Exploring Parenting" curriculum that was incorporated into all of the 9,400 U.S. Head Start Centers' existing programs in the fall of 1978. It was concluded that Exploring Parenting was not an effective treatment for changing poor minority mothers' parent attitudes, as measured by two attitude scales.

Cornish, Edward. "The Future of the Family: Intimacy in an Age of Loneliness." *Futurist* 13 (Feb. 1979): 45-58.

Examines the state of the family in today's world and constructs six possible scenarios suggesting how the family may develop in the future.

Costello, Joan. *Review and Summary of a National Survey of The Parent-Child Center National Program.* Washington, D.C.: USDHEW/OCD, 1971.

Coulson, J.M., et al. "Effects of Different Head Start Program Approaches on Children of Different Characteristics: Report on Analyses of Data from 1966-67 and 1967-68 National Evaluations." Technical Memorandum, TM-48620001/00 (Santa Monica, CA.: Systems Development Corp., August 19, 1972): ERIC #ED 0720859.

Council for Exceptional Children. *Early Childhood Intervention-Culturally Different: A Selective Bibliography.* Exceptional Child Bibliography Series No. 671. Reston, VA.: Author, 1975A.

Contains approximately 60 abstracts and associated indexing information for documents published from 1966 to 1974. References included treat aspects such as prevention, program effectiveness, parent roles, parent education, language development, cognitive development, home visits, program descriptions, curriculum, and teaching methods.

Council for Exceptional Children. *Early Childhood Intervention-Infancy: A Selective Bibliography. Exceptional Child Bibliography Series No. 670.* Reston, VA: Author, 1975B.

Provides an annotated bibliography on early childhood intervention in infancy. Contains approximately 65 abstracts and documents published from 1968 to 1974. References include aspects such as prevention, parent roles, parent education, program descriptions, language development, cognitive development, instructional materials, stimulation, teaching methods, sensory experience, home instruction, and demonstration projects for the following areas of exceptionality: learning disabilities, cerebral palsy, disadvantaged youth, mentally handicapped, multipy handicapped, visually handicapped, speech handicapped, and developmental disabilities.

Cowell, Catherine. "Nutrition Assessment of Preschool Children in Head Start Programs In and Out of Compliance with the Nutrition Performance Standard." *Dissertation Abstracts International* 44(7-B) (1983): 2114.

Examined whether children in Head Start programs in compliance with the Nutrition Performance Standard had greater gains in nutritional status of height and weight than children in programs which were out of compliance. Age adjusted height and weight data at screening were compared with growth data at follow-up six months later. The analysis of variance indicated that any gains in height or weight after adjusting the age were not due to the compliance level of the Head Start Program.

Criteria for Parent and Child Centers, Mimeo. Washington, D.C.: USDHEW/OCD, July 19, 1967 (GSA DC 68-1480).

*Crittenden, A. "We 'Liberated' Mothers Aren't." *The Washington Post* (5 February 1984): D1.

*CSR, Inc. Refer to McKey et al. 1985.

Cunningham, C., and K. Osborn. "A Historical Examination of Blacks in Early Childhood Education." *Young Children* 34 (3) (March 1979): 20-29.

Current Population Reports. *Negro Population: March 1964.* Washington, D.C.: U.S. Government Printing Office, Series P-20 No. 142, Oct. 11, 1965.

*Curtis, J. *A Guide for Working Mothers.* New York: Simon and Schuster, 1975.

*Cutright, Phillips. "Timing the First Birth: Does it Matter?" *Journal of Marriage and the Family* 35 (1973): 585-595.

Tests the assumption that timing of first birth has an enduring effect on a woman's chances for a good marital life and the number of children she will have. Shows that the risk of female headed families living in poverty 20 years after first birth is the same for all ever-married mothers whether first child was born before marriage or not. Finds no racial differences.

*Darien, Jean C. "Factors Influencing the Rising Labor Force Participation Rates of Married Women with Pre-school Children." *Social Science Quarterly* 56(4): (1976): 614-630.

Investigates factors which influence the increasing labor participation rate among white, married mothers of pre-school children from 1960-1970. Found that the young age of mothers had the greatest influence.

*Darity, W.A., and S.L. Myers. "Public Policy and the Condition of Black Family Life." *The Review of Black Political Economy* (1984): 164-187.

Darlington, R.B., J.M. Royce, A.S. Snipper, H.W.Murray, and I. Lazar. "Preschool Programs and Later Social Competence of Children From Low-Income Families." *Science* 208 (April 11, 1980): 202-204.

*Dash, Leon. "At Risk: Chronicles of Teen-age Pregnancy." *The Washington Post* (Jan. 26, 1986): Al, A12-A13; (Jan. 27, 1986): A1, A8-A9; (Jan. 28, 1986): A1, A6, A8-A9; (Jan. 29, 1986): A1, A18-A19; (Jan. 30, 1986): Al, A14-A15; (Jan. 31, 1986): A1, A16.

Series of newspaper articles which examine female-headed black families and teenage parents in a low-income residential area of Washington, D.C.

*Datta, Lois-ellin. "Head Start's Influence on Community Change." *Children* 17 (1970): 193-196.

Datta, Lois-ellin. "The Impact of the Westinghouse/Ohio Evaluation on the Development of Project Head Start: An Examination of the Immediate and Long-Term Effects and How They Came About." *The Evaluation of Social Programs*. Abt. Associates. Beverly Hills, CA: Sage, 1976.

*Datta, Lois-ellin. "Another Spring and Other Hopes: Some Findings From National Evaluations of Project Head Start." *Project Head Start*. Edited by Edward Zigler and Jeanette Valentine. New York: The Free Press, 1979, pp. 405-432.

Datta, Lois-ellin et al. *A Comparison of a Sample of Full Year and Summer Head Start Programs Operated by Community Action Agencies and Local Education Agencies*. Washington, D.C.: USDHEW, 1971.

Reanalyses data from a stratified random sample of full-year 1967-1968 and summer 1968 Head Start programs to compare centers operated by local educational agencies (LEA) and community action agencies (CAA). The analyses indicated that CAA-operated programs were more likely to report parent participation in decision making and as paid staff, while LEA-operated programs were slightly more likely to report parent participation as volunteers; the CAAs had a higher proportion of paraprofessionals and LEAs more professionals; that CAAs recruited individual volunteers from a variety of sources, and LEAs mobilized formal community organization support; that LEAs were more likely to focus on family services and job training. The differences involve structure rather than process or impact and relatively few statistically reliable differences were found.

*Dave, R. "The Identification and Measurement of Environmental Process Variables that are Related to Educational Achievement." Doctoral Dissertation. University of Chicago, 1963.

David, K., and A. Grosshard-Schectman. *Study on How Mother's Age and Circumstances Affect Children.* Los Angeles: Population Research Laboratory, University of Southern California, August 1980.

Dawkins, M.P. "Educational and Occupational Goals: Male Versus Female Black High School Seniors." *Urban Education* 15(1980): 231-242.

Examines similarities and differences in educational and occupational goals of black students. Assesses the extent to which the pattern of these relationships change when control variables are introduced in the analysis.

DeAnda, Diane. "Pregnancy in Early and Late Adolescence." *Journal of Youth and Adolescence* 12 (1982): 33-43.

Identified factors which discriminate between girls who become pregnant in early versus late adolescence suing a sample of 130 pregnant adolescents and adolescent mothers.

Deloria, D., C. Coelen, and R. Ruopp. *National Home Start Evaluation: Interim Report V. Executive Summary.* High/Scope Education Research Foundation; Abt Associates, October 15, 1974.

*Demkovich, L. "A Job for Every Welfare Mother, But What About the Kids?" *National Journal* (March 4, 1978): 341-344.

Describes conflict between child advocates and President Jimmy Carter's welfare reform plan. Carter's plan would require mothers with children ages 7-14 to accept full-time employment as a condition of their public assistance, but only if adequate day care could be found. Child advocates asked: What is adequate care? Who should provide it? How should it be paid for?

*Dittmann, L. "Project Head Start Becomes A Long Distance Runner." *Young Children* 35 (6) (September 1980): 2-9.

Dornbusch, Sanford M., J. Merrill Carlsmith, Steven J. Bushwall, Philip L. Ritter, Albert H. Hastorf, and Ruth T. Gross. "Single Parents, Extended Households, and the Control of Adolescents." *Child Development* 56 (April 1985): 326-341.

Studies the interrelationships among family structure patterns of family decision-making, and deviant behavior among adolescents.

Dryfoos, Joy. "School-Based Health Clinics: A New Approach to Preventing Adolescent Pregnancy?" *Family Planning Perspectives* 17 (March-April 1985): 70-75.

Reviews strategies for preventing adolescent pregnancies and identifies school-based clinics as a promising intervention that combines health promotion and medical treatment.

*Dryfoos, J. et al. "The Intellectual and Behavioral Status of Children Born to Adolescent Mothers, Research on Consequences of Adolescent Pregnancy and Childbearing." Final report submitted to the National Institute of Child Health and Human Development, November 30, 1979.

Dunbar, Leslie W. *Minority Report.* Pantheon Books, 1984.

Reviews the histories of blacks, Mexican-Americans, Indians, Puerto Ricans, Chinese, Japanese, and other minorities. It explains how the fundamental contours of the Constitution have been defined and accepted for these minority groups.

*Dunteman, G. et al. *A Report on Two National Samples of Head Start Classes: Some Aspects of Child Development of Participants in Full Year 1967-1968 and 1968-1969 Programs*. Research Triangle Park, N.C.: Research Triangle Institute, July 1972.

*Durham, J. "Compensatory Education: Who Needs It?" *Clearinghouse* 44 (1969): 18-22.

Eckhardt, Kenneth W., and Eldon C. Schriner. "Familial Conflict, Adolescent Rebellion, and Political Expression." *Journal of Marriage and the Family* (August 1969): 494-499.

Suggests that a positively and moderately strong relationship exists between family conflicts and male adolescent divergence from a father's political position and a weaker relationship for divergence from a mother under a condition of high parental interest in politics. No significant relationships were established for females and their departures from paternal political views under a condition of either varying conflict or parental political interests.

*Edwards, Cecile H. *Training Program for Prospective Residents of Renovated Public Housing*. Proposal Submitted to the District of Columbia Department of Housing and Community Development. Washington, D.C.: Howard University, 1982.

Elder, Glen H., Jr., Trivan Nguyen, and Aushalom Caspi. "Linking Family Hardship to Children's Lives." *Child Development* 56 (April 1985): 361-375.

Investigates the role of parental behavior (rejecting, nonsupportive) in linking economic hardship to children's lives in the Oakland Growth Study.

Elshtain, Jean Bethke. "Family Reconstruction." *Commonweal* 107 (Aug. 1, 1980): 430-436.

Advocates family reconstruction as an alternative to the pressures from all sides that are now facing the family.

Empson, Judith et al. *An Impact Evaluation of the Resource Access Projects. 1978-1979*. Washington, D.C.: Roy Littlejohn Associates, Inc., 1979.

Reviews the 1978-1979 performance of the Resource Access Projects (RAPs), a network of projects federally funded to assist handicapped children in Head Start through the development and dissemination of materials and information, and by providing training services to Head Start staff and to the families of handicapped children.

*Engram, Eleanor. "Role Transition in Early Adulthood: Orientations of Young Black Women." *The Black Woman*. Edited by La Frances Rodgers-Rose. Beverly Hills, CA: Sage, 1980, pp. 175-188.

Ensher, Gail L. et al. "Head Start for the Handicapped: Congressional Mandate Audit." *Exceptional Child* 43 (1977): 202-210.

Summarizes the findings of a national evaluation of Head Start services to the disabled during the first year of the Congressional mandate's implementation. The findings indicate reasonable progress in meeting the needs of the handicapped, but labeling of children with minor problems has increased and serious problems remain in accommodating children with severe disabilities. Recommendations for improving Head Start services to handicapped children are listed, including a suggestion for reducing society's inclination to segregate or exclude children with major differences in development.

Epstein, A.S. *Assessing the Child Development Information Needed by Adolescent Parents with Very Young Children*. Ypsilanti, MI: High/Scope Educational Research Foundation, 1980.

Erickson, Edsel L. et al. *A Study of the Effects of Teacher Attitude and Curriculum Structure on Preschool Disadvantaged Children. Annual Progress Report I.* Kalamazoo, MI: Western Michigan University, 1968.

Erickson, Eric H. *Childhood and Society.* 2nd ed. New York: W.W. Norton, 1963.

Feinstein, C. (Ed.). "Working Women and Families." *Sage Yearbooks in Women's Policy Studies Vol. 4.* Beverly Hills, CA: Sage Publications, 1979.

Includes articles on employment problems, alternative work patterns, and child care.

Ferber, M., and B. Birnbaum. "One Job or Two Jobs?: The Implications for Young Wives." *Journal of Consumer Research* 7 (December 1980): 263-271.

*Fergenbaum, I. *English Now; Teacher's Manual.* New York: Meredith Corporation, 1970.

Ferman, Louis A., Joyce L. Kronbluh, and Alan Haber (Eds.). *Poverty in America.* Ann Arbor, MI: University of Michigan Press, 1965.

Field, T. "Early Development of the Pre-Term Offspring of Teenage Mothers." *Teenage Parents and Their Offspring.* Edited by K. Scott, T. Field, and E. Robinson. New York: Grune and Stratton, 1981, pp. 145-175.

Fishel, Leo. *Employer Sponsored Child Care In Appalachia.* Washington, D.C.: University Research Corporation, 1982.

Fisher, L. "Child Competence and Psychiatric Risk." *Journal of Nervous and Mental Disease* 168(1980): 323-331.

Fisher, R.R. "Project Slow Down: The Middle Class Answer to Project Head Start." *School and Society* 98(1970): 356-357.

Flores de Apodaca, Robert et al. "Quick Socio-Emotional Screening of Mexican-American and Other Ethnic Head Start Children." *Hispanic Journal of Behavioral Sciences* 5(1983): 81-92.

Investigated the use of a standardized quick screening instrument (the AML) for detecting Mexican-American and other ethnic minority Head Start children "at risk" for later adjustment difficulties. The 38 participating teachers and their aides readily accepted the use of the scale; they found it relevant and brief, and it provided them with a set of observations through which to communicate with mental health and education professionals. Similarly, these professionals found the scale invaluable in identifying and prioritizing their consultation work with teachers and parents.

*Ford, Kathleen. "Second Pregnancies among Teenage Mothers." *Family Planning Perspectives* 15(Nov.-Dec. 1983): 268-269, 271-272.

Presents national data on the contraceptive practice of teenage mothers, pregnancy rates in the year following their first birth and the planning status of those pregnancies. Data are shown by race, age at first birth, income level and marital status.

Fox, L.H. "Report for the USOE Task Force on Gifted and Talented Education." *Gifted Child Quarterly* 22(3): (1978): 284-291.

Lists the recommendations of the task force organized by the Commissioner of Education in the fall of 1977.

Frasier, M.M. "Rethinking the Issues Regarding the Culturally Disadvantaged Gifted." *Exceptional Children* 45(April 1979): 438-442.

Focuses on issues relative to providing programs that meet the needs of the disadvantaged gifted individual, creating an effective learning environment and developing appropriate educational programs.

Freeberg, N., and D. Payne. "Parental Influence on Cognitive Development in Early Childhood: A Review." *Child Development* 38 (1967): 65-89.

*Friedman, Dana E. *Encouraging Employer Support to Working Parents: Community Strategies for Change.* New York: Carnegie Corporation, 1983.

Aims to determine: 1. the nature and extent of employer support for working parents; and 2. strategies which could facilitate additional employer support based on a study of four communities (Boston, Houston, San Francisco and Minneapolis).

The report has three sections: an analysis of the state of the art; a description of strategies used to encourage employer support to working parents; and a discussion of the obstacles to, and consequences of, employer support. The author concluded that in every community, the number of change agents far exceeds the number of corporations that have implemented family support systems in any form. She argues that the USA is now in an "education phase" characterized by information gathering and analysis. Friedman argues that the future development of employer support will depend on the formation of innovative and creative partnerships between the public, private, and voluntary sectors.

*Furstenberg, F. *Unplanned Parenthood: The Consequences of Teenage Childbearing.* New York, Free Press, 1976.

*Furstenberg, F. "Burdens and Benefits: The Impact of Early Childbearing on the Family." *Journal of Social Issues* 36(1980): 64-87.

Explores the impact of teenage pregnancy and childbearing on the families of the adolescent and examines the amount and type of support extended by the family of origin to the pregnant teenager. Analyses data from a longitudinal study of teenage childbearing in Baltimore and a series of intensive case studies of adolescents and their families done at the Philadelphia Child Guidance Clinic. Finds that a variety of services are available to the young mother. Details the various kinds of outcomes for the family, the adolescent parent, and the child. Discusses the family's relations with the father of the child, and the division of child care responsibilities.

Furstenberg, F.F., and A.G. Crawford. "Family Support: Helping Teenage Mothers to Cope." *Family Planning Perspectives* 10 (1978): 322-333.

Gaines, Rosslyn. *Helping Handicapped Children: Recommendations for Model Programs in Head Start Centers.* Los Angeles: University of California, 1979.

Identification of the handicapping condition, diagnostic assessment, social and cognitive intervention, special services for the handicapping condition and parent involvement.

*Gary, L.D. (Ed.) *Black Men.* Beverly Hills, CA: Sage Publications, 1981.

Gay, J.E. "A Proposed Plan for Identification of Black Gifted Children." *Gifted Child Quarterly* 23(3) (1978): 353-360.

Contends that traditional methods do not identify black gifted students adequately. Proposes a six step plan to identify a larger percentage of black gifted children: 1. securing commitments, 2. locating nominees, 3. setting up case studies, 4. parental contact and involvement, 5. interview and testing, and 6. group problem solving.

Geismar, Ludwig L., and Ursula Gerhart. "Social Class, Ethnicity, and Family Functioning. Exploring Some Issues Raised by the Moynihan Report." *Journal of Marriage and the Family* XXX 3(1968): 480-487.

Studies black, white and Puerto Rican families in an attempt to assess the influence of social class on the manner in which ethnic group membership affects family behavior. The researchers found that when socioeconomic status was controlled, differences in family structure and behavior which are generally attributed to race were limited.

*General Accounting Office. *Early Childhood and Family Development Programs Improve the Quality of Life for Low-Income Families*. Washington, D.C.: GAO, 1979, Report #HRD-79-40.

*General Accounting Office. *Does AFDC Workfare Work? Information Is Not Yet Available From HHS's Demonstration Projects*. Washington, D.C.: General Accounting Office, GAO/IPE-83-3, January 24, 1983.

Responds to a request from Senator Edward M. Kennedy to investigate the Community Work Experience Program (CWEP). CWEP demonstrations are intended to test innovative approaches for requiring recipients of Aid to Families with Dependent Children (AFDC) to earn their welfare benefits in jobs in the public or the private nonprofit sector. GAO concluded that CWEP had not yet produced information that could show whether workfare was effective.

General Mills Corporation. *Families At Work: Strengths and Strains*. Minneapolis, Minnesota: General Mills, 1981.

Germanis, P.G. *Workfare: Breaking the Poverty Cycle*. Heritage Foundation, July 1982.

Giele, Janet Zollinger. "Changing Sex Roles and Family Structure." *Social Policy* 9(Jan.-Feb. 1979): 32-43.

Views the effect of changes in life-styles in the role of women within the family unit, noting the increase in the number and salaries of working women.

*Gil, D.G. *Unravelling Social Policy*. Cambridge, MA: Schenkman Publishing Company, 1976.

*Gilchrist, Lawayne D., and Steven Paul Schinke. "Teenage Pregnancy and Public Policy." *Social Service Review* 57(June 1983): 307-322.

Outlines research on the scope and consequences of teenage pregnancy; reviews the history of policies and legislation that have addressed the problem; and summarizes the complexities of public involvement in teenagers' contraception, unplanned pregnancy, and parenthood.

Gilder, George. *Wealth and Poverty*. New York: Basic Books, 1981.

*Giraldo, Z.I. *Public Policy and the Family, Wives and Mothers in the Labor Force*. Lexington, MA: D.C. Heath and Co., 1980.

Gist, Noel P., and William S. Bennett, Jr. "Aspirations of Negro and White Students." *Social Forces* 42 (October 1963): 40-48.

Glasgow, Douglas G. The Black Underclass. Vintage Books, 1980.

Concentrates on a group of youths between the ages of 18 and 34 whom the author knew well. The book analyzes the reasons why a black underclass continues to exist in this country. It offers a new understanding of the aspirations and motivations of ghetto youth and adds an important dimension to the debate of race versus class.

Glass, G., B. McGaw, and M.L. Smith. *Meta-Analysis in Social Research*. Beverly Hills, CA: Sage Publications, 1981.

Glazer, Nathan, and Daniel P. Moynihan. *Ethnicity: Theory and Experience*. Cambridge, MA: Harvard University Press, 1975.

Describes a model which distinguishes seven assimilation dimensions or variables: cultural, structural, marital, identificational, attitude receptional (absence of prejudice), behavior receptional (absence of discrimination), and civic (absence of value and social conflict).

Glick, Paul C. "How American Families are Changing." *American Demographics* 6(Jan. 1984): 21-25.

Reports Census Bureau data that household growth between 1982 and 1983 was too slow to be statistically significant. The total number of households in the United States rose by only 391,000, the first time that the U.S. has gained fewer than one million households in one year since 1966-67, and the first statistically insignificant increase in two decades. Average household size increased from 2.72 to 2.73 persons per household.

*Glick, Paul, and Karen Mills. "Black Families: Marriage Patterns and Living Arrangements." Paper Presented at the W.E.B. DuBois Conference on American Blacks, Atlanta, GA., Oct. 1974.

Goldberg, Herbert. "The Psychologist in Head Start: New Aspects of the Role." *American Psychologist* 23 (1968): 773-774.

Describes the experiences of a psychological consultant to a Head Start program and the changes in conventional role behavior he found necessary to make in order to function effectively.

Goodenow, Ronald K., and Arthur O. White (Eds.). *Education and the Rise of the New South*. Boston, MA: G.K. Hall and Co., 1981.

Discusses southern educational history. Themes include the nature and impact of urbanization and the emergence of the modern political economy with its stress on education for differentiated occupational and social roles. Increased professionalism and competing influences are also presented.

Gordon, B., and K. Kammeyer. "The Gainful Employment of Women with Small Children." *Journal of Marriage and the Family* (May 1980): 327-360.

Reports longitudinal data for 735 women on reasons for working, family variables, attitudes about mothering, etc. Economic need was the predominant reason given for choosing to work.

Gordon, Edmund. "Parent and Child Centers: Their Basis in the Behavioral and Educational Sciences--An Invited Critique." *American Journal of Orthopsychiatry* 41, no.1 (1971): 39-42.

*Gordon, E.W. "Evaluation During the Early Years of Head Start." *Project Head Start*. Edited by E. Zigler and J. Valentine. New York: Free Press, 1979, pp.399-404.

Reviews the early period in the development of Head Start research and evaluation. Identified four major issues and experiences: 1. a tension between the use of small-scale controlled experiments on a large-scale field experiment and the employment of other techniques to collect and analyze mass data; 2. the hurried development of measuring instruments; 3. the development of the Head Start Research and Evaluation Centers; and 4. the emergence of an anti-evaluation and anti-testing sentiment.

*Gordon, S. *Evaluation of Project Head Start Reading Readiness in Issaguena and Sharkey Counties Mississippi*. Final Report, EDO 14319, 1966.

Gray, J.M., M.E. Schuman, H. Dunn, et al. "Motivating Today's Students: A Symposium." *Today's Education* 70(Nov.-Dec. 1981): 36-48.

Contends that teachers themselves need to be motivated in order to motivate students. Gives practical suggestions for stimulating and motivating students.

Gray, S., and R. Klaus. "An Experimental Preschool Program for Culturally Deprived Children." *Child Development* 36 (1965): 887-898.

*Greenberg, P. *The Devil Has Slippery Shoes*. London: Macmillan, 1969.

*Greenblatt, B. *Responsibility for Child Care: The Changing Role of Family and State in Child Development.* San Francisco: Jossey-Bass, 1977.

Presents a history of the relationship between publicly sponsored child care and family needs.

Grossman, A.S. "Working Mothers and Their Children." *Monthly Labor Review* (May 1981): 49-54.

Grotberg, Edith H. *Review of Research 1965 to 1969.* Washington, D.C.: OEO, 1969.

Reviews research and demonstration projects supported by OEO's Research and Evaluation Office. The categories of research and demonstration tended to:

1. Sub-population Characteristics
   - A. Language,
   - B. Cognitive, Intellectual, and Achievement Behavior,
   - C. Social-Emotional behavior and self-concept;
2. Demonstration Programs;
3. Teacher Characteristics;
4. Parent Participation;
5. Head Start and the Community; and
6. Follow-up.

Gurin, P., G. Gurin, R.C. Lao, and M. Bettie. "Internal-External Control in the Motivational Dynamics of Negro Youth." *Journal of Social Issues* 25(1969): 29-53.

Halsey, A.H. *Change in British Society.* London: Oxford University Press, 1978.

Hamilton, Marshall L. "Evaluation of a Parent and Child Center Program." *Child Welfare* 51 (April 1972): 248-258.

Hanushek, E.A. "Sources of Black-White Earning Differences." *Social Science Research* 11 (1982): 103-126.

Hare, B. "Self-Perception and Academic Achievement: Variations in a Desegregated Setting." *American Journal of Psychiatry* 137 (1980): 683-689.

Finds no significant racial differences among fifth grade students on any measures of general or area specific (i.e., school, home, peers) self-esteem when socioeconomic status is controlled for, but finds significant differences by social class on most measures when race is controlled. Highlights the need to move from the current concern with the psychological consequences of desegregation for black children toward addressing the misfit relationships between poor children and the school.

*Harmon, C., and E. Hanley. "Administrative Aspects Of Head Start." *Project Head Start*. Edited by Edward Zigler and J. Valentine. New York: Free Press, 1979, pp. 379-398.

Harrell, J.E., and C.A. Ridley. "Substitute Child Care, Maternal Employment and the Quality of Mother-Child Interaction." *Journal of Marriage and the Family* (August 1975): 556-564.

*Harrington, Michael. *The Other America: Poverty in the United States*. New York: Macmillan, 1962.

Harter, S. "A New Self-Report Scale of Intrinsic Versus Extrinsic Orientation in the Classroom: Motivational and Information Components." *Developmental Psychology* 17 (1981): 300-312.

*Harter, S. "The Perceived Competence Scale for Children." *Child Development* 58 (1982): 87-97.

Harvard Educational Review. "Perspectives on Inequality: A Reassessment of the Effect of Family and Schooling in America." *Harvard Educational Review* 43 (Feb., 1973): 33-165.

*Height, Dorothy I. "What Must be Done About Children Having Children?" *Ebony* 40 (Mar. 1985): 76,78,80,82,84.

Heinicke, C., D. Friedman, E. Prescott, C. Puncel, and J. Sale. "The Organization of Day Care: Considerations Relating to the Mental Health of Child and Family." *American Journal of Orthopsychiatry* 43 (January 1973): 8-22.

Heiss, Jerold. "On the Transmission of Marital Instability in Black Families." *American Sociological Review* XXXVII, No. 2 (1972): 82-92.

Examines whether or not marital instability is transmitted generationally in some black families. In analyzing data from a sample of black males and females, twenty-one to forty-five year olds who lived in high- and low-income communities in a Northern metropolitan area, a weak relationship was found to exist between divorce and separation in the parental home and instability in the marriages of the respondents.

Heiss, Jerold. *The Case of the Black Family: A Sociological Inquiry.* New York: Columbia University Press, 1975.

A secondary analysis of the data collected and analyzed by Robert L. Crain and Carol S. Weisman which are reported in *Discrimination, Personality, and Achievement: A Survey of Northern Negroes* (New York: Seminar Press, 1972). Heiss found that black families cannot be completely characterized by traits such as age at marriage, family size, interaction patterns, stability, kin relations, and household composition which were utilized in previous analyses.

Heiss views racism as the source of the problem in developing theories which malign black families and notes that economics alone will not solve the problem; recognition that programs are built upon deficient and racist research recommendations may be helpful in finding solutions.

Herold, E.S. "The Health Belief Model: Can It Help Us to Understand Contraceptive Use Among Adolescents?" *Journal of School Health* 53(1) 1983: 19-21.

Examines the general statement that the Health Belief Model be applied to family planning research. Shows specifically how the main concepts of the model can be applied to family planning, and especially to the use or non-use of contraception among sexually active young females.

*Herold, E.S., and M.S. Goodwin, "Premarital Sexual Adult and Contraceptive Attitudes and Behavior." *Family Relations* 30 (1981): 247-253.

Looks at the relationship between premarital sexual guilt and contraceptive attitudes for a sample of 355 sexually active single women ages 13-20. Finds significant relationship between premarital sexual guilt and last contraceptive method used.

Herskovits, Melville, J. *The Myth of the Negro Past.* Boston: Beacon Press, 1944.

Contends that African traditions, attitudes, and institutionalized forms of behavior have survived and are evident in contemporary America.

Herzog, Elizabeth. "Is There a 'Breakdown' of the Negro Family?" *Social Work* XI No. 1 (1966): 3-10.

Contends that many of the writings which describe Black families as pathological are based on fictitious assumptions rather than on factual information. This author argues that as family service practitioners plan services for poor people, their strengths should be recognized.

Herzog, Elizabeth. "Social Stereotypes and Social Research." *Journal of Social Issues* XXVI No. 3 (1970): 109-125.

Reviews stereotypes found in the social science literature. Social science literature is replete with models in which two or more separate variables have been forced into a single continuum (for example, boys from fatherless homes do not succeed). This kind of research does not evoke a clear picture of the information which is described or of that which is sought.

:rzog, Elizabeth. "Who Shall Be Studied?" *American Journal of Orthopsychiatry* XLI, No. 1 (1971): 4-12.

Calls for a different method of researching those issues which are perceived and defined as social problems. Herzog contends that groups and institutions, rather than variables or correlates of ethnicity (race) and poverty, should be the major focus of such research because groups and institutions are in the positions which obstruct the necessary societal changes. The people and institutions which need to be changed are those that control the destinies of poor and black people.

Ierzog, Elizabeth, and E. Bernstein. "Health Services for Unmarried Mothers." Washington, D.C.: Children's Bureau, USDHEW Pub. No. 425, 1964.

Iess, R.D., and V.C. Shipman. "Early Blocks to Children's Learning." *Children* 12 (1965A): 189-194.

:ss, R.D., and V.C. Shipman. "Cognitive Elements in Maternal Behavior." *Minnesota Symposia on Child Psychology, Vol. 1.* Edited by J.P. Hill. Minneapolis: University of Minnesota Press, 1967, pp. 57-81.

Iess, R.D., and V.C. Shipman. "Early Experience and Socialization of Cognitive Modes in Children." *Early Childhood Education Rediscovered.* Edited by J.L. Frost. New York: Holt, Rinehart, and Winston 1968, pp. 79-86.

ghberger, Ruth, and Helen Brooks. "Vocabulary Growth of Head Start Children Participating in a Mother's Reading Program." *Home Economics Research Journal* 1 (1973): 185-187.

Studies two groups of Head Start children: The mothers of one group read to their children at least fifteen minutes a day. The other group of children had the opportunity to take home toys from a toy library. All the children were administered the Peabody Picture Vocabulary test.

Hill, Charles H. "Head Start: A Problem of Assumptions." *Education* 92: (1972): 89-93.

Hill, Martha S. "Trends in the Economic Situation of U.S. Families and Children: 1970-1980." *American Families and the Economy*. Edited by Richard R. Nelson, and Felicity Skidmore. Washington, D.C.: National Academy Press, 1983, pp. 9-59.

Deals with the theory that poverty and welfare dependence are transmitted intergenerationally largely because values and motivations deemed vital to economic achievement are not reinformed during a childhood spent in poverty and dependence on welfare.

*Hill, Martha S., and Michael Ponza. "Poverty and Welfare Dependence Across Generations." *Economic Outlook USA* (Summer 1983): 61-64.

*Hill, Robert. *The Strengths of Black Families*. New York: Emerson Hall, 1971.

*Hill, Robert. *The Widening Economic Gap*. Washington, D.C.: National Urban League Research Department, 1979.

Hilliard, A.G., III. "Cultural Diversity and Special Education." *Exceptional Children* 46 (May 1980A): 584-588.

Argues that cultural diversity requires no special education but normal, valid professional practice should be provided to serve all children well.

Hilliard, A.G., III. "Educational Assessment: Presumed Intelligent Until Proven Otherwise." *Journal of School Health* 50 (May 1980): 256-258.

Specified key features of a general medical model and discusses whether such a model is appropriate for testing in education. Found several problems with using such a model.

Hilliard, Thomas O. et al. *Evaluation of the Child and Family Mental Health Project Phase I*. San Francisco, CA: The Urban Institute for Human Services, 1981.

Presents approaches and materials for improved management in the Head Start program in conjunction with the Grantee Management Status Report. The program's management problems are identified from the point of view of the Head Start Director in the grantee organization.

Hofferth, S.C. "Day Care in the Next Decade: 1980-1990." *Journal of Marriage and the Family* 41 (1979): 649-658.

Estimates level of demand and preferences for different types of child care.

Collins, E.R. "The Marva Collins Story Revisited: Implications for Regular Classroom Instruction." *Journal of Teacher Education* 33(Jan.-Feb. 1982): 37-40.

Discusses the relationship between the curriculum and pupil's cultural experiences as a significant factor in Ms. Collins' success.

olmes, Monica, Douglas Holmes, and Dorie Greenspan. *Case Studies of the Seven Parent-Child Centers Included in the Impact Study. Atlanta, Detroit, Harbor City, Menemonie, Mount Carmel, Pasco and St. Louis. Vol. 1.* Center for Community Research, Nov. 1972 (EDO84034).

olmes, Monica, Douglas Holmes, Dorie Greenspan, and Donna Tapper. *The Impact of the Head Start Parent-Child Centers on Children: Final Report.* Center for Community Research, Dec. 1973.

ome Start and Child and Family Resource Program: Report of a Joint Program, March, 1974. Washington, D.C.: USDHEW/OHD/OCD (OHD-74-1072), 1974.

e Home Start Demonstration Program: An Overview. Washington, D.C.: USDHEW/OCD, 1973.

me Start and Other Programs for Parents and Children, Report of a National Conference, March 1975. Washington, D.C.: USDHEW/OHD-76-31089, 1976.

The Home Start Program: Guidelines, December 1971. Washington, D.C.: USDHEW/OCD, 1971.

Honig, Alice. *Parent Involvement in Early Childhood Education.* Washington, D.C.: National Association for the Education of Young Children, 1975.

Hoskins, Linus A. "Black Youth Unemployment: A Step Toward An Understanding of the Crisis in the Black Family." Paper presented to the Biennial Meeting of the Society for Research in Child Development, Toronto, Canada, April 27, 1985.

Reviews the literature on black youth unemployment and reports the findings of a study of the attitudes of minority businesses and academics toward a conceptual approach to black youth unemployment. Hoskin's survey of 94 minority business owners in Los Angeles, Chicago, and Washington, D.C. found that negative views of the youth, were held; the youth were blamed for their plight; and a sub-minimum wage for youth was supported. The 77 academicians interviewed in Los Angeles, Chicago, and Washington, D.C. argued that schools were not preparing the youth for employment and that minority businesses should hire more youth.

**Hospital and Community Psychiatry*. "Predictors of Repeat Pregnancies Among Low-Income Adolescents." *Hospital and Community Psychiatry* 35 (July 1984): 719-723.

Found that female attitudes toward contraception did not predict contraceptive use. The authors suggest that parental support of contraception plays a more important role in preventing repeat pregnancies than does the adolescents' reported attitudes toward contraception.

*Houston, S.H. "A Reexamination of Some Assumptions About the Language of the Disadvantaged Child." *Child Development* 41 (1970): 947-963.

Asserts that study and commentary on linguistic diversity has developed a body of misconception and mythology centering around the notion of linguistic deprivation.

ubbell, R. *A Review of Head Start Research Since 1970.* Washington, D.C.: CSR, Inc., 1983.

uell, B. *A Model for Developing Programs for Black Children.* Washington, D.C.: National Black Child Development Institute, 1976.

man Development News. Washington, D.C.: USDHHS/OHDS April 1983.

mphrey, H. *Federal Food Program-1973, Hearings Before the Senate Select Committee on Nutrition and Human Needs.* Washington, D.C.: Government Printing Office, 1973.

unt, J. McVicker. *Intelligence and Experience.* New York: Ronald Press, 1961.

unt, J. "Towards the Prevention of Incompetence." *Research Contributions from Psychology to Community Mental Health.* Edited by J. Carter. New York: Behavioral Publications, 1968, pp. 19-45.

nt, J. McVicker. "Parent and Child Centers: Their Basis in the Behavioral and Educational Sciences." *American Journal of Orthopsychiatry* 41, no. 1 (1971): 13-38.

linek, J. "The Role of the Parent in a Language Development Program." *Journal of Research and Development in Education*, 8 (1975): 14-23.

encks, Christopher, Marshall Smith, Henry Acland, Mary Jo Bane, David Cohen, Herbert Gintis, Barbara Heyns, and Stephan Michelson. *Inequality -- A Reassessment of the Effect of Family and Schooling in America.* New York: Basic Books, 1972.

Suggests that many popular explanations of economic inequality are largely wrong. Economic inequality cannot be blamed primarily on the fact that parents pass along their disadvantages to their children, neither can economic inequality be blamed on differences between schools, since schools have little effect on any measurable attribute of those who attend them.

*Jensen, A.R. "How Much Can We Boost IQ and Scholastic Achievement?" *Harvard Educational Review* 39 (1969): 1-123.

*Johnson, Kay, Sara Rosenbaum, and Janet Simons. *The Data Book: The Nation, States and Cities*. Washington, D.C.: Children's Defense Fund, 1985.

As part of the Children's Defense Fund's "Adolescent Pregnancy Prevention: Prenatal Care" Campaign, this report presents national facts and state rankings on prenatal care, infant mortality and adolescent pregnancy.

*Johnson, L.B. "Remarks of the President at Howard University -- To Fulfill These Rights - June 4, 1965." *The Moynihan Report and The Politics of Controversy*. Edited by L. Rainwater and W.L. Yancey. Cambridge, MA.: MIT Press, 1967, pp. 125-132.

*Johnson, Richard H. *Letter of Transmittal to the Office of the Commissioner from the National Parent Involvement Task Force*. Washington, D.C.: USDHHS, OHDS, ACYF, March 11, 1986.

*Joint Center for Political Studies. *A Framework for Racial Justice*. Washington, D.C.: Author, 1983.

*Jones J., and J. Fowler. *The Head Start Program-- History, Legislation, Issues and Funding--1964- 1982. Report No. 82-93 EPW*. Congressional Research Service, Washington, D.C.: 1982.

Jones, Reginald L., editor. *Black Psychology*. New York: Harper and Row, 1972.

Presents philosophical and empirical work by black psychologists and other behavioral and social scientists. This book highlights those issues which pertain to blacks in the psychological literature which need clarification and reinterpretation.

Juarez and Associates, Inc. *An Evaluation of the Head Start Bilingual Bicultural Curriculum Development Project Final Report.* Los Angeles, CA: Author, 1982A.

Four models for bilingual, bicultural Head Start programs were tested in eight centers. This evaluation study is based on the third year of curriculum development activities. Results are given for language measurement tests administered to Spanish-preferring and English-preferring children.

Juarez and Associates, Inc. *An Evaluation of the Head Start Bilingual Bicultural Curriculum Models. Final Report. Executive Summary.* Los Angeles, CA: Author, 1982B. HS200788.

Evaluates the impact of eight bilingual, bicultural Head Start programs in a three-and-one-half-year study. Findings show greater improvement in both Spanish and English for Spanish-preferring children, and in English for English-preferring children.

Kagan, J. "The Child -- His Struggle for Identity." *Saturday Review* December, 1968, pp. 80-87.

Kahn, A., and S.B. Kamerman. *Not for the Poor Alone: European Social Services.* Philadelphia: Temple University Press, 1975.

*Kahn, A., and S.B. Kamerman. *Helping America's Families.* Philadelphia: Temple University Press, 1982.

Kahn, A., S.B. Kamerman, and B.G. McGowan, *Child Advocacy: Report of a National Baseline Study.* New York: Columbia University Press, 1972.

Kamerman, S.B. *Parenting in an Unresponsive Society. Managing Work and Family Life.* New York: Free Press, 1980.

*Kamerman, S.B., and C. Hayes (Eds.). *Families that Work: Children in a Changing World.* Washington, D.C.: National Academy Press, 1982.

*Kamerman, S.B., and A. Kahn (Eds.). *Family Policy: Government and Families in Fourteen Countries.* New York: Columbia University Press, 1978.

Kamerman, S.B., and A. Kahn. "The Day Care Debate: A Wider View." *The Public Interest* (Winter 1979): 76-93.

Discusses several points of misinformation on child care need, quality, and cost. Discusses alternative to out-of-home child care for working parents.

Kamerman, S. B., and A. Kahn. *Child Care, Family Benefits, and Working Parents.* New York: Columbia University Press, 1981.

Offers the results of a six country study of child care: France, Hungary, Sweden, The United States, The Federal Republic of Germany, and The German Democratic Republic. Implications for the industrialized world are analyzed.

The USA was the only country in the group with no statutory maternity-related benefits, no universal child rearing benefits and no universal maternal and child health service benefits. Moreover, the USA is the only country in which the basic income support program (AFDC):

1. assures no uniform minimum cash benefit,

2. is restricted almost completely to single parent, female-headed families, and

3. is designed primarily to support mothers who are not in the labor force, although it is believed that two-thirds of the mothers may be employed. Initially, most Head Start mothers did not work.

*Kamerman, S.B., and A. Kahn. "Company Maternity Leave Policies." *Working Women* (February 1984): 79-84.

Argues that employer accommodation to childbearing is still very far from being a worker's right. Only 40 percent of employed women are entitled to a paid six-week disability leave at the time of childbirth.

*Kamerman, S.B., and P.W. Kingston. "Employer Responses to the Family Responsibilities of Employees." *Families That Work.* Edited by S.B. Kamerman, and C. Hayes. Washington, D.C.: National Academy Press, 1982, pp. 144-208.

Kandel, D. "Race, Maternal Authority, and Adolescent Aspiration." *American Journal of Sociology* 76 (1967): 999-1004.

*Kanter, R. *Work and Family in the U.S.: A Critical Review and Agenda for Research and Policy.* New York: Sage Foundation, 1977.

Kardiner, A., and L. Ovesey. *The Mark of Oppression: Explorations in the Personality of the American Negro.* New York: Norton, 1951. (Cleveland, Ohio: World, 1962. Paperback.)

*Katzell, R.A., and Daniel Yankelovitch. *Work, Productivity and Job Satisfaction.* New York: Psychological Corporation, 1975.

Kellam, S.C., R.G. Adams, C.H. Brown, and M. E. Ensimger. "The Long-Term Evolution of the Family Structure of Teenage and Older Mothers." *Journal of Marriage and the Family* 44(1982): 343-359.

*Keniston, Kenneth, and the Carnegie Council on Children. *All Our Children: The American Family Under Pressure.* New York: Harcourt Brace Jovanovich, 1977.

Explored the cognitive development of very young children with disadvantaged backgrounds. Concentration was placed on the time span from conception to about age nine. The book described some of the anxieties, worries, and obstacles that a changing society has created for American parents and children.

Keyserling, M.D. "Economic Status of Women in the U.S." *Journal of the American Economic Association* (May 1976): 205-212.

Khatena, J. "President's Message." *Gifted Children Quarterly* 22(3) (1978): 265-266.

Makes observations from personal experiences in Singapore in terms of identifying and aiding gifted minority students.

Khatena, J. *Music, Art, Leadership and Psychomotor Abilities Assessment Records.* Starkville, MS.: Allan Associates, 1981.

Future assessment procedures for gifted students should expand to include leadership ability, visual/performing arts ability, and psychomotor ability.

Kilpatrick, J.J. "Even Well-Heeled Children Helped by School Lunches." *Durham Morning Herald,* November 22, 1983

*Kirschner Associates. *A National Survey of the Impacts of Head Start Centers on Community Institutions.* Albuquerque, N.M.: Kirschner Associates, May 1970.

Klaus, R., and S. Gray. "The Early Training Project for Disadvantaged Children: A Report after Five Years." *Monographs of the Society for Research in Child Development,* 1968, 33 Ser. No. 120.

Klausner, S.Z., et al. *The Workplace Reaches Out: A Study of Organization Impropriation. V. I and II.* (NTIS #PB-236 186 and PB 236 187/1ST.) Philadelphia: Center for Research on the Acts of Man, 1974.

Studied services offered by employers which usually were provided by community or family in 106 Delaware Valley companies. Included recommendations for development of work-related health services and child care.

Klein, Jerry W. "Mainstreaming the Preschooler." *Young Children* 30 (July 1975): 317-326.

*Knitzer, J. "Parental Involvement: The Elixir of Change." *Early Childhood Development Programs and Services: Planning for Action.* Edited by Dennis N. McFadden. Washington, D.C.: National Association for the Education of Young Children, 1972, pp. 83-95.

*Knudsen, D.S. "The Declining Status of Women: Popular Myths and the Failure of Functionalist Thought." *Social Forces* 48 (1969): 183-193.

Examines data from the U.S. census 1940-1964 and finds a persistent decline in women's occupational, economic, and educational achievements compared to that of men.

Kochman, T. *Black and White Styles in Conflict.* Chicago: University of Chicago Press, 1981.

Examines black and white interactions in an attempt to reconstruct the cultural factors that shape the attitudes that blacks and whites bring with them to the interaction process.

Kohlberg, Lawrence. "Development of Moral Character and Moral Ideology." *Review of Research in Child Development Vol. 1.* Edited by L.W. Hoffman and M. Hoffman. New York: Russell Sage Foundation, 1964, pp. 383-431.

Kohn, M. *Social Competence, Symptoms, and Under-Achievement in Childhood: Longitudinal Perspectives.* Silver Spring, Maryland: V.H. Winston and Sons, 1977.

Kohn, M., and B.L. Rosman. "A Social Competence Scale and Symptom Checklist for the Preschool Child." *Developmental Psychology* 6 (1972): 430-444.

Koldin, L.C. *The Welfare Crisis.* New York: Exposition Press, 1971.

Koos, E.H. *The Health of Regionville, New York.* New York: Columbia University Press, 1964.

*Kovar, Mary Grace. *Variations in Birthweight, Legitimate Live Births, U.S. 1963*. Washington, D.C.: Vital and Health Statistics, Series 22 No. 8, National Center for Health Statistics, USDHEW, 1968.

*LaBarre, M. "The Strengths of the Self-Supporting Poor." *Social Casework* XLIX (1968): 459-466.

*Labov, W. *Language in the Inner City: Studies in Black English Vernacular*. Philadelphia: University of Pennsylvania Press, 1972.

*Ladner, Joyce. "Adolescent Pregnancy: A National Problem." *New Directions: The Howard University Magazine* (January 1985): 16-21.

Lantz, H.R. "Family and Kin as Revealed in the Narratives of Ex-Slaves." *Social Science Quarterly* 60 (1980): 667-675.

Examines 1,735 WPA narratives of ex-slaves and 537 narratives of children of ex-slaves in order to determine the extent to which each group could identify their parents, siblings, and kin. Concludes from data of the 1850s and 1860s that while maternal mortality is higher for black women than white women, the maternal mortality figure is about two percent for black women. Finds also that non-slaves are able to identify parents and kin; and non-slaves had a lower rate of broken homes.

*Laosa, Luis. "School, Occupation, Culture, and Family: The Impact of Parental Schooling on the Parent-Child Relationship." *Journal of Educational Psychology* 74 (1982): 791-827.

Hypothesizes that among the enduring effects of schooling on the individual are certain behavioral dispositions that determine how he or she will behave as a parent. Finds that the linkages between parental schooling and the parent-child relationship can be taken as plausible explanations of the frequent scholastic failure observed among the members of certain ethnic minorities in the U.S. Presents a theoretical model that links parental schooling, family interaction processes, and children's scholastic performance.

aosa, Luis. "Social Policies Toward Children of Diverse Ethnic, Racial and Language Groups in the United States." *Child Development and Social Policy*. Edited by H.W. Stevenson, and A.E. Siegel. Chicago: University of Chicago Press, 1985, pp. 1-109.

Traces the major trends in the evolution of social policies toward children that bear directly on issues of ethnic, racial, and language diversity. Laosa also examines the public attitudes, the intellectual assumptions, and the sociodemographic trends that have accompanied these policy developments. The impact of social scientists in these policies is also explored.

sh, T., H. Segal, and D. Dudzinski, *The State of the Child: New York City II*. New York: Foundation for Child Development, 1980.

wrence, Margaret M. *Young Inner City Families: Development of Ego Strength Under Stress*. New York: Behavioral Publications, Inc., 1975.

Questions whether or not psychoanalytic techniques are applicable to low-income families who live under stress (i.e., no resources, desertion, illiteracy, etc.). Using her own clinical experience as a child psychiatrist and a review of the literature, the author concludes that the ego-psychological and developmental approaches of treatment are valid.

zar, Irving, and R.B. Darlington. "Lasting Effects of Early Education." *Monographs of the Society for Research in Child Development* 47 (2-3 Serial No. 195) (1982).

Assesses the long term effects of early childhood education experience on poor children based on the work of 12 independent investigators. The results show long-term effects in four areas: school competence, developed abilities, children's attitudes and values, and impact on the family.

Lazar, Irving, R. Darlington, H. Murray, J. Royce, and A. Snipper. "Lasting Effects of Early Education." *Monographs of the Society for Research in Child Development* 47 (1-2 Serial No. 194) (1982).

*Lazar, Irving, V.R. Hubbell, H. Murray, M. Rosche, and J. Royce. *The Persistence of Preschool Effects: A Long-Term Follow-Up of Fourteen Infant and Preschool Experiments.* The Consortium on Developmental Continuity, Education Commission of the States. Final Report to the Administration on Children, Youth and Families, Office of Human Development Services (Grant No. 18-76-07843). Washington, D.C.: U.S. Government Printing Office, 1977.

Lazar, Irving, et al. *A National Survey of the Parent-Child Center Program.* Los Angeles: Kirschner Associates, Mar. 1970 (EDO48933).

Leepson, Marc. "Coping with Inflation." *Congressional Quarterly* 2 (1980): 507-524.

Discusses the effects of the economy on family life and life-styles.

Lein, L. "Parental Evaluation of Child Care Alternatives." *Urban and Social Change Review* 12:1 (1979), 11-16.

Reviews findings from several studies on patterns of use and preferences for different types of child care.

*Lerner, G. (Ed.) *Black Women in White America: A Documentary History.* New York: Random House, 1973.

LeRose, B. "A Quota System for Gifted Minority Children: A Viable Solution." *Gifted Child Quarterly* 22 (1978): 394-403.

Lester, B., and C. Coll. "Relations between Teenage Pregnancy and Neonatal Behavior." Final Report submitted to the National Institute of Child Health and Human Development, Center for Population Research, n.d.

Levine, Edward M. "Middle-Class Family Decline." *Society*. 18(Jan.-Feb. 1981): 72-78.

Argues that the sociocultural and economic conditions that have done so much to improve our standard of living and enrich life by extending independence and personal fulfillment have also undercut the middle-class nuclear family's efforts to achieve stability and happiness.

Levine, S., F.F. Elzey, and M. Lewis. *California Preschool Social Competency Scale*. Palo Alto, CA: Consulting Psychologists Press, 1969.

Levitar, S. *What's Happening to the American Family?* Baltimore: Johns Hopkins University Press, 1981.

Levitar, S., and Richard S. Belous. "Working Wives and Mothers: What Happens to Family Life?" *Monthly Labor Review* 104 (Sept. 1981): 26-30.

Reflects concern about the survival of the family given the increase of working women: most women can combine work with marriage and motherhood, and handle or better share the resulting household responsibilities.

Levy, Frank. *The Intergenerational Transfer of Poverty. Working Paper 1241-102*. Washington, D.C.: The Urban Institute, January 1980.

Lewis, Jerry M., and John G. Looney. *The Long Struggle-Well-Functioning Working-Class Black Families*. Brunner/Mazel Publishers, 1983.

Looks at well-functioning middle-class black families in the inner city. The interest here is the impact of the socioeconomic context on family competence as revealed in family structure and function.

Lewis, Oscar. *A Study of Slum Culture: Backgrounds for LaVida*. New York: Basic Books, 1968.

*Lincoln, R. "Editorial." *Family Planning Perspectives* 15(1983): 104.

*Lourie, Reginald S. "Head Start, A Retrospective View: The Founders." *Project Head Start*. Edited by Edward Zigler and Jeanette Valentine. New York: Free Press, 1979, pp. 97-102.

Discusses the early efforts to get Head Start moving. Explains how a national program for 100,000 children between 4 and 5 years in poverty areas was set up within seven months. Points out the priorities of the program, the most important of which were the health of the children, and approaches to solving family problems. Shows how the program expanded through the years.

*Macauley, Jacqueline. "Stereotyping Child Welfare." *Society* (January/February 1977): 47-51.

*MacIntyre, D.M. *Public Assistance: Too Much or Too Little?* New York: New York State School of Industrial Relations, Cornell University, Bulletin, 53-1, December 1964.

Mackler, B. "Blacks who are Academically Successful." *Urban Education* 5 (1970): 210-237.

Reviews the literature from the early 1960's on black academic achievement. Documents different patterns of social and personal development and relates these patterns to scholastic performance among disadvantaged children.

*Maggard, Heather Fairburn. "Teen-age Pregnancy: Passing Controversial Legislation." *State Legislatures* 12(Feb. 1986): 12-16.

Reviews state legislative efforts in Connecticut, New York, and Wisconsin.

Magidson, Jay, and Dag Borbom. "Adjusting for Confounding Factors in Quasi-Experiments: Another Reanalysis of the Westinghouse Head Start

Evaluation." Paper presented at the Annual Meeting of the American Statistical Association. Houston, Texas, August 9-12, 1980.

Evaluations of social programs based upon quasi-experimental designs are typically plagued by problems of nonequivalence between the experimental and comparison group prior to the experiment. In such settings it is extremely difficult, if not impossible, to isolate the effects of the program from the confounding effects associated with the relevant preexisting differences between the groups. A classic occurrence of the problem is revealed in the Westinghouse Report. A portion of the data using Sorbom's statistical adjustment is reanalyzed. This approach improves upon previous analyses in the following ways: 1. it recognizes that the Head Start and comparison groups are separate and distinct populations; 2. it offers a statistical test of the null hypothesis that the two groups are equal on a latent factor called the socio-economic advantage; and 3. a goodness of fit statistic providing an overall test of the assumptions of model indicates that the model fits the data better than any previous model. Results do not support the strong inferences drawn by the original evaluators.

Makinson, Carolyn. "The Health Consequences of Teenage Fertility." *Family Planning Perspectives* 17(May-June 1985): 132-139.

Summarizes the consequences of teenage pregnancy and childbirth in the United States, Canada, Britain, France, and Sweden.

Malone, Margaret. *Child Care Tax Credit*. Washington, D.C.: Congressional Research Service, August 7, 1980.

Malone, Margaret. *Child Day Care: The Federal Role*. Washington, D.C.: Congressional Research Service, 1981.

Malone, Margaret. *Selected Federal Programs Which Fund Child Care and Related Services*. Washington, D.C.: Congressional Research Service, March 31, 1980, updated November 2, 1981.

Lists nearly all federally funded child day care programs along with its authorizing legislation; a brief description of its general purpose; and budget authorization levels and federal expenditures.

Mandell, B.R. (Ed.) *Welfare in America.* Englewood Cliffs, N.J.: Prentice-Hall, Inc., 1975.

*Mann, A.J., A. Harrell, and M. Hurt. *A Review of Head Start Research Since 1969 and an Annotated Bibliography* (DHEW Publication No. 78-31102). Washington, D.C.: U.S. Department of Health, Education, and Welfare, 1977.

Reviews Head Start research and provides an annotated bibliography of literature relating to the Head Start program. Briefly summarized are the findings and extent of research related to the impact of Head Start in the following five areas: child health, social development of the child, cognitive development of the child, the family, and the community.

Mann, Edward T., and C. Courtney Elliott. "Assessment of the Utility of Project Head Start for the Culturally Deprived: An Evaluation of Social and Psychological Functioning." *Training School Bulletin* 64 (1968): 119-125.

Represents the first phase of longitudinal research dealing with the effects of Project Head Start on affective and cognitive functioning of disadvantaged children in the rural Southwest.

*Marsiglio, William. "Confronting the Teenage Pregnancy Issue: Social Marketing as an Interdisciplinary Approach." *Human Relations* 38, No.10: (1985): 983-1000.

Reviews research on attitudes and behaviors on contraceptive use among teenagers and advocates social marketing as a good approach to increasing responsible teenage contraception.

Martin, Carolyn J. *The Politics and Process of Social Program Evaluation: The Head Start Example.*

Bloomington, Indiana: Indiana University IDPYC Program, School of Education, 1977.

Critiques evaluations of Head Start for their emphasis upon measurable program effects and insufficient attention to quality indicators. Chapters cover the social and political context of Head Start, the history of the program, the politics of evaluation, the meaning of evaluation and the methodology of this investigation. Changes in the structure of the Office of Child Development, DHEW, are proposed, along with an evaluation model which is designed to allow for input from interest groups for appeal of decisions.

Martin, E.P., and J.M. Martin. *The Black Extended Family*. Chicago: The University of Chicago Press, 1978.

Masnick, G., and M.J. Bane. *The Nation's Families: 1960-1990*. Cambridge, MA.: Joint Center for Urban Studies of MIT and Harvard, 1980.

Matney, William C., and Dwight L. Johnson. *America's Black Population 1970 to 1982*. Washington D.C.: U.S. Department of Commerce, 1983.

*Maxwell, Joan Paddock. *No Easy Answers: Persistent Poverty in the Metropolitan Washington Area*. Washington, D.C.: Greater Washington Research Center, December 1985.

Brings together information from the 1970 and 1980 censuses about poverty in the Washington, D.C. area. Particular emphasis was placed on black persons living in the District of Columbia who suffered most intensely from poverty.

Mbiti, J.S. *African Religions and Philosophies*. Garden City, N.Y.: Anchor Books, Doubleday, 1970.

McAdoo, Harriette Pipes. "The Impact of Upward Mobility of Kin-Help Patterns and the Reciprocal Obligations in Black Families." *Journal of Marriage and the Family* 40(1978): 761-776.

McAdoo, Harriette Pipes. "Youth, School, and the Family in Transition." *Urban Education* 16 (Oct. 1981A): 261-277.

Describes some of the transitions now occurring in urban families and shows how the economic and social forces at play within the urban setting are leading to transitions on all fronts.

*McAdoo, Harriette Pipes (Ed.). *Black Families*. Beverly Hills, CA: Sage Publications, Inc., 1981B.

Deals with the presumed inability of Black families to fulfill societal prerequisites. Argues that researchers appear to have abandoned the cultural deviant perspective of Black families and that more culturally relevant empirical studies should emerge.

McAdoo, Harriette P., and John L. McAdoo (Eds.). *Black Children: Social, Educational, and Parental Environments*. Beverly Hills, CA: Sage Publications, 1985.

A collection of twenty papers which address major issues, theories, and empirical findings on the diverse life experiences of black families.

McCray, Carrie Allen. "The Black Woman and Family Roles." *The Black Woman*. Edited by La Frances Rodgers-Rose. Beverly Hills, CA: Sage Publications, 1980, pp. 67-78.

Examines the role of black women in their families; calls for continued research from a more balanced and unbiased perspective which neither denigrates black women for their functional roles nor idealizes them in the process of black family survival.

McCroskey, J. "Working Mothers and Child Care: The Context of Child Care Satisfaction for Working Women with Preschool Children." D.S.W. Dissertation. UCLA, 1980.

Relates satisfaction with child care arrangements to work satisfaction for women in professional/managerial versus clerical/technical work.

McDonald, R. Robin. "Head Start in Jeopardy?" *The National Center Reporter* 8 (1978): 8-9, 30.

Discusses the National Head Start Association conference in Cleveland, May 24-27, 1978. The primary concern was President Jimmy Carter's proposal to transfer the administration of Head Start to the Department of Education. Marion Wright Edelman, a keynote speaker at the conference, accused the Carter Administration of turning the program over "to the various school systems whose failures necessitated Head Start in the first place." Opposition to this transfer was also based on the comprehensive nature of the program and the influence of parents.

McDonald, Valerie B. "Parent Involvement In Project Head Start: Philosophy and Program Implementation." Master's Thesis. Goddard College, 1980.

Concluded that at the basis of effective parent involvement is an understanding and acceptance of every parent and a willingness by parents to involve themselves on a level that is meaningful to them. This study found that decentralization of parent involvement at the local Head Start center level is more effective.

*McGraw, Onalee. *The Family, Feminism and the Therapeutic State.* Washington, D.C.: The Heritage Foundation, 1980.

Discusses several issues such as: The meaning and purpose of the family; the family versus the cult of self; defending the family from the helping professionals; and the family, human rights and the courts.

*McKey, R.H., I. Condelli, H. Ganson, B. Barrett, C. McConkey, and M. Plantz. *The Impact of Head Start on Children, Families and Communities.* Washington, D.C.: CSR, Inc., June 1985.

McMillan, David W., and Robert W. Hiltonsmith. "Adolescents at Home: An Exploratory Study of the Relationship Between Perception of Family Social Climate, General Well-Being, and Actual Behavior in the Home Setting." *Journal of Youth and Adolescence* 11 (1982): 301-315.

Investigated the relationship between behavior in the home environment and perception of family social climate and personal well-being in a socialecological perspective.

*Mecklenburg, Marjory E., and Patricia G. Thompson. "The Adolescent Family Life Program as a Prevention Measure." *Public Health Reports* 98 (Jan.-Feb. 1983): 21-29.

Describes the two objectives of The Adolescent Family Life Program as care services for which only pregnant and parenting adolescents are eligible, and prevention services which are aimed at preventing adolescent sexual relations and which are available to any adolescent. The program also funds projects that demonstrate and evaluate innovative services.

*Mediax Associates, Inc. *Measures of Development Among Young Children: Socio-Emotional Domain.* Westport, CT.: Author, 1978.

Discusses the measurement of behavioral and attitudinal aspects of young children's socioemotional development and briefly describes a variety of instruments designed to measure such development.

*Mediax Associates, Inc. *An Overview of a Project to Develop Head Start Profiles of Program Effects on Children.* Westport, CT.: Author, 1979.

Provides an overview of a project to develop Head Start measures of program effects on children 3 to 7 years of age. The program approach is distinctive in emphasizing evaluation of all aspects of children's development that may affect their overall competence in reflecting the concerns, views, and values of a broad range of persons, and in recommending that the proposed measures be processed differently with children from different backgrounds in order to generate a plurality of scales of development.

*Mediax Associates, Inc. *Accept My Profile: Perspectives for Head Start Programs on Children.* Westport, CT: Mediax Associates, Inc. 1980.

*Mediax Associates, Inc. *Instruments Developed in the Head Start Program Effects Measurement Project.* Westport, Conn., Mediax Associates, 1983.

*Menken, J. "Health Consequences of Early Childbearing." Paper Given at the Conference on Consequences of Adolescent Pregnancy. Washington, D.C., October 1975.

Menken, J. "The Health and Social Consequences of Teenage Childbearing." *Teenage Sexuality, Pregnancy and Childbearing*. Edited by F. Furstenberg, R. Lincoln, and J. Menken, Philadelphia, PA.: University of Penna. Press, 1980, pp. 167-183.

Mercer, J.R., and J.F. Lewis. *System of Multicultural Pluralistic Assessment.* New York: Psychological Corporation, 1979.

Meyers, C.E., R. Ninira, and A. Zetlin. "The Measurement of Adaptive Behavior." *Handbook of Mental Deficiency: Psychological Theory and Research.* Edited by N.R. Ellis. Hillsdale, N.J.: Erlbaum Associates, 1979.

Midco Educational Associates, Inc. *Perspectives on Parent Participation in Project Head Start: An Analysis and Critique.* Denver, CO: Midco, 1972.

Describes a project which investigated the impact of Head Start parent participation on the program's quality, on institutional changes in the community, on the Head Start children, and on the Head Start parents themselves. Two types of parent participation were investigated: 1. parents in decision-making roles, and 2. parents in learner roles. Another type of involvement in which parents were paid employees in Head Start programs was also studied.

*Midco Educational Associates, Inc. *Investigation of the Effects of Parent Participation in Head Start*. (Non-Technical Report) Washington, D.C.: USDHHS/ACYF, 1972.

Mifflin, Ruth E. *Enhancing Parental Teaching and Interaction Skills with Young Children*. Provo, Utah: Brigham Young University, 1980.

Evaluated the effectiveness of a parent education program designed to enhance parent's verbal interaction skills. Seventeen families of preschool children participated in 4 weekly parent workshops, while 16 control group families did not. Experimental group mothers, fathers, and sets of parents modeled significantly more positive self-statements than did control parents. The program was effective at changing parent's behavior in a short time.

*Miller, Walter B. "Focal Concerns of Lower Class Culture." *Poverty In America*. Edited by Louis A. Ferman, Joyce L. Kornbluh, and Alan Haber. Ann Arbor, MI: University of Michigan Press, 1965, pp. 261-269.

Molnar, Thomas. "The Destruction of the Family." *Human Life Review* 9 (Winter 1983): 25-37.

Describes the "ideologically-motivated dismantling and de-structuring of the family."

Moore, Kristin A. "Teenage Childbirth and Welfare Dependency." *Family Planning Perspectives* 10 (July-August, 1978): 233-235.

*Moore, Kristin A., and Martha R. Burt. *Private Crisis, Public Cost: Policy Perspectives on Teenage Childbearing*. Washington, D.C.: Urban Institute Press, 1982.

Moore, Kristin A., and S.L. Hofferth. "Women and their Children." *The Subtle Revolution. Women at Work.* Edited by R.E. Smith. Washington, D.C.: The Urban Institute, 1979.

*Moore, Kristin A., and Richard F. Wertheimer. "Teenage Childbearing and Welfare: Preventive and Amelioratives Strategies." *Family Planning Perspectives* 16 (Nov.-Dec. 1984): 285-289.

Gives the results of the computer-simulation research project which compared the effects of seven hypothetical strategies, or scenarios, on the incidence and cost of welfare dependency among young women. These scenarios project a range of possible outcomes resulting from interventions to either decrease adolescent childbearing or break the childbearing poverty.

Moore, Kristin et al. "Teenage Childbearing: Consequences for Women, Families, and Government Welfare Expenditures." *Teenage Parents and Their Offspring*. Edited by K. Scott, T. Field, and Ed Robertson. New York: Grune and Stratton, Inc., 1981.

Moore, S. G. "ETS-Head Start Longitudinal Study of Factors Related to High and Low Achieving Young Black Children." *Young Children* 33 (1978): 74-77.

Found that High and Low children showed different degrees of readiness for school as early as four years of age, prior to attendance in any preschool or Head Start program.

Morgan, Carolyn Stout. "Interstate Variations in Teenage Fertility." *Population Research and Policy Review* 2(Feb. 1983): 67-83.

Examines the wide variation among states in adolescent childbearing using indicators that request high or low modernity, i.e., percent urban, percent fundamentalism, percent black, and region (South--non-South); the intermediate variables of factors affecting exposure to intercourse (percent married females 15 to 19); and the deliberate fertility control factor of induced abortion (the state abortion-to-live birth ratio).

Morgan, H. "How Schools Fail Black Children." *Social Policy* 10 (Jan.-Feb. 1980):49-54.

Examines some theories which deal with ways in which learners process new information. Finds that there is a high degree of socialization and teacher-child interaction where the classroom is defined as an efficient workroom and where the child's play is viewed as work. Shows that the social interaction models found in the lower grades provide an atmosphere within which black children as a group can do well. Argues that there appears to be a steady decline in group-measured academic achievement for black children once the early childhood period has passed.

*Moroney, R. *The Family and the State*. New York: Longman Group Limited, 1976.

Moroney, R. *Families, Social Services, and Social Policy: the Issue of Shared Responsibility*. Washington, D.C.: U.S. Government Printing Office, 1980.

Morris, Jeanne B. "Indirect Influence on Children's Racial Attitudes." *Educational Leadership* 38 (January 1981): 286-287.

Morrow, B. "Elementary School Performance of Offspring of Young Adolescent Mothers." *American Educational Research Journal* (Fall 1979): pp. 423-429.

*Moynihan, Daniel Patrick. "Employment, Income, and the Ordeal of the Negro Family." *Daedalus* 94(1965): 745-770.

*Moynihan, Daniel Patrick. *The Politics of a Guaranteed Income*. New York: Random House, 1973.

*Moynihan, Daniel Patrick. *Family and Nation*. Harcourt Brace Jovanovich, Publishers, 1986.

Looks at the disintegration of the American family. Argues that if the family suffers, the young suffer most.

*Muenchow, Susan, and Susan Shays. *Head Start in the 1980's. Review and Recommendations. A Report Requested by the President of the United States.* Washington, D.C.: U.S. Department of Health and Human Services, Office of Human Development Services, ACYF, Head Start Bureau, September 1980.

A 15th Anniversary Report on Project Head Start. The report is divided into five sections: an inventory of Head Start programs and demonstration projects; a review of the success of Head Start programs; a presentation of problems in the Head Start programs; a presentation of policy options for the 1980's; and a list of recommendations.

*Murray, Charles. *Losing Ground. American Social Policy 1950-1980.* New York: Basic Books, Inc., 1984.

Explains why the problems of the black, poor people have become worse despite enormously increased expenditures on education for the poor, welfare, on-the-job training, food stamps and other programs instituted by the government.

Murray, Harry W. "Early Intervention in the Context of Family Characteristics." Paper Presented at the Annual Meeting of the American Orthopsychiatric Association, New York, NY., April 12-16, 1977.

Compares results from 11 longitudinal studies to determine whether preschool education improves the IQ of low income children when their family situations are taken into account and if so, how long the effects last. The results indicate that there is a significant probability that lower-class children who attend a preschool will have higher IQ's than those who do not for at least 3 years after preschool. Findings also show that for lower-class populations, significant correlations exist between mother's education, social class, family size, and birth order, and IQ, but that the combined effect of these variables on the percent of variance explained for IQ is slight. Finally, little evidence is found that preschools affect the correlations between family variables and IQ.

Murray, Kathleen. *Legal Aspects of Child Care as an Employee Benefit.* San Francisco, CA: Child Care Law Center, 1980.

National Commission on Working Women, National Manpower Institute. *National Survey of Working Women. Perceptions, Problems, and Prospects.* Washington, D.C.: Author, 1979.

Summarizes national survey of 80,000 working women concentrated in lower paying, low status jobs--80 percent of all working women. Includes discussion of problems, satisfaction, and dissatisfaction with work.

Nazzaro, Jean. "Head Start for Handicapped--What's Been Accomplished?" *Exceptional Children* 41 (1974): 103-106.

Discusses the accomplishments of Head Start in serving handicapped children, with emphasis on the issue of unnecessary labeling to fill "handicapped" spaces. In order to meet the Congressional mandate, there was concern that children were being improperly classified.

*NCSS (National Center for Social Statistics). Social Rehabilitation Service, U.S. Department of Health, Education and Welfare. *Public Assistance Statistics.* Washington, D.C.: U.S. Government Printing Office, December, 1977.

Neel, Ann F. "Preschool Education: Lessons Learned-Questions Asked." *Child Welfare* 54 (1975): 487-494.

Discusses the immediate and long-term gains produced by compensatory education programs including Head Start. It is suggested that further research is needed with the aim of targeting child development programs in ways most likely to produce benefits.

Nelson, Linden, and Millard C. Madsen. "Cooperation and Competition in Four-Year-Olds as A Function of Reward Contingency and Subculture."

Developmental Psychology 1 (1969): 340-344.

Cultural differences in cooperation and competition were measured in black and white pairs and between middle-class and Head Start children. No significant differences were found.

Nelson, Richard R., and Felicity Skidmore. *American Families and the Economy -- The High Costs of Living*. Washington, D.C.: National Academy Press, 1983.

Concerned with marshaling information about what the changing climate has meant for the economic welfare of families with children.

New York Times. "Migrants with Head Start." Sun., Aug. 28, 1977.

Nihira, K., R. Foster, M. Shelhaur, and H. Leland. *AAMD Adaptive Behavior Scale*. Washington, D.C.: American-Association of Mental Deficiency, 1974.

Nixon, R.M. "President's Statement on the Establishment of an Office of Child Development." *Head Start Newsletter* 4(1969A): 1.

Nixon, R.M. "Statement by the President on the Establishment of an Office of Child Development." *Young Children* 24 (1969B): 262-264.

Nixon, R. (1971, December 9). *Veto Message*, as reported in the Public Papers for 1972, pp. 1174-87.

Nobles, Wade W. "Toward an Empirical and Theoretical Framework for Defining Black Families." *Journal of Marriage and the Family* 4 (1978): 679-687.

Norman, Michael. "The New Extended Family: Divorce Reshapes the American Household." *New York Times Magazine* (Nov. 23, 1980): 27-28, 44, 46, 53-54, 147, 162, 166, 173.

Describes how divorce and remarriage are forcing families to create new relationships between the parents and children.

Novak, Michael. "The American Family: An Embattled Institution." *Human Life Review* 6 (Winter 1980): 40-53.

Warns that there is a huge family establishment growing in the United States. It is powerfully institutionalized through all the family service agencies of the government with a strong vested interest in understanding the family in a certain way. Suggests that many of the ideas, images, and cultural messages of our society are radically hostile to the values on which strong families depend.

Nye, Barbara Ann. "The Impact of the Minimum Wage Upon Head Start Budgets: Implications for Service Delivery." *Dissertation Abstracts International* 44 (2-A) 1983: 348.

Conducted a wage comparability survey and a 5-year budget analysis on Head Start programs. Cost analysis techniques were used to determine the effect of the minimum wage on compensation rates and budget levels for service delivery. Findings disclosed the impact of the minimum wage and inflation on the compensation structure and service delivery levels in Head Start. The minimum wage was judged to be deleterious to Head Start budgets by compressing the wage structure and thus, reducing pay differentials and the influence of staff experience and education. Levels of component services were indirectly reduced due to personnel cost increases which in part resulted from a 46 percent increase in the minimum wage over the previous 3 years.

*Nye, I.F. *School Age Parenthood. Extension Bulletin 667.* Pullman, WA: Cooperative Extension Services, Washington State University, 1976.

ffice of Child Development, Delegation of Authority to Secretary of Health, Education and Welfare, Head Start Memorandum of Understanding. *Head Start Newsletter* July 2-8, 1969.

ffice of Child Development (USDHEW). *Head Start Services to Handicapped Children, First Annual Report of the U.S. Department of Health, Education, and Welfare to the Congress of the United States on Services to Handicapped Children in Project Head Start.* March 1973.
Second Annual Report. Apr. 1974.
Third Annual Report. June 1975.
Fourth Annual Report. Dec. 1976.
Fifth Annual Report. Dec. 1977.

ffice of Child Development. Transmittal Notice: Announcement of the Head Start/Medicaid Early and Periodic Screening, Diagnosis and Treatment Program. OCD-HS-73-14, Dec. 1973.

Office of Economic Opportunity. *Catalog of Federal Assistance Programs.* The Office of Economic Opportunity, Washington, D.C., June 1, 1967, 554.

gbu, John U. *Minority Education and Caste - The American System in Cross-Cultural Perspective.* New York: Academic Press, 1978.

Looks at the impact of school integration on black academic achievement, the social, constitutional, political, and ethical justifications are all rejected.

Ogbu, John U. "Origins of Human Competence: A Cultural-Ecological Perspective." *Child Development* 52 (1981): 413-429.

'Keefe, Ruth Ann. "Head Start: Partnership with Parents." *Children Today* (Jan.-Feb. 1973): 12-16.

Describes the 16 Home Start demonstrative programs that served 2,500 children. Various aspects of Home Start are outlined, including the nutrition component; the health component; psychological and social services; intellectual and physical development; home visitors; the use of community resources; and project evaluation.

O'Keefe, A. *What Head Start Means to Families*. Washington, D.C.: U.S. Government Printing Office, USDHEW Publication No. OHDS 79-31129, 1979.

Reports that Head Start parents allow their children to help more with household tasks, read to their children more, and show more interest in their children's reading and writing skills.

*Omwake, E.B. "From the President." *Young Children* 25 (1970): 130-131.

Omwake, E.B. "Assessment of the Head Start Preschool Education Effort." *Project Head Start*. Edited by Edward Zigler and Jeanette Valentine. New York: Free Press, 1979, pp. 221-230.

Argues that evaluation efforts experienced many problems because of inadequate and constantly shifting funding levels; frequent personnel changes; conflict around goals and approaches; and bureaucratic interference. Explains that by 1970, the preschool program became stronger after a reorganization of the curriculum when IQ change and achievement test scores were not regarded as the primary goal of Head Start. Finds that a pressing problem of the program is short-term training for inexperienced staff.

Orton, R. "Letter to Parents and Staff." *Head Start Newsletter* 4 (1969): 1.

*Orton, R. "Head Start: A Retrospective View: The Founders." *Project Head Start*. Edited by Edward Zigler and Jeanette Valentine. New York: Free Press, 1979, pp. 129-134.

*Osofsky, H.J., J.W. Hagen, and P.W. Wood. "A Program for Pregnant School Girls -- Some Early Results." *American Journal of Obstetrics and Gynecology* 100 (1968): 1020.

Oyemade, U.J. "Socialization Patterns and Behavioral Outcomes in Black Adolescents." Paper Presented at the Annual Meeting of the National Council of Family Relations (October, 1982).

Oyemade, U.J. "The Rationale for Head Start as a Vehicle for Upward Mobility of Minority Families." *American Journal of Orthopsychiatry* (Oct. 1985): 591-602.

Critiques premises that guided the develop culture-of-poverty theory: the concept of transgenerational poverty; the assumption of education as a vehicle for upward mobility; and the assumption that the child could serve as a vehicle for the economic mobility of the family.

*Oyemade, U.J., E. Kane, M. Dejoie-Smith, and H. Laryea. *Black Family Coping Styles and Adolescent Behaviors: Final report.* (No. 90-C-1763). Washington, D.C.: Department of Health and Human Services, 1983.

Padilla, Raymond V. (Ed.) *Bilingual Education and Public Policy in the United States. Ethnoperspectives in Bilingual Education Research. Volume I.* Ypsilanti, MI: Eastern Michigan University, 1980A.

Includes several papers on each of the legal aspects of bilingual education, the politics of implementing bilingual programs, the role of the community in establishing and maintaining bilingual programs, and bilingual program models.

Padilla, Raymond V. (Ed.) *Theory in Bilingual Education: Ethnoperspectives in Bilingual Research, Volume II.* Ypsilanti, MI: Eastern Michigan University, 1980B.

Part II of a three-volume text that presents the three basic factors of the bilingual educational equation--public policy, theory, and technology. This volume focuses on the theoretical aspects of bilingual education.

Palmer, E.L. "Can Television Really Teach?" *American Education* 5(1969): 2-6.

*Palmer, F.H., and L.W. Anderson. "Long Term Gains From Early Intervention: Findings From Longitudinal Studies." *Project Head Start*. Edited by E. Zigler and J. Valentine. New York: Free Press, 1979, pp. 433-466.

Compares the gains which may be derived from Head Start and early-intervention studies and concludes that the two types of studies are not synonymous. Explains that Head Start was designed to include maximum community input with respect to services and educational components, while the intervention studies were designed to test the impact on the children involved. Contends that early-intervention programs have been found to work for poor children who went to school. Suggests ways in which Head Start, though slightly different, can also work.

*Parker, Seymour, and Robert J. Kleiner. "Social and Psychological Dimensions of the Family Role Performance of the Negro Male." *Journal of Marriage and the Family* XXXI. No. 3(1969): 500-506.

Found that social class was not related to differences in how a sample of urban black males functioned as husbands in both the psychological and the breadwinning role. Those men who perceived of themselves as "failures" as husbands also felt that they could not hope for success in their jobs. It is thought that this kind of life view is not definitive of a subcultural pattern in terms of either race or class. The authors conclude that the societal problems which confront men may result in inadequate performance as husbands and fathers.

*Pasamanick, Benjamin, and Hilda Knobloch. "The Contribution of Some Organic Factors to School Retardation in Negro Children." *Journal of Negro Education* 27 (February 1958): 4-9.

Patterson, James T. *American Struggle Against Poverty 1900-1980* Cambridge: MA: Harvard University Press, 1981.

Explores the changing perspectives, especially of reformers, toward poverty and welfare. The text focuses mainly on the period from 1930 to 1980 since these were years of increasing governmental involvement in social welfare. The book tries to integrate intellectual history and analysis of public policy.

Payne, James S., Ruth A. Payne, Cecil D. Mercer, and Roxana G. Davison. *Head Start: A Tragicomedy with Epilogue*. New York: Behavioral Publications, 1973.

Pearce, Diane. "The Feminization of Poverty: Women, Work, and Welfare." *The Urban and Social Change Review* Vol. II (1977): 28-36.

Looks at the way poverty is becoming a female problem and examines the impact of the marketplace and the welfare system on the incidence of poverty among women as family heads.

erlman, Nancy. *What is Health Start? Profiles of Selected Projects*. Washington, D.C.: Urban Institute, April 1972 (EDO68182).

erry, K.S. *Child Care Centers Sponsored by Employers and Labor Unions in the United States*. Washington, D.C.: U.S. Department of Labor, 1980A.

erry, K. "Survey and Analysis of Employer Sponsored Day Care in the United States." Doctoral Dissertation. University of Wisconsin in Milwaukee, 1980B.

Identified 105 company child care centers in 1978 (see Burud, Aschbacher, and McCrosky for more recent estimates).

'eters, Donald L. "Social Science and Social Policy and the Care of Young Children: Head Start and After." *Journal of Applied Developmental Psychology* (1980): 1 (1): 7-27.

Reviews the relative influence of social science research in the formulation of social policy through historical case studies of Head Start and federally funded day care. It is concluded that economic, social, and political factors are the principal initiators of broad program efforts and that social science research is influential in specifying the problem and in "fine-tuning" solution alternatives. The subjectivity of social science research is addressed by analyzing both the nature of the research questions asked and the advocacy role played by social scientists.

Phi Delta Kappan. "A Study of Head Start." 50 (1969): 591.

The Westinghouse Report is the subject of this editorial which first appeared in *The New Republic*. The author finds the major fault of the study to be the over-generalizations made from limited evaluative research. Among the study limitations identified by the author are: 1. the failure to measure the medical and nutritional effects of Head Start; 2. the lack of effort expended in ascertaining differences in quality among various Head Start programs; 3. the measurements taken were completely post-hoc, i.e., children were tested one to three years after their Head Start experience; and 4. the income and status of Head Start parents were not recorded. The author warned that the Westinghouse Report could be used to eliminate Head Start funding.

Phillips, Bertrand P. "Head Start Parents in Participant Groups: III. Community Trainer as Link to Social Change." *Journal of Applied Behavioral Science* 10 (1974): 259-263.

Investigated whether parent involvement achieved harmony among child, family, parent group, Head Start, and school groups.

Phillips, Deborah. "Continuity of Care: Theory, Evidence and Policy Applications." *International Journal of Mental Health* 12 (Winter 1983-84): 5-21.

Pierson, D.E., D.K. Walker, and T. Tivnan. "A School-Based Program from Infancy to Kindergarten for Children and their Parents." *The Personnel and Guidance Journal* (April 1984): 448-455.

Provides evidence of the effectiveness of good preschool programs for middle-class children.

*Placet, P.S., and G.E. Hendershot, "Public Welfare and Family Planning: An Empirical Study of the Broad Son Myth." *Social Problems* 21 (1976): 658-673.

*Plave, M. "Family Day Care: The Solution for Dallas Corporations." *Human Development News* (Oct-Nov. 1983): 1-2.

Describes a two-year federally funded program to develop and manage a family day care home system for corporation employees and their children, primarily infants and toddlers.

Postman, N. "The Disappearing Child." *Educational Leadership* 40 (March 1983): 10-17.

Compares child-actors from the days of "Leave it to Beaver" with those of the time of Gary Coleman and argues that the simplicity of childhood has disappeared from those children appearing in the media. Contends that the perception of children as miniature adults is reinforced by their criminal activities and a high level of sexual activity among children. The author feels that the media is, in part, responsible for this.

Powell, Douglas R. *Finding Child Care: A Study of Parents' Search Processes.* Detroit, MI: Merrill Palmer Institute, June 1980.

Pratt, Grade K. "Ethical Imperatives for Head Start." *Educational Forum* 36 (1972): 215-219.

Presser, H. B. *The Social and Demographic Consequences of Teenage Pregnancy for Urban Women.* College Park, Maryland: The University of Maryland Press, 1979.

Presser, H. B., and W. Baldwin. "Child Care as a Constraint on Employment: Prevalent Correlates and Bearing on the Work and Fertility Nexus." *American Journal of Sociology* 85 (5) (March 1980): 1202-1213.

Presser, H. B., and Linda Salsberg, "Public Assistance and Early Family Formation: Is there a Pronatalist Effect?" *Social Problems* 23 (1975): 226-241.

Examines the relationship between public assistance and fertility with a focus on time of early family formation. Found that welfare recipients want fewer children than non-recipients and suggests that welfare may be a consequent of an untimely birth rather than a stimulus.

**Project Developmental Continuity: Guidelines for a Planning Year*. Mimeo. USDHEW, Office of Child Development, 1974.

**Project Developmental Continuity: Guidelines for an Implementation Year*. Mimeo, USDHEW, Office of Child Development, 1975.

**Project Developmental Continuity: A Head Start Demonstration Program Linking Head Start, Parents, and the Public School*. Washington, D.C.: USDHEW, Office of Child Development, 1977 (GPO 917-327).

Puglisi, D.J., and A.J. Hoffman. "Cultural Identity and Academic Success in a Multicultural Society: A Culturally Different Approach." *Social Education* 42 (1978): 495-498.

Argues that an educational model currently exerting significant influence on the character of educational programs, curricular materials and classroom strategies has contributed to the discord and frustration among some ethnic groups. Suggests that an alternative model for working with minority group children offers a greater opportunity for success than one predicated on assimilation at the expense of cultural identity.

Quinn, Jane Bryant. "Federal Help on Day Care Shifted From Poor to Middle Class." *Washington Post* (November 23, 1981): 39.

*Radke-Yarrow, M. "The Elusive Evidence." *Newsletter, Division of Developmental Psychology, American Psychological Association*, Fall, 1963.

*Rainwater, Lee. "Theoretical Issues in Poverty Research." *The Journal of Social Issues* 26 (Spring 1970): 149-167.

Deals with the knowledge required to guide programs of social change more effectively. It further suggests that understanding the problem of poverty may be dependent upon increased understanding of behavior in general, and in particular upon empirical and theoretical advances in understanding the problems of the relationship between the environment and behavior.

Rainwater, Lee. "The Problem of Lower Class Culture." *Journal of Social Issues* 26 (1970): 133-148.

Raizen, Senta et al. *Design for a National Evaluation of Social Competence in Head Start Children.* Santa Monica, CA.: Rand Corp., 1974.

Specifies the design for a national evaluation of the effects of Head Start programs on the total child, defined in terms of the child's social competence. This report is not meant to be construed as a recommendation that a national evaluation be undertaken.

Randolph, Linda A. et al. "Head Start Dental Health Services: A Blueprint for Preschool Children's Dentistry in the U.S.A." *International Dental Journal* 30 (1980): 39-48.

Describes the Head Start dental health program. The program provides children with dental examinations, restorative and other treatment services and prophylactic and preventive services. Dental health education, including nutrition education, is provided for children, parents and staff. The basic health services goal of the program is to link the child and family to an on-going source of health care beyond the usual one-year period the Head Start child is enrolled in the program. Such a goal necessitates a close working relationship between private practice and government-funded dental practitioners at the community level to make maximum utilization of dental health resources. A major focus of the program is to balance the competing priorities of treatment and prevention services within a finite, limited and often inadequate dental budget.

Raspberry, W. "Why Push to Move Head Start?" *Young Children* 33 (1978): 15.

Criticizes President Carter's proposal to move Project Head Start from under the jurisdiction of the Department of Health and Human Services to the newly formed Department of Education. Mr. Raspberry believes that Head Start is "...doing fine as it is and that the proposed transfer involves unnecessary risks."

Reidford, P., and M. Berzonsky. "Field Test of an Academically Oriented Preschool." *Elementary School Journal* 29 (1969): 271-276.

*Reiss, I.C. *The Social Context of Premarital Sexual Permissiveness*. New York: Holt Rinehart and Winston, 1967.

Rhine, W. Ray (Ed.). *Making Schools More Effective: New Directions From Follow Through*. New York: Academic Press, 1981.

Acquaints readers with the major characteristics of Project Follow Through. Reviews the beginnings of Head Start and other events that gave rise to Follow Through and examines its two guiding strategies: 1. "planned variation"; and 2. "sponsorship." Describes the Follow Through models -- Parent Education Model, Direct Instruction Model, Behavior Analysis Model, High/Scope Cognitively Oriented Curriculum Model, and the Bank Street Model. Discusses the impact of Follow Through.

*Richmond, Julius R., Deborah J. Stipek, and Edward Zigler. "A Decade of Head Start." *Project Head Start*. Edited by Edward Zigler and Jeanette Valentine. New York: Free Press, 1979, pp. 135-152.

Shows how Head Start, an effort of several groups, was organized to help the nation's disadvantaged children and their families. Discusses the goals and components of Head Start, Head Start's mandate and funding, and innovative Head Start demonstration programs. Tries to clear up any misconceptions about Head Start and offers a candid evaluation.

*Riley, Clara M.D., and Frances M.J. Epps. *Head Start, in Action*. New York: Parker Publishing Company, Inc., 1967.

Rivera-Casale, Cecilia, Lorraine V. Klerman, and Roger Manela. "The Relevance of Child-Support Enforcement to School-Age Parents." *Child Welfare* 63 (Nov.-Dec. 1984): 521-532.

Asks whether fathers of children born to school-age mothers be expected to support their offspring. Reviews recent studies and analyzes policies in several states.

*Rivlin, Alice M. "Forensic Social Sciences." *Harvard Educational Review* 43 (1973): 61-75.

*Rivlin, Alice M., and P.M. Timpane (Eds.). *Planned Variation in Education*. Washington, D.C.: Brookings Institution, 1975.

Roberts, W. "Review of Greenberg, P., 'The Devil Has Slippery Shoes.'" *Saturday Review* 160 (1969): 12-13.

Robinson, Bryan E., and Robert L. Barret. "Teenage Fathers." *Psychology Today* 19 (Dec. 1985): 66-70.

Argues that many teenage fathers care about their babies, whether or not they walk or are pushed away from fatherhood.

*Robinson, James L., and Willa Barrie Choper. "Another Perspective on Program Evaluation: The Parents Speak." *Project Head Start*. Edited by Edward Zigler and Jeanette Valentine. New York: Free Press, 1979, pp. 467-479.

Assesses parent's contribution to the Head Start program. Finds that parents are proud of the changes made to their lives through the program. Discusses some of the benefits of the program, such as gains in cognitive development, improved health, and the positive attitude of parents toward their children.

Rodgers, Harrell. *The Cost of Human Neglect --America's Welfare Failure*. New York: M.E. Sharpe, Inc., 1982.

*Rodgers, Harrell. "Youth and Poverty: An Empirical Test of the Impact of Family Demographics and Race." *Youth and Society* 16 (1985): 421-437.

Examines the extent of poverty among American youth between 1959 and 1982.

*Rodgers, Harrell. *Poor Women, Poor Families -- The Economic Plight of America's Female-Headed Households*. New York: M.E. Sharpe, Inc, 1986.

Traces the rise in poor households headed by women over a number of years. Compares the U.S. social welfare system with that of Europe, and makes suggestions for reform.

*Rodgers-Rose, L.F. (Ed.) "The Black Woman: A Historical Overview." *The Black Woman*. Edited by L.F. Rodgers-Rose. Beverly Hills, CA: Sage, 1980, pp. 15-25.

Outlines the history of black American women, including their African heritage, the legacy of slavery, and the post-slavery period. Contends that the African women were raised in an environment that stressed the importance of motherhood. They were independent and earned their own living. Shows that during slavery, though women were separated from their children, the bond of motherhood remained strong. Finds that life for the black slave was difficult, but their African socialization help them to remain strong in the face of all their perils. Argues that after slavery black women had to deal with many hardships because of economic structure. Shows that many of them are the heads of their families and this results in poverty for a large number of them.

Rodman, Hyman, and Patricia Voydanoff. *Social Class and Parent's Aspirations for Their Children.* Detroit, MI: Merrill Palmer Institute, 1968.

Interviewed parents of black children enrolled in Head Start in regard to their aspirations for education, occupation, and income of their children. It was found that the social class of the parents was inversely related to the width of the range of aspirations, but that the peak of the lower class was the same as that of the middle class.

*Rogers, S. "Situational Factors Affecting Language Usage of Low-Income Black Preschool Children." Doctoral Dissertation. Catholic University, 1976.

Rollock, Barbara. *The Black Experience in Children's Books.* New York: The Dial Press, 1974.

Catalogues books which are suitable for children of all ages and some for adults to share with children.

*Romaine, M.F. *Testimony on Behalf of the Zale Corporation Before the Committee on Labor and Human Resources.* U.S. Senate. 16 November 1983.

Testified about the child care center at the Zale corporation home office which opened to serve 70 families in January 1979. The center has improved employee morale and created bonds among the parents; in five years of operation, not a single negative event has surfaced. Romaine further stated that as the need for child care continues to grow, they hope that there is not an attempt to provide universally available, public-supported child care in this country.

Roman, Virginia. "Statement for the Record." *Oversight Hearing of the Head Start Program, Subcommittee on Human Resources of the Committee on Education and Labor, House of Representatives.* Government Printing Office, Washington, D.C., February 23, 1982, pp. 76-78.

Rosario, Jose, and John M. Love. *Evaluations of Bilingual Programs: Examples of the Reproductive Functions of Evaluative Research, Bilingual Education Paper Series. Volume 4. No. 7.* Los Angeles: California State University, April 1979.

Contrasts examples of bilingual research and describes the Head Start Strategy for Spanish Speaking Children.

*Rosenbaum, Sara. *Providing Effective Prenatal Care for Pregnant Teenagers.* Washington, D.C.: Children's Defense Fund, 1983.

*Ross, Catherine J. "Early Skirmishes with Poverty: The Historical Roots of Head Start." *Project Head Start: A Legacy of the War on Poverty.* Edited by Edward Zigler and Jeanette Valentine. New York: Free Press, 1979, pp. 21-42.

Looks at the development of formal education in the U.S. from the early 1800s through the 1900s. Discusses the care of indigent children, kindergartens, and preschool health programs. Examines the early involvement of the Federal government in day care programs in the 1930s. Shows how this led to more involvement of the government, thus giving birth to Project Head Start.

Ross, Heather L., and Isabel V. Sawhill. *Time of Transition -- The Growth of Families Headed by Women.* Washington, D.C.: The Urban Institute, 1975, pp. 9-96.

Deals with the single-parent family, a phenomenon that has grown at a very rapid rate. Suggests that changing economic conditions, and shifts in government policy is creating more female-headed families, and that this explains the rates of female headship which are much higher for some subgroups than for others.

*Rosser, P.L., and U.J. Oyemeade. "Development in Black Children." *Advances in Behavioral Pediatrics*, 1 (1980): 153-179.

Rejects the assumption that black children are deficient in their behavior. Hypothesizes that the behavior of black children is logical and valid and that a variety of stimuli may have the same effect on the development of the child though it may be manifested in different ways. Finds support for these ideas in the works of several writers such as Piaget. Discusses certain developmental areas, e.g., intellectual, language, in order to support the hypothesis.

Roth, R.W. "The Effects of 'Black Studies' on Negro Fifth Grade Students." *Journal of Negro Education* 38(1969): 435-439.

Investigates the change in students' black pride and self-concept after being exposed to "Black Studies."

*Royster, E.C., J.C. Larson, T. Fer, S. Fosburg, M. Nauta, B. Nelson, and G. Takata. *A National Survey of Head Start Graduates and Their Peers*. Cambridge, MA: Abt Associates, Inc. Report No. AAI-77-54, 1978.

Rudd, N.M., and P.C. McHenry. "Working Women: Issues and Implications." *Journal of Home Economics* (Winter 1980): 26-29.

Ruopp, R., J. Travers, F. Glantz, and C. Coelen. *Children at the Center. Summary Findings and Their Policy Implications. Final Report of the National Day Care Study*. Cambridge, MA: Abt Associates, 1979.

*Ryan, Sally (Ed.). *A Report on Longitudinal Evaluations of Preschool Programs, Vol. 1*. Washington, D.C.: USDHEW, Publication No. (OHD) 74-24, 1974.

Attempts to assess the impact of preschool intervention programs by reviewing the findings of small, controlled long-term evaluations of programs in various parts of the USA. Eight researchers with available longitudinal data contributed to this volume. All of the articles report an immediate impact of preschool intervention on a short-term basis.

*Ryan, W. *Blaming the Victim*. New York: Pantheon Books, 1971.

Saikowski, Charlotte. "A Time for Families." *Christian Science Monitor* (July 22, 1980): 12-14; (July 23, 1980): 12-13; (July 25, 1980): 12-13.

Sandoval-Martinez, Steven. "Findings from the Head Start Bilingual Curriculum Development and Evaluation Effort." *Journal of the National Association for Bilingual Education* 7 (1982): 1-12.

Bilingual children who received bilingual preschool services made greater preschool gains than comparison group children who received regular English-language preschool services. In addition, English-preferring children who were placed in bilingual classrooms achieved the same developmental gains over the preschool year as those who were placed in regular English-language preschool classrooms.

Sato, I.S. "The Culturally Different Gifted Child-The Dawning of His Day?" *Exceptional Children* 40 (May 1974): 572-576.

Proposes a definition for the term culturally gifted child. Re-examines the identification procedure and calls for more research with an emphasis on environmental and sociological variables. Discusses the need for qualitatively differentiated program provision.

Sawhill, Isabel. "Discrimination and Poverty Among Women Who Head Families." *Women and the Workplace: The Implications of Occupational Segregation*. Edited by Martha Blaxall, and Barbara Reagan. Chicago: University of Chicago Press, 1976.

Examines the reasons for the growth in families headed by women. Suggests that labor market discrimination and occupational segregation contribute to the existing poverty among many of these families.

cales, P. *Sex Education and the Prevention of Teenage Pregnancy -- An Overview of Policies and Programs in the United States*. Washington, D.C.: Family Impact Seminar, George Washington, University, n.d., p. 6.

Scanzoni, John A. *The Black Family in Modern Society*. Boston: Allyn and Bacon, Inc., 1971.

Examines the premise, posited by E. Franklin Frazier, that there is a strong link between black family structure and economic resources. The concluding recommendation of this study is that black families at every class level will become structurally indistinguishable from the dominant form of family in this society if the promise of the American Dream is permitted to become a reality for them. Scanzoni recommends job mobility and equality of occupational opportunity.

Scanzoni, John A. *Sex Roles, Life Styles, and Child Bearing*. New York: The Free Press, 1975.

Scanzoni, John A. *The Black Family in Modern Society: Patterns of Stability and Security*. Chicago: University of Chicago Press, 1977.

canzoni, John A. *Sex Roles, Women's Work, and Marital Conflict*. Lexington, MA: DC Heath and Co., 1978.

Scanzoni, John A. "Family: Crisis or Change?" *Christian Century* 98 (Aug. 12-19, 1981): 794-799.

Scarr, Sandra. "Needed: A Complete Head Start." *Elementary School Journal* 69 (5)(1969): 236-241.

Discusses the social and biological deprivations associated with poor children.

Schaefer, E.S. "Converging Conceptual Models for Maternal Behaviors for Child Behavior." *Parental Attitudes and Child Behavior*. Edited by J.C. Gildewell. Springfield, IL: Charles C. Thomas, 1961.

*Schiller, Bradley R. *The Economics of Poverty and Discrimination*. Englewood Cliffs, N.J.: Prentice-Hall, Inc., 1980.

Discusses important developments in poverty and discrimination. Offers an initial statement of the problem, a detailed analysis of possible causes, and a review of present and potential policies.

Schwarz, J. Conrad, Marianne L. Barton-Henry, and Thomas Pruzinsky. "Assessing Child-Rearing Behaviors: A Comparison of Ratings Made by Mother, Father, Child, and Sibling on the CRPBI." *Child Development* 56 (April 1985): 462-479.

Looks at the reliability and validity of scales from the Child's Report of Parental Behavior (CRPBI). Data are also presented on the utility of aggregating the ratings of multiple observers.

Schweinhart, Lawrence J. *Early Childhood Development Programs in the Eighties: The National Picture*. Ypsilanti, MI: High Scope Press, 1985.

Schweinhart, Lawrence J., and Steven Barrett. *South Carolina's Early Childhood Programs Are A Good Investment*. Ypsilanti, MI: High/Scope Educational Research Foundation, 1984.

Reports to the Governor evidence on the effectiveness of South Carolina's early childhood programs in helping children achieve greater success in first grade. Specifically, it states that these programs for low-income families help to: 1. improve intellectual performance and scholastic achievement; 2. reduce unnecessary special education placements; 3. reduce high school drop out rates; 4. prevent some juvenile delinquency and teenage pregnancy; and 5. improve employability and decrease the need for welfare assistance.

hweinhart, Lawrence J., and D.P. Weikart. *Young Children Grow Up: The Effects of the Perry Preschool Program On Youths Through Age 15.* Ypsilanti, MI.: High/Scope Educational Research Foundation, 1980.

chweinhart, Lawrence J., and David P. Weikart. "What Do We Know So Far? Do Head Start Programs Work?" *High Scope Resource Magazine* 5 (Winter 1986): 1,20, 22-23.

Critiques the report of the Head Start Evaluation, Synthesis, and Utilization Project by CSR, Inc. (see McKey, Condelli, Ganson, Barrett, McConkey and Plantz, 1985). The authors argue that this report draws conclusions without adequate evidence; fails to consider all of the relevant evidence available; overgeneralizes the findings of studies; and fails to distinguish between low quality of design and high quality of design studies.

ott, Ralph. "Home Start: Family-Centered Preschool Enrichment for Black and White Children." Psychology in the Schools 10, no.2(1973): 140- 146.

lect Committee on Children, Youth and Families. *Teen Pregnancy: What is Being Done? A State by State Look.* Washington, D.C.: U.S. Government Printing Office, Dec. 1985.

Reports on the incidence of teenage pregnancy and the efforts of 49 states to deal with this problem.

Senderowitz, Judith, and John M. Paxman. *Adolescent Fertility: Worldwide Concerns*. Washington, D.C.: Population Reference Bureau, 1985. (Population Bulletin, v. 40, no.2.)

*Seymour, H., and C.M. Seymour. "Black English and Standardized American English Contrasts in Consonantal Development of Four and Five Year Old Children." *Journal of Speech and Hearing Disorders* 46 (1981): 274-280.

Shapiro, S. "Parent Involvement in Day Care: Its Impact on Staff and Classroom Environments." *Child Welfare* 56 (1977): 749-760.

*Shipman, V.C. *Disadvantaged Children and their First School Experiences: Demographic Indexes of Socioeconomic Status and Maternal Behaviors on Attitudes*. Princeton, N.J.: Educational Testing Services, 1972, ERIC ED069424.

*Shortridge, K. "Working Poor Women." *Women: A Feminist Perspective*. Edited by J. Freeman. Palo Alto, CA: Mayfield Publishing Co., 1976.

Shreve, Anita. "Careers and the Lure of Motherhood." *The New York Times Magazine* (November 21, 1982): 38.

Shreve, Anita. "The Working Mother as Role Model." *The New York Times Magazine* (Sept. 9, 1984): 39-43, 50, 52, 54.

Argues that as increasing numbers of women enter the work force, researchers are beginning to study the psychological and social effects this may have on their children.

*Shriver, Sargent. "The Origins of Head Start." *Project Head Start*. Edited by E. Zigler and J. Valentine. New York: Free Press, 1979, pp. 49-67.

Shure, M.B. "Social Competence as a Problem-Solving Skill." *Social Competence*. Edited by J.D. Wine and M.D. Smye. New York: Guildford Press, 1981.

Skerry, Peter. "The Charmed Life of Head Start." *Public Interest* 73 (1983): 18-40.

Reviews a series of challenges that Head Start has weathered throughout its existence to foster the claim that Head Start has had a "charmed" existence. Skerry argues that one reason Head Start has endured is because it has managed to be many things to many constituencies -- for example, a compensatory education program, a provider of health services, a catalyst for community change. While Head Start has never lived up to its original claims, Head Start has been able to deliver something to just about everyone.

kolnick, Arlene. "The Family and its Discontents." *Society* 18 (Jan.-Feb. 1981): 42-47.

Divides theories about the family into two groups: 1. that which sees the family as a timeless entity; and 2. that which sees only crisis and disintegration in contemporary family. Suggests that the latter is more popular today. Argues that these is much evidence for it as seen in the high divorce rates and the changes in sex roles and division of labor within the family.

aughter, Diana T. "Maternal Antecedents of the Academic Achievement Behaviors of Afro-American Head Start Children." *Educational Horizons* (1969): 24-29.

aughter, Diana T. "Relation of Early Parent-Teacher Socialization Influences to Achievement Orientation Among Low Income Black Children." *The Social Context of Learning and Development.* Edited by J. Glidewell. New York: Gardner, 1977, pp. 101-131.

ughter, Diana T. "Parental Potency and the Achievements of Inner-City Black Children." *American Journal of Orthopsychiatry* 40 (1970): 433-440.

*Slaughter, Diana T. "What is the Future of Head Start?" *Young Children* (March 1982): 3-9.

Argues that Head Start has accomplished everything but what it was originally expected to accomplish: equal educational opportunity. As a primary prevention program, Head Start's accomplishments surpass the limited, rather naive, early expectations. Head Start instigated some crucial dialogues between people of highly diverse social backgrounds who cared about poor children.

*Small, Gloria. "Remote Battlegrounds: The Office of Special Field Projects." *Project Head Start.* Edited by E. Zigler and J. Valentine. New York: Free Press, 1979, pp. 339-348.

Discusses the widening influence of the Head Start program in such places as federal Indian reservations, Puerto Rico, the U.S. Virgin Islands, and the U.S. Territory of the Pacific Islands. Talks about the problems which had to be overcome. Evaluates the programs in the above territories.

Smith, A.D., A.E. Fortune, and W.J. Reid. "WIN, Work, and Welfare." *Social Service Review* 49(1975): 396-404.

Reveals that a number of people are still on welfare after being on the WIN program for about 18 months. Found that women gain more from WIN in terms of education and training, while men are encouraged to return quickly to work though mainly unskilled jobs.

Smith, Barbara Lester. "An Investigation of a Parent Intervention Model on Changing Attitudes of Head Start Mothers." *Dissertation Abstracts International* (1980): 41(10): Section A. 4278.

Measures parent attitude change related to child rearing and locus of control brought about by a discussion treatment program. A focused parent education curriculum was used as a discussion guide. After the treatment, observed behaviors of the experimental group parents indicated that they were feeling much more able to control their environments and intervene for themselves and their children.

Smith, C. "Poor Head Start and its Children." *The New Republic* 160 (1969): 11-13.

*Smith, Marshall S., and Joan S. Bissell, "Report Analysis: The Impact of Head Start." *Harvard Educational Review* 49 (Feb. 1970): 51-104.

*Social Research Group, George Washington University. *A Review of Head Start Research Since 1969 and an Annotated Bibliography.* Washington, D.C.: Social Research Group, 1977.

*Sorenson, Robert. *Adolescent Sexuality in Contemporary America.* New York: World Publishing Co., 1973.

Sorkin, A.S. "On the Occupational Status of Women, 1870-1970." *American Journal of Economist Sociology.* 32(1973): 235-243.

Sponseller, D.B., and J.S. Fink. "Early Childhood Education: A National Profile of Early Childhood Educator's Views." *Education and Urban Society* 12 (February 1980): 163-173.

Sponseller, D.B., and J.S. Fink. "Public Policy Toward Children: Identifying the Problems." *Young Children and Social Policy.* Edited by W.M. Bridgeland, and E.A. Duane. Beverly Hills, CA: Sage, 1982., pp. 14-20.

Identifies four problems with America's response to children: the substitution of talk for action; inability to form consensus goals; attention to the needs of some children, but not to the needs of others; and the promotion of indirect, rather than direct, solutions. Explanations for these problems are offered as: individualistic/family oriented cultural values impinge on social action; economic priorities influences action direction; crisis-oriented approach to change; and inexperienced child advocates.

*Stack, C.B., and H. Semmel. "Social Insecurity: Welfare Policy and the Structure of Poor Families." *Welfare In America*. Edited by B.R. Mandell. Englewood Cliffs, N.J.: Prentice-Hall, Inc., 1975, pp. 89-103.

Stack, C.B. All Our Kin. New York: Harper and Row, 1974.

Staines, C., J.H. Place, L.J. Shepard, and P. O'Conner. "Wive's Employment Status and Marital Adjustment: Yet Another Look." *Psychology of Women Quarterly* 3 (1978): 90-120.

Found that the negative effects of wives' employment on wives' reports of marital adjustment restricted specifically to mothers of preschool children, and to wives with less than a high school education.

Stanford Research Institute International. *An Analysis of Government Expenditures Consequent on Teenage Pregnancy*. Menlo Park, CA: Stanford Research Institute International, 1979.

Staples, Robert. "Public Policy and the Changing Status of Black Families." *The Family Coordinator* XXII, No. 3 (1973): 345-351.

Reviews the methods in which governmental policies have historically denigrated the functioning of black families. A review of the literature concerning government policy formulations for families with no and low incomes and description of the Moynihan Family Assistance Program (with its "workfare" requirement) are summarized and critiqued. Through utilizing this material, Staples proposes a public policy for low income black families based upon what he has determined to be the changing status of black families.

State of Families. New York: Family Service of America, 1984.

Provides data on what is happening to families, including number and location, changing values and life situations, and who gets the economic rewards.

**The Status of Handicapped Children in Head Start Programs: Seventh Annual Report of the U.S. Department of Health, Education and Welfare to the Congress of the United States on Services Provided to Handicapped Children in Project Head Start.* Washington, D.C.: USDHEW, February, 1980.

*Steady, F.C. (Ed.) *The Black Women Cross-Culturally.* Cambridge, MA: Schenkown Publishing Company, 1981.

Brings together a body of literature on the black women, as she is seen in Africa, the Caribbean, South America and the United States of America. Examines the effects of colonialism on the status of African women. Tries to redefine the traditional concepts of "family" and "household" in the Caribbean context. Discusses the spread of capitalism and the images of women in South America, and the influence of racism and class in the lives of black women in the U.S.

Stein, Harry. "The Case for Staying Home." *Esquire* 101(June 1984): 142-144.

Argues that a mother's place is not necessarily in the home. The issue is whether women can work and have a child without suffering. The conclusion of some liberated men and women is: now that woman can have it all, her family has a lot to lose.

Steiner, Gilbert Y. *The Children's Cause.* Washington, D.C.: The Brookings Institution, 1976.

Examines the apparatus for making children's policy, and evaluates policy proposals against the background of tension between proponents of public, rather than private, responsibility. Contends that the divisiveness of public relief politics is largely attributable to the growth in the number and cost of dependent children.

*Steiner, Gilbert Y. *The Futility of Family Policy*. Washington, D.C.: The Brookings Institution, 1981.

*Stengel, Richard. "The Missing-Father Myth." *Time*. 126(December 9, 1985): 90.

*Stephan, S. *Head Start Issues in FY 1986: Funding, Administration, and Recent Evaluations*. Washington, D.C.: Congressional Research Service, January 15, 1986.

Reviews the background of Project Head Start including federal administration issues, local administration issues, and program evaluation reports.

*St. Pierre, M. "Black Female Single Parent Family Life: A Preliminary Sociological Perspective." *The Black Sociologist* 9(1982): 28-47.

Stern, Carolyn. *Teacher Ratings of Behavioral Objectives as Related to Performance of Children on Specific Tasks*. Los Angeles: University of California, 1980.

Examines the relationship between Head Start children's test performance and the objectives of Head Start teachers. The children tested scored highest on those items the teachers had rated high in importance and lowest in those rated low in performance. The author suggests that one of the reasons for the negative findings of the Westinghouse Study (1969) might be a lack of correspondence between the objectives of Head Start teachers and the types of instruments used in achievement testing.

*Stevens, J.H. "Child Development Knowledge and Parenting Skills." *Family Relations* 33(1984): 237-244.

Looks at the relationship between parents' knowledge about child development and their ability to provide a quality home learning environment. 243 black and white mothers of infants were studied. Controlling for income and eduction, mothers who were more knowledgeable about critical environmental factors and infant normative development scored higher on the parenting skill measure.

*Stevens, J.H., and B.N. Duffield, "Age and Parenting Skill Among Black Women in Poverty." *Early Childhood Research Quarterly* 1 (1986): 221-235.

Examined the relationship between mothers' age and measures of maternal behavior using a sample of 158 poor black mothers and their infants. When education was controlled, the mothers' age was positively correlated with general parenting ability and with verbal responsivity and nonpunitiveness. However, mothers aged 21 and older who became pregnant while teachers demonstrated less optimal parenting and had infants who showed less optimal development.

Stine, O.C., R.V. Rider, and E. Sweeney, "School Leaving Due to Pregnancy in an Urban Adolescent Population." *American Journal of Public Health* 54 (1964): 1-6.

Examines the incidence of pregnancy among school-age girls in Baltimore, Maryland, and found a large number of premature births and infant mortality related to mothers under 16.

*Stipek, D.J., Jeanette Valentine, and E. Zigler. "Project Head Start: A Critique of Theory and Practice." *Project Head Start. A Legacy of the War on Poverty.* Edited by Edward Zigler and Jeanette Valentine. N.Y.: Free Press, 1979, pp. 477-494.

Appraises the theories behind Head Start and the problems encountered in their implementation.

Stone, J. "General Philosophy: Preschool Education Within Head Start." *Project Head Start. A Legacy of the War on Poverty.* Edited by Edward Zigler and Jeanette Valentine. N.Y.: Free Press, 1979, pp. 163-174.

Describes how the educational component of Head Start emerged out of a ten-week education program for poor children in New Haven, Connecticut. Points out that the program began with the publication of a curriculum manual which presents a philosophical overview of education for young children. Explains how the program was planned, how families were informed about it, and how children were recruited. Discusses how the first lessons were executed, and the reactions of the children.

*Subcommittee of Human Resources of the Committee on Education and Labor, House of Representatives. 1980, *Oversight of Head Start: Lasting Effects.* Washington, D.C.: Government Printing Office, February 20, 1980.

*Subcommittee on Human Resources of the Committee on Education and Labor, House of Representatives. *Oversight Hearing on the Head Start Program.* Washington, D.C.: Government Printing Office, February 23, 1982.

*Subcommittee of Human Resources of the Committee on Education and Labor, House of Representatives. *Authorizations for Head Start, Follow Through, Community Services, and Establish Child Care Information and Referral Services.* Washington, D.C.: Government Printing Office, March 21, 1984.

Taylor, D.L. (Ed.) *Nature of Communication Disorders in Culturally and Linguistically Diverse Populations.* San Diego, CA: College-Hill Press, 1986.

Focuses on background issues pertaining to cultural and linguistic diversity. Deals with language variations within the U.S. and language acquisition in Black Americans. Discusses the prevalence and nature of communication disorders in Black Americans, Hispanic Americans, Native Americans and other indigenous peoples of North America.

Thomas, Susan B. *Research on Approaches to Early Education: An Abstract, Bibliography.* Urbana, Illinois: ERIC Clearinghouse on Early Childhood Education, 1974.

Contains 157 citations which include studies of parental involvement, research on the long-term effects of educational intervention programs, and research on specific program models and model comparisons.

Thomas, William V. *Two-Income Families*. Washington, D.C.: Editorial Research Reports, 1979, v. 2, no. 2.

Discusses America's new economic elite; wives in the U.S. workforce; and the impact of dual earner families on families and society.

Thompson, Donald L. "Head Start at Home: A Model for Rural Areas." *Appalachia* 5 (Jan. 1972): 17-19.

Thompson, Roger. "Sexual Revolution Reconsidered." *Congressional Quarterly* (1984): 511-527.

*Thorman, M.S. "An Exploratory Investigation of the Childbearing Attitudes in a Population of Teenagers." *Dissertation Abstracts International* University Microfilm No. 8129885, 1982, 42 3021A.

*Thornburg, H. *Teenage Pregnancy: Have They Reached Epidemic Proportions?* Phoenix, Arizona :Governor's Council on Children, Youth, and Families, 1979.

Thornton, Arland, and Deborah Freedman. "The Changing American Family." Washington, D.C.: Population Reference Bureau, 1983. Population Bulletin, v. 38, no. 4.

Documents recent changes in American family patterns resulting both from long-term trends in urbanization, industrialization, and economic growth and the disruption of the Great Depression and World War II, as well as changed attitudes toward marriage, parenthood, divorce, and the roles of women.

Tilly, A., and J.W. Scott. *Women, Work and Family*. New York: Holt, Rinehard and Winston, 1978.

Presents historical and anthropological perspectives on the impact of social and economic changes on women's work.

**Time*. "Children Having Children." (December 9, 1985): 78-90.

Torrance, E.P. "Dare We Hope Again?" *Gifted Child Quarterly* 22 (1978): 292-312.

Examines efforts made between 1958-1978 to help gifted minority students. Found no consistent plan for the development of the gifted.

*Travers, J.R., and R.J. Light (Eds.). *Learning From Experience: Evaluating Early Childhood Demonstration Programs*. Washington, D.C.: National Academy Press, 1982.

*Treiman, D., and K. Terrell. "Sex and the Process of Status Attainment: A Comparison of Working Men and Women." *American Sociological Review* 40 (1970): 174-200.

Compares the process of educational, occupational and income attainment of working men and women ages 30-44. Finds that while the process of educational and occupational attainment is the same for men and women, women still earn less controlling for experience and hours worked.

*Trickett, P.K. "Career Development in Project Head Start: A Legacy of the War on Poverty." *Project Head Start*. Edited by Edward Zigler and Jeanette Valentine. New York: The Free Press, 1979, pp. 315-338.

12,000 Head Start parents have received college training for credit through the Head Start program, and well over 1,000 have received A.A. or B.A. degrees.

*Troutman, D.E., and J.S. Falk. "Speaking Black English and Reading: Is There a Problem of Interference?" *Journal of Negro Education* 51 (1982): 123-133.

Turner, Ralph R., and Linda K. Boulter. "Predicting Social Competence: The Validity of the PIPS." Paper Presented at the 89th Annual Meeting of the American Psychological Association, Los Angeles, CA, August 24-28, 1982. 16p.

Concludes that the ICPS model may prove to be an important assessment and training tool for developing social competence in young children. The measures used are appended.

Turner, Ralph R., David B. Connell, and Arthur Mathis. "The Preschool Child or the Family? Changing Models of Developmental Intervention." *Life Span Developmental Psychology: Intervention.* Edited by Ralph R. Turner, and Wayne W. Reese. New York: Academic Press, 1980.

Umansky, Warren. "On families and the Re-Valuing of Childhood." *Childhood Education* 59 (Mar.-Apr. 1983): 259-266.

Discusses the evolution of today's family and examines issues and solutions that may contribute to a re-valuing of the child's place in society.

U.S. Bureau of the Census. *Divorce, Child Custody and Child Support.* Current Population Reports, U.S. Department of Commerce, 1979, No. 84.

U.S. Bureau of the Census. *Marital Status and Living Arrangements. Current Population Report.* (Series P-20. No. 52.) Washington, D.C.: Author, 1981A.

U.S. Bureau of the Census. *Trends in Child Care Arrangements of Working Mothers. Current Population Report.* (Series P-23, No. 117.) Washington, D.C.: Author, 1982.

U.S. Bureau of the Census. *Money Income and Poverty Status of Families and Persons in the United States.* (Series P-60 No. 145.) Washington, D.C.: Author, 1983A.

U.S. Bureau of the Census. *Statistical Abstract of The United States: 1982-1983.* Washington, D.C.: Author, 1983B.

*U.S. Bureau of the Census. *Current Population Surveys*. U.S. Department of Commerce, 1985.

*U.S. Congress. House Committee on Education and Labor, Subcommittee on Human Resources of the Committee on Education and Labor. *Oversight Hearings on the Head Start Program*. Washington, D.C.: U.S. Congress, 1982.

Reviews and discusses the Reagan administration's plans for Project Head Start as presented in the controversial and widely disseminated policy paper entitled "Head Start: Directions for the Next Three Years." Outlines objectives established for Head Start and the policy options and actions that could be used to reach those objectives. The five major objectives outlined in the strategy paper focus on enrollment, program quality, training and technical assistance, coordination with community groups, and program management and administration. Special attention is given to the proposal for converting parent and child centers to regular Head Start programs and descriptions of the work of such centers are included in the text. Appended materials include the ACYF policy paper, related news articles, and many responses to the paper from parents, centers, legislators, agencies, and organizations.

*U.S. Congress. House Committee on Energy and Commerce. Subcommittee on Health and the Environment. *Pregnancy-Related Health Services*. Hearings, 99th Congress, 1st Session. Washington, D.C. Government Printing Office, 1985. Serial no. 99-13.

Hearings on the prevention of low birthweight, Feb. 25, 1985; Adolescent Pregnancy and Reauthorizaiton of Adolescent Family Life Act--H.R. 927, Mar. 21, 1985; Family Planning Act Reauthorization, Mar. 27, 1985.

*U.S. Congress. House Committee on Post Office and Civil Service. Subcommittee on Census and Population. *Demographics of Adolescent Pregnancy in the United States*. Joint Hearing, Subcommittee on Census and Population of the Committee on Post Office and Civil Service, and Subcommittee on Health and the Environment of the Committee on Energy and Commerce, House of Representatives, 99th Congress, 1st session. Apr. 30, 1985. Washington, D.C.: Government Printing Office, 1985.

Serial no. 99-5 (Committee on Post Office and Civil Service); Serial no. 99-8 (Committee on Energy and Commerce).

*U.S. Congress. House Committee on Ways and Means. Subcommittee on Public Assistance and Unemployment Compensation. *Administration's Proposed Savings in Unemployment Compensation, Public Assistance, and Social Services Programs.* 97th Congress, 1st Session, March 11-12, 1981. Washington, D.C.: U.S. Government Printing Office.

*U.S. Congress. House Committee on Ways and Means. Subcommittee on Oversight and Subcommittee on Health and the Environment of the Committee on Energy and Commerce. *Impact of Budget Cuts on Children.* Washington, D.C.: Government Printing Offices, March 3, 1982.

*U.S. Congress. House Committee on Ways and Means. Subcommittee on Public Assistance, and Unemployment Compensation. *Teenage Pregnancy Issues.* Hearing, 99th Congress, 1st session. May 7, 1985. Washington, D.C.: Government Printing Office, 1985. Serial 99-33.

*U.S. Congress. House Select Committee on Children, Youth, and Families. *Teen Parents and their Children: Issues and Programs.* Hearing, 98th Congress, 1st Session. July 20, 1983. Washington, D.C.: Government Printing Office, 1984.

*U.S. Congress. House Select Committee on Children, Youth, and Families. *Teen Pregnancy: What is Being Done? A State-by-State Look; Report Together with Additional and Minority Views.* Washington, D.C.: Government Printing Office, 1986.

*U.S. Congress. Public Law 88-452: *Economic Opportunity Act of 1964*. Aug 20, 1964, 78 stat. 508.

*U.S. Congress. Senate Committee on Labor and Human Resources. Subcommittee on Family and Human Services. *Adolescents in Crisis: Parental Involvement*. Hearing. 98th Congress, 2nd session. Washington, D.C.: Government Printing Office, February 1984.

*U.S. Department of Commerce. Bureau of the Census. Current Population Reports, Series P-20, No. 198. *Daytime Care of Children: October 1974 and February 1975*. Washington, D.C.: Government Printing Office, October 1976.

*U.S. Department of Commerce. Bureau of the Census. Current Population Reports, Series P-60. No. 120. *Money Income and Poverty Status of Families and Persons in the United States: 1978 (Advance Report)*. Washington, D.C.: U.S. Government Printing Office, 1979, Table 18.

*U.S. Department of Commerce. Bureau of the Census. Current Population Reports, Series P-60, No. 127. *Money Income and Poverty Status of Families and Persons in the United States: 1980*. (Advance data from the March 1981 Current Population Survey.) Washington, D.C.: Government Printing Office, 1981A.

*U.S. Department of Commerce. Bureau of the Census. Current Population Reports, Series P-20, No. 365. *Marital Status and Living Arrangements: May 1980*. Washington, D.C.: Government Printing Office, October 1981B.

*U.S. Department of Commerce. Bureau of the Census. *Statistical Abstract of the United States 1981*. Washington, D.C.: Government Printing Office, 1981C.

*U.S. Department of Commerce. Bureau of the Census. *Current Population Survey*. 1984 and 1985.

*U.S. Department of Health, Education, and Welfare. *Perspectives on Human*

Deprivation: Biological, Psychological, and Sociological. Washington, D.C.: U.S. Government Printing Office, 1968.

*U.S.D.H.E.W. *Health, United States, 1976-1977.* Washington, D.C.: U.S. Government Printing Office, 1977. National Center for Health Statistics, 1977A.

*U.S.D.H.E.W. *Hospital and Surgical Insurance Coverage, United States -- 1974.* Hyattsville, MD.: National Center for Health Statistics, Series 10, No. 117, August 1977B.

*U.S.D.H.E.W. *Preliminary Report: U.S. Immunization Survey, 1978.* Atlanta, GA.: Public Health Service, Center for Disease Control, 1980.

*U.S. Department of Health and Human Services. *Annual Summary for the United States, 1978: Births, Deaths, Divorces, and Marriages.* Hyattsville, MD.: National Center for Health Statistics, Monthly Vital Statistics Report, Vo. 27 No. 13, August 13, 1979A.

*USDHHS. *The Status of Children, Youth, and Families 1979.* Washington, D.C.: Government Printing Office, 1979B. Publication number (OHDS) 80-30274.

*USDHHS. Monthly Vital Statistics Report. Vol. 29, No. 1, *Final Natality Statistics 1978.* Hyattsville, MD: National Center for Health Statistics, April 28, 1980.

*USDHHS. *Head Start: Directions for the Next Three Years.* Washington, D.C.: ACYF, 1981.

Provides a "discussion draft" of the objectives that ACYF established in its three-year plan for Head Start. ACYF identifies five major objectives for Head Start: 1. maintaining and increasing Head Start enrollment; 2. improving program quality; 3. improving and streamlining the delivery of training and technical assistance; 4. strengthening relationships with other public, private and voluntary agencies and organizations; and 5. improving administration and management.

*USDHHS. Office of the Inspector General, Region X. *Head Start National Program Inspection*. Washington, D.C.: USDHHS, March 1984A.

Reports on the enrollment and attendance issues within Head Start. The report rated deficiencies in calculating, reporting and monitoring enrollment and attendance; and noted the underrepresentation of whites in Head Start; and the overrepresentation of minorities in Head Start.

*USDHHS. Office of Human Development Services, Administration for Children, Youth, and Families. Head Start Bureau. *Head Start Program Performance Standards (45-CFR 1304).* Washington, D.C.: U.S.D.H.H.S. Publication No. (OHDS) 84-31131, November 1984B.

Sets out the goals of Project Head Start as they may be achieved by the program components, with emphasis on the performance standards.

*USDHHS. Office of the Inspector General. *A Program Inspection of Head Start, Unemployment Insurance Cost.* Washington, D.C.: USDHHS, February 1985A.

Reports that about three-fourths of all Head Start grantees surveyed drew unemployment compensation during the summer, contrary to the primary intent of unemployment insurance laws.

*USDHHS. Office of the Inspector General. *A Program Inspection of Head Start. Wage Comparability to Day Care Agencies.* Washington, D.C.: USDHHS, February 1985B.

Reports data from 62 Head Start projects and 188 day care agencies located in nine regions (18 states). The study found that hourly wages are higher, and annual wages are lower, within Head Start. Head Start staff had more extensive duties and responsibilities than day care staff.

*USDHHS. OHDS. ACYF. Head Start Bureau. *Project Head Start Statistical Fact Sheet.* Washington, D.C.: USDHHS, December 1985C and January 1987.

Lists a number of facts about Head Start: budget, number of programs, enrollment, racial/ethnic composition, ages of children, location of sites, number of sites, cost per child, number of staff, number of volunteers, and other facts.

*USDHHS. (1987.) See USDHHS, 1985C.

U.S. Department of Housing and Urban Development. Office of Policy Research and Development. Washington, D.C.: Government Printing Office, August 1980, p. 52.

*U.S. Department of Labor. *U.S. Working Women: A Data Book.* Washington, D.C.: Author, 1977.

U.S. Department of Labor. Employment and Training Administration. *Employment and Training Report of the President 1980*, Table G-9, Washington, D.C.: Government Printing Office, 1980.

*U.S. Department of Labor. *Employers and Child Care: Establishing Services Through the Workplace.* Washington, D.C.: U.S. Department of Labor, The Women's Bureau Pamphlet 23, 1982.

Reports of the Women's Bureau's initiative to establish employer-sponsored child care systems throughout the country. The book outlines the child care needs and services available; describes employer/labor involvement in programs that support working parents; discusses how to analyze the costs and funding resources for each program; conveys general tax issues related to employer-sponsored child care services; and provides information on the program components of a child care center, including resources to guide planners in program development and implementation. The appendix is a list of employer-sponsored child care programs in the United States.

*Valentine, Jeanette. "Program Development in Head Start: A Multifaceted Approach to Meeting the Needs of Families and Children." *Project Head Start: A Legacy of the War on Poverty.* Edited by Edward Zigler and Jeanette, Valentine. New York: Free Press, 1979, pp. 349-366.

Claims that Head Start has experimented with a number of approaches to meet the needs of children and families in poverty. Discusses comprehensive sevices to families and children, Health Serivce delivery demonstrations, and special programs for targed groups as part of a review of programs tried over the years. Examines the coordination of Head Start with other agencies serving disadvantaged children and looks at directions for the future.

*Valentine, Jeanette, C.J. Ross, and E. Zigler. "Epilogue." *Project Head Start.* New York: Free Press, 1979, pp.509-516.

Gives an overview of the Head Start program. Looks at the problems it had to overcome and the successes it has had. Argues that the involvement of parents may, in the long run, be more important than the children's performance. Sees the present status of the program as a national laboratory that offers a combination of educationl, health, and social welfare services to the nation's children. Looks to the future and concludes that the flexible nature of the program should allow it to adopt to change in the future.

*Valentine, Jeanette, and Evan Stark. "The Social Context of Parent Involvement in Head Start." *Project Head Start.* Edited by Edward Zigler and Jeanette Valentine. New York: Free Press, 1979, pp.291-314.

Contends that there were conflicting ideas on parent involvement in Head Start -- some saw parents as participating in education programs, while others saw parents as decision makers. Described four dimensions of parent involvement as set out by Head Start: 1. making decisions about programs; 2. volunteering; 3. planning parent education; and 4. receiving home visits from Head Start staff.

*Ventura, S.J. "Recent Trends and Differentials in Illegitimacy." *Journal of Marriage and the Family* 31(1969): 447-450.

Veroff, J., E. Douvan, and R.A. Kulka. *The Inner American: A Self-Portrait from 1957 to 1967*. New York: Basic Books, 1981.

*Verr, V. "One Step Forward -- Two Steps Back: Child Care's Long American History." *Child Care: Who Cares?* Edited by P. Roby. New York: Basic Books, 1973, pp.157-171.

Vicerky, J. "Women's Economic Contribution to the Family." *The Subtle Revolution. Women at Work*. Edited by R.E. Smith. Washington, D.C.: The Urban Institute, 1979.

*Vogt, Leona M., Thomas White, Garth Buchanan, Joseph Wholey, and Richard Lamoff. *Health Start: Final Report of the Second Year Program*. Washington, D.C.: Urban Institute, Dec. 1973A, Urban Institute Working Paper 964-6. (EDO92235).

*Vogt, Leona M. et al. *Health Start: Summary of the Evaluation of the Second Year Program*. Washington, D.C.: Urban Institute, Dec. 1973B, Urban Institute Working Paper 964-5. (EDO92236).

*Vogt, Leona M., and Joseph Wholey. *Health Start: Final Report of the Evaluation of the First Year Program*. Washington, D.C.: Urban Institute, Dec. 29, 1972. (EDO71760).

Waldman, A., S. Grossman, H. Hayghe, and B.L. Johnson. "Working Mothers in the 1970's: A Look at the Statistics." *Monthly Labor Review* (October 1979): 39-49.

Wallerstein, Judith S., and Joan Berlin Kelly. *Surviving the Breakup -- How Children and Parents Cope with Divorce*. New York: Basic Books, Inc., 1980.

Deals with changes in parent-child relationships. The unfamiliar structure of the postdivorce family contributed to the anxiety of both parents and children. Parents were often unaware of the changes taking place in their relationships with their children and were acutely troubled by the absence of role models for a divorce family.

*Wallis, Claudia. "Children Having Children." *Time*, 126 (Dec. 9, 1985): 78-82, 84, 87, 89-90.

Contends that the high rate of unmarried adolescent parents represents a distressing flaw in the social fabric of America. An accompanying article by Richard Stengel addresses "The Missing-Father Myth."

*Washington, Anita C. "A Cultural and Historical Perspective on Pregnancy-Related Activity Among U.S. Teenagers." *The Journal of Black Psychology* 9(August 1982): 1-28.

Examines data on recent changes in birth rates, sexual activity, abortion, illegitimacy, and adoption rates among white and non-white adolescents.

Washington, R.O. "Toward a Theory of Social Competence: Implications for Measuring the Effects of Head Start Programs." *Urban Education* 10(1) (1975): 73-85.

Presents the motivational aspects and sociocultural dimensions of social competence in order to stress the value-laden nature of the concept.

*Washington, Valora. "Implementing Multi-Cultural Education: Elementary Teachers Attitudes and Professional Practice." *Peabody Journal of Education* 59(1982): 190-200.

Studies 3,017 elementary school teachers in 69 public school systems in North Carolina to determine their attitudes about, access to, and use of multicultural teaching materials and methods. Found that while teachers indicated a commitment to equal treatment and equal opportunities, they did not have access to the materials to enable them to act in accordance with their beliefs. Most teachers did not use multicultural materials or methods at all, or their use of these techniques was neglible. These findings for elementary schools contrast sharply with efforts to promote cross-cultural understanding as stated in the Head Start performance standards.

*Washington, Valora. "Continuity of Care in American Support for Dependent Children. The AFDC Example." *International Journal of Mental Health* 12(1984, Winter): 59-77.

Examines the history, current status, and future needs of the AFDC program. Uses the concept of "Continuity of Care" to discern how well the program serves children and families. Found discontinuities in the definition of AFDC in previous links of eligibility to parental conduct; in the manner in which benefits are calculated; and in the way services are provided during the prenatal, preschool and adolsecence periods of development.

*Washington, Valora. "Head Start: How Appropriate for Minority Families in the 1980's?" *American Journal of Orthopsychiatry* 55(October 1985A): 557-591.

Questions Head Start's continuing relevance for minority group children and their families. Argues that the challenge of Head Start in the 1980's is to maintain, advocate for, and monitor program quality.

*Washington, Valora. "Social and Personal Ecology Influencing Public Policy for Young Children: An American Dilemma." *Young Children in Context: Impact of Self, Family and Society on Development*. Edited by Caven S. McLoughlin, and Dominic F. Gullo. Springfield, Illinois: Charles C. Thomas, 1985B, pp.254-274.

Reviews American attitudes and responses to public attention for children through historical and philosophical perspectives, and through a review of existing children's policies and programs. The future of children's policy is discussed.

Washington, Valora. "Social Policy, Cultural Diversity, and the Obscurity of Black Children." *Journal of Educational Equity and Leadership* 5(Winter 1985C): 320-335.

Illustrates the view that cultural diversity is ignored in the formulation of social policy. As a result, the needs and interests of black children are obscured in two ways: 1. by the emphasis on economic deprivation as opposed to race and racism in the formulation of social policy; and 2. by the implementation of social policy in ways that undermine survival strategies of poor black families.

*Washington, Valora, and Blanche Glimps. "Developmental Issues for Adolescent Parents and Their Children." *Educational Horizons* (Summer 1983): 195-199.

Reviews the effects of adolescent parenting on children, and explores issues related to the children's physical and cognitive functioning and to their material support and nurturing. The authors argue that society has a responsibility to help adolescents prevent pregnancies and to mitigate the consequences when preventive measures fail.

Washington, Valora, and Courtland Lee. "Teaching and Counseling the Black Child: A Systemic Analysis for the 1980's." *Journal of Non-White Concerns in Personnel and Guidance* 9(1981): 60-67.

Identifies areas of divergence between the black community and educational institutions, and presents a systemic analysis of this divergence as it relates to teaching and counseling. Six areas of divergence are highlighted: sex roles, language, service orientation, reference group orientation, achievement expectations, and problem origination.

*Washington, Valora, and Courtland Lee. "Teaching and Counseling Black Males in Grades K to 8." *Black Caucus Journal of the National Association of Black Social Workers* 13(1) (Spring 1982): 25-29.

Argues that four variables impede successful interaction between black boys and school settings: 1. the attitudes and behavior of school personnel; 2. biased curriculum content and models; 3. the absence of black male role models; and 4. community-school divergence regarding valid male role-models. Provides teaching and counseling strategies to counteract these four variables.

*Washington, Valora, and Ura Jean Oyemade. "Employer-Sponsored Child Care: A Movement or a Mirage?" *Journal of Home Economics* (Winter 1984): 11-15, 27.

Examines current status of employer-sponsored child care by reviewing: 1. trends in family life-styles that affect the workplace; 2. corporate changes that affect both employee expectations and family life; 3. the prevalence, relative success, and limitations of the employer-sponsored child care options; and 4. government initiatives to support corporate action.

*Washington, Valora, and Ura Jean Oyemade. "Changing Family Trends; Head Start Must Respond." *Young Children* (September 1985): 12-19.

Discusses the impact of four family trends on Project Head Start: the feminization of poverty, the rise in teen parenting, the surge in the number of mothers of preschool children in the workforce, and the increasing challenge of poor families to attain economic self-sufficiency. Recommendations are offered as to how Head Start can better serve children and families affected by these trends. This article served as the basis for this book.

*Washington, Valora, and Roberta Woolever. "Training Teachers for Diversity: An Urban Necessity." *Perspectives on Urban Affairs in North Carolina.* Edited by W.J. Wicker. Chapel Hill, N.C.: UNC Urban Affairs Institute, 1979, pp.57-66.

Argues that teachers and teacher educators are not prepared for the reality of cultural diversity, although support for multicultural education is growing. This paper expresses some philosophies and goals for multicultural teacher education and assesses how multicultural education is being fostered. The paper also proposes methods for achieving multicultural education and for evaluating those efforts in terms of teacher skill and attitudes.

*Weikart, D.P. "Preschool Education for Disadvantaged Children." *Learning from Experience: Evaluating Early Childhood Demonstration Programs.* Edited by J.R. Travers, and R.J. Light (Eds.). Washington, D.C.: National Academy Press, 1982, pp.197-202.

*Weisberg, H.I., and W. Haney. *Longitudinal Evaluation of Head Start Planned Variation and Follow Through.* Cambridge, MA: Huron Institute, 1977.

*Weitzman, Lenore J. "The Economics of Divorce: Social and Economic Consequences of Poverty, Alimony, and Child Support Awards." *UCLA Law Review* 28 (1980): 1181.

Looks at the financial aspects of divorce, and examines the social and economic consequences for husbands and wives, as well as for children.

Weitzman, Lenore J. *The Divorce Revolution: The Unexpected Social and Economic Consequences for Women and Children in America.* New York: The Free Press, 1985.

Found that attempts to correct an outmoded legal code that was degrading and humiliating to all parties have had traumatic economic and social consequences. Divorced women and their children are becoming a new underclass, suffering a decline of 73 percent in their standard of living after divorce. The sharpest drop and most severe deprivation are suffered by older homemakers and women with young children due to the assumption that such people will become self-sufficient in a short period of time. Even more troubling is a child support system that routinely awards pitifully inadequate amounts, and then fails to enforce its own standards. Sixty to 80 percent of all fathers, rich as well as poor, do not comply with court orders. Under the new laws as under the old, 90 percent of all custodial parents are women, although some gender-neutral provisions now force women to fight (often by bargaining away support) for what use to be their right. For children, Weitzman recommends income-sharing, to equalize the standards of living in the custodial and non-custodial households. She also urges more effective techniques to enforce those awards, including wage assignments, income tax intercepts, national collection services, property liens, and bonds and jail.

*Westinghouse Learning Corporation. Ohio University, Athens, Ohio. *The Impact of Head Start: An Evaluation of the Effects of Head Start on Children's Cognitive and Affective Development. Volumes I-II and Executive Summary*, 1969.

Examines differences between Head Start first, second, and third graders and non-Head Start first, second, and third graders in intellectual and social-personal development. The major conclusions drawn from these data were: 1. Summer programs are ineffective in producing lasting gains in affective and cognitive development; 2. full-year programs are ineffective in aiding affective development and only marginally effective in producing lasting cognitive gains; 3. all Head Start children are still considerably below national norms on tests of language development and scholastic achievement, while school readiness at grade one approaches the national norm; and 4. parents of Head Start children voiced strong approval of the program.

While full-year Head Start is somewhat superior to summer Head Start, neither could be described as satisfactory. Further research aimed at the development of an effective preschool program is recommended.

The report was published in two volumes. Volume I contains the text of the report and supporting appendices A through E. Volume II contains Appendices F through J which are made up entirely of back-up statistical data.

*Westney, Ouida E., Renee R. Jenkins, June Dobbs Butts, and Irving Williams. "Sexual Development and Behavior in Black Preadolescents." *Adolsecence* XIX (75) (Fall 1984): 557-568.

Assesses sexual maturation and sociosexual behaviors in a sample of 101 nine- to eleven-year-old middle- and low-income boys and girls. Girls were more advanced than boys in the process of sexual maturation. Genital development in boys was significantly related to their sexual behavior; no association was found for girls or for income level.

*Westney, Ouida E., Renee R. Jenkins, Irving C. Williams, and June Dobbs Butts. "Pubertal Development and Sexual Behavior in Black Preadolescents." *Adolescence*, (1983): 10-20.

*Westoff, C.F., G. Colott, and A.D. Foster. "Teenage Fertility in Developed Nations: 1971-1980." *Family Perspectives* 15(3) (1983): 105-110.

Examines trends in adolescent fertility during the 1970's for 32 countries. Found that U.S. teenage fertility rates, while declining, are still high compared with other counties. Found extreme cases of high teenage fertility among U.S. blacks and Japanese.

White, Burton L. *Making Sense Out of Our Education Priorities*. Massachusetts Laboratory of Human Development, Harvard University, 1973, Ed 085 087.

*Willensky, H. "Orderly Careers and Social Participation: The Impact of Work History on Social Interaction in the Middle Class." *American Sociological Review* 26(4) (1961): 521-539.

Tests Durkheim's and Manheim's ideas about careers as a source of social integration among 678 white males. Found that retreat from work and community life is due to chaotic work experiences.

*Willhelm, S.M. "Black-White Equality: The Socioeconomic Conditions of Blacks in America, Part II." *Journal of Black Studies* 14 (1983): 151-184.

Williams, L.R. "Mending the Hoop: A Study of Roles, Desired Responsibilities, and Goals for Parents of Children in Tribally Sponsored Head Start Programs." *Dissertation Abstracts International* 1975, 36(3-A): 1361.

Develops a set of instructional objectives for a training program for parents in tribally-sponsored Head Start Programs based on the present and desired roles of parents and the Federal policy guidelines for the involvement of parents in local Head Start programs.

Williams, Terry, and William Kornblum. *Growing Up Poor.* New York: Lexington Books, 1985.

Introduces some of the teenagers who are trapped in poverty, and shows how some succeed in the struggle to get out and how others finally give up trying.

William, W., and J.W. Evans. "The Politics of Evaluation: The Case of Head Start." *Annals of the American Academy of Political and Social Science* 385 (1969): 118-132.

Traces the controversy generated by the Westinghouse Report in order to look at implications for future policy.

Willmon, Betty J. "Reading Readiness as Influenced by Parent Participation in Head Start Programs." *International Reading Association Conference Proceedings, Part 1.* (April 1968): 617-622.

Discusses the influence of parent participation on the reading readiness of Head Start participants.

Willmon, Betty J. "Parent Participation as a Factor in the Effectiveness of Head Start Programs." *Journal of Educational Research* 62(9)(1969): 406-410.

Indicates that the influence of higher active parental involvement in Head Start appeared to serve as an intervening variable which influenced academic motivation.

Wilson, Ellen. "Home Truths." *Human Life Review* 6, (Summer 1980): 19-20.

Draws out some of the distinguishing characteristics of the family and shows how the family serves its members and society.

Wilson Quarterly. "The American Family." 4 (Summer 1980): 113-149.

Contains several articles: Psychologist Arlene Skolnick looks at the family in American history; sociologist Graham Spanier provides an overview of the latest academic research into family matters; and specialists Mary Jo Bane, Lee Rainwater, and Martin Rein examine the evolving government-family partnership.

*Wilson, William J. "The Black Community in the 1980s: Questions of Race, Class and Public Policy." *Annals. AAPSS*, 454 (March 1981): 26-41.

*Wilson, W.J., and K.M. Neckerman. "Without Jobs, Black Men Cannot Support Families." *Point of View: The Congressional Black Caucus Foundation* 2 (1985, Fall): 1,3-5.

Wolfe, Linda. "The New York Mother." *New York Times* 17(Sept. 10, 1984): 32, 34-39.

Discusses the complexities and concerns of mothers, particularly those who work in New York City.

*Woloch, N. *Women and the American Experience.* New York: Alfred A. Knopf, 1984.

Women's Bureau. *The Earnings Gap Between Women and Men.* Washington, D.C.: U.S. Department of Labor, 1979.

Describes factors related to women's persistent disadvantage in earnings that are unexplained by differences in ability and experience.

*Work, Henry H. "Parent-Child Centers: A Working Reappraisal." *American Journal of Orthopsychiatry* 42, no.4 (July 1972): 582-595.

Yando, R., V. Seitz, and E. Zigler. *Intellectual and Personality Characteristics of Children: Social Class and Ethnic Group Differences.* Hillsdale, N.J.: Erlbaum, 1979.

Found that when children were examined across a variety of problem solving situations, no one group performed uniformly better than any other group. Children can be better understood by devising measures and defining situations that allow all their competencies to emerge.

*Yarrow, M., J. Campbell, and R. Burton. *Childrearing: An Inquiry into Research and Methods.* San Francisco, Jossey-Bass, 1968.

*Yong, K.C. "A Comparative Study of Knowledge and Attitude of Child Growth and Development Among Teenage Mothers and Adult Mothers." *Dissertation Abstracts International* 42 1474A University Microfilms No. AAD 81-21572, 1981.

*Zelnik, Melvin, and John F. Kantner. "Sexual Activity, Contraceptive Use, and Pregnancy Among Metropolitan Area Teenagers: 1971-1979." *Family Planning Perspectives* (Sept./Oct. 1980): 230-237.

Zelnik, Melvin, and Young J. Kim. "Sex Education and its Association with Teenage Sexual Activity, Pregnancy and Contraceptive Use." *Family Planning Perspectives* 14(May-June 1982): 117-119, 123-126.

Argues that young people who have had sex education are no more likely to have sexual intercourse than those who have never taken a course. However, sexually active young women who have had sex education are less likely to have been pregnant than their counterparts who have had no such instruction.

Zigler, Edward. "The Environmental Mystique: Training the Intellect Versus Development of the Whole Child." *Childhood Education* 46(1970): 402-412.

*Zigler, Edward. "Project Head Start: Success or Failure?" *Learning* 1, no. 7(1973): 43-47.

Zigler, Edward. "Has it Really Been Demonstrated that Compensatory Education is Without Value?" *American Psychologist* 30 (1975): 935-937.

*Zigler, Edward. "Project Head Start: Success or Failure?" *Project Head Start.* Edited by E. Zigler, and J. Valentine. New York: Free Press, 1979, pp. 495-507.

Examines the different objectives of Project Head Start -- social competence, health, intellectual ability, social and emotional development, family involvement and community change --in reference to the disadvantaged child. Discusses elements which lead to an overly cognitive emphasis in evaluations of Head Start and other remedial programs. Argues that the broad-based goals of Project Head Start makes it a success.

*Zigler, Edward. "Assessing Head Start at 20: An Invited Commentary." *American Journal of Orthopsychiatry* 55(October 1985): 603-609.

Critiques articles by Valora Washington (1985A) and Ura Jean Oyemade (1985). Highlights the accomplishments of Head Start over two decades as well as some of its limitations.

Zigler, Edward, W. Abelson, and V. Seitz. "Motivational Factors in the Performance of Economically Disadvantaged Children on the Peabody Picture Vocabulary Test." *Child Development* 44 (1973): 294-303.

Zigler, Edward, and Karen Anderson. "An Idea Whose Time Had Come: The Intellectual and Political Climate for Head Start." *Project Head Start.* Edited by Edward Zigler, and Jeanette Valentine. New York: The Free Press, 1979, pp.3-19.

Zigler, Edward, and S. Kagan. *Child Development Knowledge and Educational Practice: Using What We Know.* Chicago: Eighty-First Yearbook of the National Society of the Study of Education, 1982.

Zigler, Edward, and Mary E. Lang. "Head Start: Looking Toward the Future." *Young Children* 38(1983): 3-6.

Examines the strengths and accomplishments of the Head Start program and suggests directions for future program development. The authors stress the need for attention to program quality, staff-child ratios, class size, and teacher salaries/benefits.

Zigler, Edward, and Leslie Rescorla. "Social Science and Social Policy: The Case of Social Competence as a Goal of Intervention Programs." *Psychology Research, Public Policy and Practice: Toward A Productive Partnership.* Edited by Richard A. Kassochau, Lyn P. Rehmm, and Leonard P. Ullmann. New York: Praeger, 1985, pp.62-94.

Presents the case of social competence as the appropriate goal for early intervention programs and describes the authors' efforts to conceptualize and operationalize the concept of social competence.

Zigler, Edward, and P. Trickett. "IQ, Social Competence, and Evaluation of Early Childhood Intervention Programs." *American Psychologist* 33(9) (1978): 789-798.

Zigler, Edward, and Jeanette Valentine. (Eds.) *Project Head Start: A Legacy of the War on Poverty.* New York: Free Press, 1979.

PART F:

AUTHORS AND NAMES INDEX

PART G:

SUBJECT INDEX